BURIED MEMORIES

A VULNERABLE GIRL AND HER STORY OF SURVIVAL

Katie Beers
with Carolyn Gusoff

**BEAUFORT
BOOKS**

Copyright © 2013 Carolyn Gusoff and Katie Beers

FIFTH EDITION

Library of Congress Cataloging-in-Publication Data on File

For inquiries about volume orders, please contact:

Beaufort Books
27 West 20th Street, Suite 1102
New York, NY 10011
sales@beaufortbooks.com

Published in the United States by Beaufort Books
www.beaufortbooks.com

Distributed by Midpoint Trade Books,
a division of Independent Publishers Group
www.midpointtrade.com
www.ipgbook.com

Printed in the United States of America

Interior design by Megan Trank
Cover Design by Mark Karis

ISBN: 9780825307782

I'd like to dedicate this book to my amazing parents, Barbara and Tedd; my loving husband, Derek; and my two beautiful children, Logan and Halee.

—Katie Beers

To my parents, Ileen and Gerry Gusoff, with gratitude and love.

—Carolyn Gusoff

CONTENTS

Actual names have been used. In some cases, last names are absent to protect the privacy of those who have not previously been identified publicly.

"When the 'action of telling a story' has come to its conclusion, the traumatic experience truly belongs to the past."

—Judith Herman, M.D.
Trauma and Recovery: The Aftermath of Violence—
from Domestic Abuse to Political Terror

INTRODUCTION

THE DRIVE EAST was therapeutic. Not in a meditative way: I didn't have time for that. It took me back, literally. Because for me and most others of my species, the Long Island Expressway is as much Memory Lane as it is the world's longest parking lot. In Hollywood, they give bus tours of movie stars' homes. On Long Island, reporters like me could drive you up and down the roads and narrate their twisted and tragic tales. Due south at Exit 37—that's where a crazed gunman opened fire on a commuter train; Exit 41 to the end, just before you reach the canals—the split level where a teenaged Amy Fisher put a bullet in Mary Jo Buttafuoco's head; Exit 53 south—here's where a nurse poisoned patients and then feigned coming to their rescue, but never did in time; Exit 68 to the sea—that's where TWA flight 800 plunged into the Atlantic; Exit 64 to the Sound—that's where a wealthy couple was butchered, their son sent to prison for two decades for the double murder, of which he was later cleared.

These are invisible landmarks, faded like scars that are still evident only to those who seek them out. They are like markers on a map of suburban turmoil, with so many pushpins it's hard to make out the land mass. Exit 71—The Hamptons—wineries, farm stands, ocean breezes. But for me and others like me, it's simply Katie Beers territory.

I had little company on the solitary stretch of road to East Hampton, and the almost summer sun in a big sky cast dark green shadows on wavy fields of corn and sod. My mind was cluttered with my usual morning fare—getting the kids off to school while pitching and setting up news stories, always a nerve-splitting juggle. Children need to be fed and so do news managers, and I don't know which are more impatient for their morning meal. As I raced out the door pounding the keys of my Blackberry, the cell rang. It was the school—I had forgotten to send my little one a picnic lunch for her fourth grade field day. Already I needed to make a detour, and I was late.

The two-hour drive slowed me down and took me back to a place in my memory I hadn't visited for many years. I pulled into a parking space in front of the East Hampton movie theater, put the car in park and put my mind into reverse. I tried to remember her face, which I had only seen up close once, in court, when she was ten years old. And as I straightened out the wheel, in front of me a young couple emerged from a rusty Jeep. The girl was in her mid-twenties, with shaggy brown hair, and baggy jeans. We made eye contact and I held my breath for a moment. I stared into her eyes for some sign of recognition, but there was none. The couple grabbed hands and took off down Main Street.

They were not the ones I had come to see. That would be the man sitting on a bench in front of the movie theater. I knew it instantly, even though I had never laid eyes on him. He fit his name perfectly.

"Tedd?" I asked, knowing the answer.

"Yes, Carolyn, nice to meet you," he said, extending a suntanned hand with a strong grip. He stood up, revealing an impeccably dressed man who looked well-suited for early retirement at sixty. Khaki shorts, worn leather flip flops from many healthy strolls on the beach, and the requisite Oxford-striped button-down shirt. Tedd was a man of few words by email, but in person he was welcoming. I knew immediately I was not on hostile turf.

We crossed the street to Starbucks and sat on the teak benches that line Main Street, coffees in hand, talking about an event that had occurred sixteen years earlier. We spoke of the timing that had brought us together. Earlier that year, John Esposito had come up for parole after serving fifteen years in prison, and the child he kidnapped, Katie Beers, spoke at his parole hearing. There wasn't a dry eye in the house, Tedd told me. "She remembers everything."

Tedd was the kind of man who could star in the movie version of his own life, with blond hair, astounding blue eyes, and perfectly aligned white teeth that emerged with a warm grin. The grins came often because here we were, years after one of the most disturbing events in New York's criminal history, and there appeared to be a happy ending.

"Being kidnapped," he told me, "was the best thing that ever happened to Katie."

We spoke for about an hour. He told me he had wanted to meet with me first, before he asked Katie to join us. I told him I felt a sense of maternal protectiveness for her, and I meant it. Her disappearance was a rare test for

INTRODUCTION

a reporter. Not only did it evolve into a national obsession, with a media frenzy surrounding every grain of information, but it crept into my heart in a way few stories do. I couldn't help but take it home with me and keep it, forever.

Almost daily during the ordeal, I found myself talking to people in the big tent of Katie's circus-like cast of characters, all seemingly distraught about her disappearance, but never entirely convincingly. I choked back smoke at the kitchen table of Katie's godmother, Linda Inghilleri, who would let cigarettes burn out, as I watched her fingers nearly ignite, and then light another one without missing a drag. She would hit "play" on the tape recorder next to the overstuffed ashtray and, as the Disney tune, "A Whole New World," wafted up with the smoke, tell the assembled reporters it was Katie's favorite song. The interviews invariably ended with her tears dropping onto the vinyl tablecloth and a towering pile of twisted butts.

It was my seventh year in the television news business, and 1992 was like no other. I was simultaneously covering the other big headline grabber of the year, the Amy Fisher/Joey Buttafuoco scandal, splitting my time between two mega stories and Mount Sinai Hospital. There, my fifty-seven-year-old father, athletic, strong and full of life, found out he was dying.

"Dad's in the hospital. Come quick," my sister announced on what was then a brick-sized cell phone. I instantly reversed my direction on the parkway, and by the time I made it to the emergency room on the Upper East Side, my family's faces were ashen. My husband, then a medical resident at Mount Sinai, told me that Dad's CT scan showed there was something very wrong—something dark and opaque that doesn't belong in a brain had showed up on the illuminated view box. Dad's doctor explained that tangled in the crevices were cells growing out of control: a brain tumor.

Weeks later, the eight-inch gash stapled closed on his bald spot marked where the neurosurgeon had entered to scoop out tumor cells growing like mold between cauliflower florets. I imagined it would be an ugly scar, but it never had the chance to heal—my father wouldn't live long enough. I didn't know it then, but it was impossible to remove the entire tumor without taking with it vital brain circuitry, like speech and hand-eye coordination—little functions dentists need. Seeing my father suddenly lose his hand control, his dental practice, then his speech, and finally his life, was my backdrop while I covered other people's tragedies.

I was subletting an apartment in Manhattan with my new husband—there were no children of our own yet. When Katie disappeared, it was the news story of the day. When she failed to show up, the effort to find her became an epic mission.

To now hear Tedd, the man who had raised her after her rescue, tell me that Katie had gone well beyond survival and had flourished, was a rare moment for a journalist. When you tell a different story every day in ten sentences or less, you seldom get the satisfaction of knowing the ending. With a sparkle in his crystal blue eyes, he told me this story was mine to help tell.

The email screamed for my attention from the daily flurry of digital dialogue: police trumpeting the round-up of unsuspecting johns, politicians hoping to get their two cents in during the evening news about the latest downturn in the market, and pitches from PR houses that think they're clever using your name in the salutation—as if you won't realize it's a mass mailing. And then there was the one with a simple subject line—"Introduction." In the "sender" column, a person I knew so well, yet not at all: Katie Beers.

It was the first correspondence from a girl who had an almost fictional quality in my mind—or was she now a woman? I did the math quickly. She was kidnapped in 1992, so she would now be twenty-six. What would she look like? All I could imagine was the frail, mousey figure being hurried away from television cameras, wrapped in a blue, polyurethane slicker the night we, in the news media and the rest of a mesmerized public, learned she was alive. Was I there or had I simply seen the video so many times it was etched in my memory? Suddenly, I wasn't sure.

I speed-read, scanning for potential disappointment. How many times over the last two decades had I worked for an exclusive of this magnitude? But I'd waited on this one, remembering the words of the late James Catterson, the Suffolk District Attorney who implored news reporters to let Katie grow up in peace.

INTRODUCTION

"Give Katie a Chance!" he had printed on poster board at his news conference after her rescue. I agreed with the sentiments behind the request and abided. But a decade and a half had passed, and Katie had grown up. The wounds would be sealed by now, I reasoned, the scars long faded, or at least settled into their final form.

It seemed so odd—someone I had intentionally avoided for so many years, kept outside the perimeter of privacy, was suddenly knocking at my inbox. I was surprised she was even using the same name, and I was uneasy as I opened it.

"I guess it's time," she announced, "for us to meet."

She wanted to finally tell her story. "I have been hesitant to speak to any reporters before," she wrote, "because it always seems like they exploit people, and I have been exploited too much in my young life."

Yes, the email was my proof she had survived—but how? Living is one thing; surviving is another. I had a ten-year-old who couldn't get past the cyclone scene in *The Wizard of Oz*. What child could survive a real-life trip to a place far scarier than Oz, with a flesh-and-blood cast of human monsters? Surely there would be lasting psychological effects. She couldn't be normal, I thought. If there was one thing I knew as a mother, even more than a journalist, it was that love was an essential ingredient when creating a well-balanced child. Skimp on the parenting, and the dough won't rise or something catastrophic like that. Over the years, I had seen the recipe fail many times. I expected an older Katie, but given the missing ingredients, how could she have turned out? What, I wondered, could be left of her?

———

Panera Bread in Allentown, Pennsylvania was unexpectedly mobbed. We chose the spot as a midpoint between Long Island and Katie's current home in rural Pennsylvania. Three hours from metropolitan New York, this surprised me. College kids were huddled around laptops. Elderly couples stared into space sipping soup and navigating shaky hands around giant paninis. The line snaked around the front tables, and customers were squeezing inside to stay out of the driving rain. I wondered how on earth I would locate in this crowd someone I hadn't seen in almost twenty years, and then only as a child.

The thought was short-lived. As I carved a path through the lunchtime crush and my eyes scanned the busy eatery, they rested on a young woman seated across from a young man. She was in her mid-twenties with shoulder length, amber-colored straight hair, parted in the middle. Her skin was white and unblemished and absent of any hint of makeup.

But it was her eyes that I recognized instantly. Brown almond slivers looked up and met mine. It was Katie Beers, the little girl whose name had become synonymous with abuse, neglect and disappearance. Now, here she was, all grown up—and ready to speak to a reporter for the very first time.

It amazed me that she looked exactly like the little Katie Beers of her fourth grade picture, the one plastered on the "Missing" posters and in all my news reports. It occurred to me that I had never waited longer to hear a *real story* behind the headlines.

My instinct was to hug her, but she didn't really know me at all, so we shook hands and smiled. Her husband, sitting across from her at the table, was endearingly protective. At twenty-eight, Derek was too young to remember the media frenzy his wife of two years had generated. But he grasped the concept that she had protected her story for long enough and was not going to hand it over to be cheapened.

She wanted it told, he informed me, with truth and dignity. Much had been written about her ordeal—much of it was "speculation," he said, merely a collection of newspaper accounts. She was the only one who knew what had happened to her, and she had waited to tell it properly.

As we ate, a small piece of apple from my Waldorf salad landed on Derek's sweater. "Put that in the book!" he chuckled. I told him I certainly would, and then I knew we were going to get along just fine.

Katie told me she had used the name "Katie Beers" up until her marriage and now deliberately withheld her married name. She revealed that she had gone to college and was a data programmer; Derek was a computer programmer. She didn't sound enthusiastic about her job, from which she had recently been laid off. And she was pregnant.

She spoke of forgiveness, but didn't want her intentions misinterpreted. "I never want to see him free. I want him in prison for as long as legally possible." She told me she had been raped and didn't know how to tell that part of the story, but I assured her we would find an appropriate way and create something that could help other people—something that could put years of nightmares to rest.

Her hands were young and full. A small diamond adorned her ring finger, and hot pink nails were the only embellishment—those and the diamond necklace with three small round stones that dangled around her neck. When we opened the calendar and made our next date, January 13, Katie reminded me that it would be the anniversary of her rescue.

"If it were not for the kidnapping," she laughed, "I'd be living in Mastic Beach with six children by now, driving a taxi."

"But seriously," she added straight-faced, "my life would have been a much different story."

So began my dialogue with Katie. She would always speak to me as if she were rewinding a tape—scanning for notes and chords she insisted were all still there—precisely recorded in her buried memories. Her answers were at times detached, usually matter-of-fact, and sometimes she even laughed when she spoke about the most skin-crawling tidbits of her dark childhood.

But never, it astounded me to see, were there tears.

The drive home was wet and gray. The clouds hung over the autumn palate like smoke over fire. Brown sticks of trees and evergreens were all that remained in the late fall landscape. The day seemed to define "gloomy," and it seemed appropriate. I was about to dive into a different kind of gloom—the darkest memories of a tortured child.

By four-thirty, the sky was so dark it felt as if someone had dimmed the lights. Mist hovered over New Jersey's marshes near Newark airport. I hated this time of year; it made me sleepy and dreading the winter, when fingers freeze around the metal microphone in blizzard live-shots and words struggle to be spit out of frozen lips. This is a northeastern reporter's most dreaded time of year, especially for a working mother—getting home at an hour when it seemed the kids should be already sleeping, and then starting my second job.

My kids were ten and thirteen. I thought of them as I began to construct the questions that would become Katie's narrative. And I began to ponder how on earth anyone recovers from a childhood in hell.

Katie Beers and I meet for the first time in Allentown, PA at a Panera Bread in late 2008. Katie always wanted to share her story but waited for recovery and adulthood. (Photo by Derek)

FADED SCARS

MUCH OF IT COMES back to me in vivid, saturated memories: the manila tan of egg-crate soundproofing, the putrid smells of my own waste, and the plastic taste of after-dinner mints that still make me gag. Then there are parts that are hazy, like a foggy south shore morning, and still there are parts I don't remember at all. Sometimes it even seems it all happened to someone else. But no, it happened to me—I have the hole in my left cheek to prove it. And the cigarette burn on my arm. And the deeper scars no one can see.

I would say that I didn't really know how bad my situation was until I was out if it. Like getting used to a chilly lake. You tread water and after a while you warm up, even though the water temperature hasn't changed at all. Looking back, I can feel the icy waters. But then, I didn't have the means to take the temperature of my environment. I had only two childhood friends. I saw how their lives were. I knew that my life wasn't like theirs. I was alone, floating face down in a deadly current and didn't know it.

People would say that I seemed sad. I don't remember being sad. I don't recall crying. Except for after the sexual abuse—which started long before I knew the name for it.

I'm trying to regain the memories, but it's hard to do after blocking them out for so long and trying to forget them. I would block them out and try not to think about them, because if I thought about it, it would happen more. If it was something that was present in my head, if it was something I was thinking about, it could happen again. If I didn't think about it, maybe I could will it away. But that didn't work.

John Esposito was always in the picture. My mother, Marilyn Beers, picked up his mother in the taxi she drove. John's mother started talking about her son, who she said was part of the Big Brothers program. He wasn't actually a part of the organization, but Marilyn didn't think to check that out, since John Beers, my half-brother, needed a male figure in his life. We called them "Big John" and "Little John" and Marilyn allowed

Big John to take Little John off on play-dates to go to the batting cage, to go to his house to play video games, stuff like that.

When I was older, I got to go on the outings too. I liked him. Whenever he would come see me, he would give me a toy—like a Barbie doll—and a big hug.

Big John's house was a toy store, candy store, and amusement park all in one. He converted his family garage into an apartment. That's where he lived, and that's where any kid with a sweet tooth and a video game habit would end up. The downstairs had two garage stalls, and then a door that led into his living room. A little further back was his kitchen and eating area, and a staircase in the kitchen that led upstairs. It was there that all the neighborhood kids would spend hours after school, up the stairs and down the hallway in John's bedroom. It was a huge open room with a walk-in closet that was wall-to-wall games. Any game imaginable. Board games, toys, Nintendo, Sega.

And then, in one corner, he had a little punching bag hanging from the ceiling. And a basketball hoop. And his room led to yet another room that had ping pong and arcade games lining the walls and another basketball game—this one electronic. Being in those two rooms was any kid's dream. Not to mention the candy and sweets and soda. I remember he had a little refrigerator in his bedroom always stocked with cans of soda.

Someone told Marilyn that Big John touched Little John in a bad way. So Marilyn said I was no longer allowed to see him or go to his house. But Aunt Linda, my godmother, didn't go along with that. She had no problem letting me be with Big John. She told me she thought he was a nice man.

December 26, 1992, is one of the heavily saturated days. My memories come back to me in dark reds and black—the colors of Big John's Nissan pickup truck.

They begin with the knock at the back door of the place in Mastic Beach I was calling home. It was the only door that worked, really. The little tan converted garage apartment was falling apart, and the front door was rotted shut. The back door opened into a dingy kitchen with food-caked dishes stacked in the sink—crusty because no one ever thought to wash them.

In came Ann Butler, Linda's mother. Ann liked everyone to call her "Mom." She drove the half hour from Bay Shore to Mastic Beach because we had no telephone. My "real" mother, Marilyn, was out of work. Marilyn invited Mom inside. When I came out to say "hi," Ann asked me if I wanted to go see Aunt Linda for my tenth birthday, which was in four days.

I really didn't want to visit with Aunt Linda because I used to be her slave. I cleaned the bathrooms, cooked dinner, vacuumed, and did the laundry. Linda liked to have me around to do all her housework because she was lazy, and later because she didn't have a left leg. The gangrene got to it because of her diabetes. So she had me to boss around. I couldn't exactly say "no" to her demands. Sal, Linda's husband, was even scarier than she was, and he had ways to make me do whatever he and Linda wanted.

Marilyn instructed me to leave the room. I ducked into the side bedroom that I shared with my mother and grandmother and pressed my ear up against the back of the door, which was so cardboard thin I could hear every word. Marilyn was telling Ann that I was not allowed to visit Aunt Linda because of Sal and Big John. Ann assured her I wouldn't see Sal or John. Sal, she said, wasn't living in the house with Aunt Linda anymore, and she promised that Big John would not be there either.

"Please, honey," Ann almost begged. "Linda has a whole birthday party planned for Katie."

"All right," Marilyn finally gave in, "but I want her back for her birthday."

Marilyn came into the bedroom and delivered the verdict. I would be going to Aunt Linda's for a few days to celebrate my birthday, but if Sal was at the house, or if Big John showed up, I was told to call her or the police immediately. I was not allowed to see them. I dutifully headed with "Mom" to Bay Shore, home of Linda and Sal Inghilleri.

Linda planned a birthday party for the next day and invited her family. "The Party is Here!" read the giant Mylar sign on the door of the tiny yellow shingled house on Ocean Avenue. I wore a black, floppy "Blossom" hat because it hid my boy-short hair, which had been lopped off after a stubborn case of head lice got me kicked out of elementary school. Having my waist-long hair chopped bothered me, but I was even more upset that I couldn't go to school. I knew that lice was something other kids get because my next door neighbor had it and so did some other kids in my class. I tried to sneak to school often, but the teacher would always send me to the nurse to have me re-checked for lice, and when they found them, either Grandma Helen would have to walk to the school to get me or Marilyn would have to come from work. I was praying that the haircut would get the lice out because I wanted desperately to go back to school. It had always been the safest place for me.

So I plopped the floppy hat onto my head, and Linda let me put on a little bit of make-up because it was going to be my tenth birthday—double digits. I told her that since I was going to be ten, I wanted to be called Katherine. "Happy Birthday Katherine" was scrawled in pink script on the supermarket birthday cake.

Big John dropped off a Barbie Dream House for me. It was my Christmas and Birthday all-in-one. That's why December birthdays stink. He dropped it off and told me he would come by the next day to put it together. Linda said that was fine and I remember reminding her that I wasn't allowed to see him.

She said, "It's fine! He's a nice person. He's coming!"

She then added, "We won't tell Marilyn."

John returned the next day, sat down at the dining room table, and asked Linda if, for my birthday, he could take me to Spaceplex, the giant game arcade in Nesconset about fifteen minutes away. She said, "Sure."

I leaned into Linda and whispered that Marilyn made me swear I wouldn't go anywhere with Big John, and she had told Ann that I was not allowed to. Linda dismissed me with a pointed finger in my face and said emphatically, "It's okay. He's just taking you to Spaceplex. You'll be home in a few hours."

I was getting that tight, sick feeling in my stomach—the one I had when Sal would come for me in the middle of the night and do dirty things to me. Marilyn had gotten a restraining order against Sal. But not John. Big John had never touched me.

Big John said that he was going to leave and give me time to get ready, and that he also needed to get ready. I think I was still in my pajamas. *Ready for what?* I wondered. I thought we were just going to Spaceplex. I put on my black denim skirt, a white turtleneck (one with Scottie dogs all over it), a pair of black cowboy boots, and the ever-present Blossom hat.

Big John was always polite when he would come get me, telling Linda he knew all the rules. Like a date. With the instructions all laid out—mail two letters, phone if late, and home by dinner—we were off.

Big John's house was a toy store, candy store and amusement park all in one. (Suffolk County Crime Lab)

Big John's bedroom was filled with junk food, soda and games. It's where any kid with a sweet tooth and a video game habit would end up.
(Suffolk County Crime Lab)

A GIANT

I N ONE OF OUR first meetings, Katie straightened her arm, twisting her elbow to get a better view, scanning the back for the marks she told me she knew were there.

"I know it's here somewhere. I can't believe it's faded, so I can't even find it!" she giggled. "Well, I'm sure it's here. Trust me!"

"Linda," she explained, "put out a cigarette on my arm."

Her hands then began exploring her smooth cheeks. "There's a scar here, too," she said, "used to be a hole in my cheek."

I remember the police description: White female, straight dirty blonde hair. Small hole in left cheek. It was one of those passed-over details in a news story that never seems to make much sense, but you bury it in the story anyway and privately question its significance.

Linda thought it was a wart, Katie now explained to me. Marilyn thought it was a pimple. Her two mother figures fought over the origin of the facial defect and each had her way with it. Linda burned it off with wart-removing salicylic acid, and Marilyn squeezed it between her plump fingers until it bled. The result was a hole in Katie's cheek, something she figured she would wear for the rest of her life. But now, as I scoured her face, I couldn't find a trace of it.

To our meetings, she lugged an overstuffed dark blue vinyl binder. In it were one hundred and eleven double-sided clear archive sleeves, each neatly filled with folded newspaper pages, yellowed clippings, and national magazines, compiled by someone who could obviously foretell the impact of the events and understood that the little waif at the center of the media storm would one day want to remember.

Katie told me her mother had been assembling it for years, and I understood she was not referring to Marilyn Beers. Barbara, her foster mother, had been following the kidnapping in the news and kept every article even before she knew she would end up raising the child who had vanished.

Missing from the binder, though, was the first communication that went out via fax, notifying seventy news agencies from Manhattan to Long Island on December 29, 1992. It declared in the most understated of subject lines: UNUSUAL INCIDENT[1]:

> *The Suffolk County Police Department is asking the public for their assistance in locating Kattie Beers, a nine-year-old Bayshore resident, missing under circumstances evincing an abduction.*
>
> *Kattie was last seen on Monday, December 28 at approximately 4:30 P.M. at the Spaceplex family Center, Rte 25, Nesconset.*
>
> *She is a white female, 4 feet tall, 50 pounds, light complexion, brown eyes, with straight dirty blonde hair. She had a small hole in her left cheek from minor surgery. When last seen, Kattie was wearing a dungaree skirt, white shirt with black Scottie dogs, and black boots.*
>
> *Anyone with information concerning the whereabouts of Kattie Beers can contact the Fourth Squad detectives...or the juvenile/missing persons section.*

The fax that Tuesday morning ended up in my hands. I was the News 12 Long Island early morning reporter. Some folks dread an early shift, but for me it was essential. It was the only way to live in Manhattan and beat the hour-and-a-half rush-hour traffic to Woodbury, Long Island, where News 12 is based. I could leave my apartment on East 82nd Street at 6:25 a.m., fly across the Queensboro Bridge, thus avoiding a toll which I couldn't afford on a reporter's salary, and be in the newsroom by seven sharp. I would show up with a soaking wet head and *au natural* face. I was working ten-hour shifts with barely a break in the day for the bathroom, so doing my hair and makeup on company time was an ounce of justice.

But on this day, I wished I had come to work ready to roll. The press release handed to me by the assignment editor looked routine enough—a missing child—and I was certain she would turn up quickly. In fact, most stories that involve missing people seem to resolve before the end of the work day, negating all the effort of putting together a news report. The victim usually turns out to be not missing at all, either taken by a family member or friend without permission, or voluntarily off somewhere hoping not to be found.

But this one instantly tripped the radar. "Nine-year-old" *Kattie* Beers, it said. Nine-year-olds don't usually run away from home, no matter how hellish the home.

I also knew there would be competition. A lot of it. All of the New York City stations covered Long Island with satellite news bureaus—in most cases, one reporter assigned to the entire island of nearly three million residents. Suffolk County, home to half of those residents, is a sprawling spread of terrain on the eastern side of the fish-shaped island. Surrounded by water on two shores, Suffolk is the belly and the flat end of the fishtail, and its inhabitants provide no shortage of salacious, scandalous, and at times, wacky news stories. Long Island could always be counted on to provide an interesting array of news choices. With some of the nation's most expensive zip codes, there are also pockets of the population that can barely pay inflated metropolitan-area rents and mortgages.

Bay Shore, the missing girl's hometown, according to the police release, fell somewhere in the middle. Its history reads like much of the Island's: wealthy city families had flocked to expansive beaches to build seaside mansions. Decades later, working class families from the boroughs also came east, buying their first homes here, turning farmland into suburbia.

Harvey Milk had graduated from Bay Shore High. Joe Namath had a summer spread, and the Entenmann family baked millions of boxes of beloved crumb coffee cake here. Bay Shore made news for less celebrated reasons, too: the shuttering of Main Street stores after malls invaded, and the exodus of homeowners after a flood of psychiatric patients were released from Pilgrim State Hospital.

For the most part, though, folks here took care of their kids and didn't lose track of them.

The Long Island story of the day was often the source of heated morning debate. On any given day, there could be a dozen options. The pile of overnight faxes with story pitches and breaking news could be an inch thick. With each one garnering a few seconds of perusal, the pile was then whittled down to the top ten or so. News judgment varies, but often the collective decision boiled down to balance. Too much crime turns viewers off. Too many features put viewers to sleep. Internal newsroom debates often ended with the three network affiliates and several independent TV stations heading off in opposite directions.

But once in a while, the story of the day is indisputable. There is one obvious "lede" story, editorial slang for the word "lead." Such was the case on December 29, 1992. A missing girl in a game arcade was what we call in the news business "a giant."

There was no hesitation. I knew the stations and live trucks would descend upon Bay Shore to seek out the girl's parents and neighbors, teachers and friends—and I also knew the early bird catches the worm. You snooze you lose—worn-out clichés in news because they are true. I needed to get going fast.

Tony Mazza was already geared up, sitting in the Crown Victoria in the parking lot behind News 12's studios. Tony, a cameraman, was always upbeat, never grumpy, a rarity in the business, especially at that hour. But first thing in the morning, we rarely exchanged much conversation. I gave him the address: 1083 Ocean Avenue, Bay Shore, and knew I had a good thirty minutes of shut-eye while he looked it up in the Hagstrom's and silently headed east.

We pulled up to a small house on the right side of a street without sidewalks. We weren't the first news vehicle to park, and that set off the adrenaline. Dingy yellow shingles framed a wooden front door with a big sign that read, "The Party's Here!"

Inside was what we call "one stop shopping." The missing girl's mother, a godmother, a grandmother, and the cops. I could, temporarily, relax. Everyone important to the story was present in the tiny cape, or so I thought.

Suffolk police detectives were swarming around the kitchen area. Marilyn Beers, who I quickly learned was the missing girl's mother, was standing and smoking next to a red princess phone that hung from the kitchen wall. One of the detectives asked Marilyn if the tape was real. What tape? I listened hard.

"Yeah, it's real." Marilyn showed little emotion. "I'm going crazy," she told a reporter. "Every time the phone rings, we all jump."

A GIANT

Marilyn explained to the growing gathering of reporters in the cramped kitchen that she got wind of the "situation" after a phone call to her next-door neighbor from Linda Inghilleri, her daughter's godmother.

"She went with John Esposito after I specifically told her she was not to go with John," Marilyn fumed.

Marilyn explained that Linda had played a tape from her answering machine over the phone, and she had no doubt it was authentic. Katie was crying hard and it certainly didn't sound to her as if she was playing games. Marilyn had jumped in a friend's car—her car was dead in the driveway—and rushed to West Bay Shore, twenty-five miles west of Mastic Beach, where she said she lived.

Linda, who explained she was "like a mother to Katie," wore a housecoat and a hint of pink pearl lipstick. But there was nothing to conceal the dark circles under her markedly wide-set eyes on a strikingly flat face. She said she was thirty-eight years old, but life had taken more of a toll on her than that number of years could possibly have.

She sat in a wheelchair at the kitchen table, chain-smoking as the song "A Whole New World" played on a tape recorder. The sweet lyrics wafted above the heavy, smoke-filled air emanating from the overflowing ashtray.

Katie, she said, was looking forward to going with a family friend to pick out a birthday present and then to a game arcade, but the outing turned into a tragedy.

Have you heard from her?

"She called me at a quarter after five on my answering machine and by the time I picked it up she had hung up, and I replayed the message, and the message said she was kidnapped by a man with a knife and here he comes. She was crying hysterical. I just couldn't believe what I was hearing. I had to play it back ten more times to make it sure it was real," Linda confided.

"'Please,' Katie had said, 'I've been kidnapped by a man with a knife. Oh, my God. He's coming back!'"

Who is this John Esposito, the man Katie was with?

"He was a big brother to a lot of children for mothers—that's how they raised their kids—alone. He was trusted by a lot of mothers. He told me that he just turned his back for a second to buy tokens, and she was gone. He had her coat and hat but that was the last he saw of her."

BURIED MEMORIES

I soon learned this was Linda's house, but Katie had a bedroom here. It was a cheerful little room with *101 Dalmatian* bedding and a *Little Mermaid* nightgown folded on the bed. Linda wheeled herself out from behind the table and gestured to the doorway, inviting us to videotape whatever we wanted in the bedroom. It was now clear why she couldn't walk. She was missing a leg.

"Diabetes," she said, noticing my glance. "God-dammed diabetes."

Marilyn was fielding questions in another part of the cramped kitchen, standing so close to an artificial counter-top Christmas tree that I was concerned her cigarette would spark a fire.

"She's smart, she's friendly, but she knows not to speak to strangers. She was brought up that way," Marilyn said, exposing a missing tooth on the bottom. "I don't know what else," she shook her head, "I just know I want my daughter back." Her eyes welled up.

Is it normal that she would call Linda if she needed help?

"The first person she would call is Linda, that's her godmother. She calls her 'Aunt Linda.' Next she would call her grandmother. I don't have a phone, so she would call my next-door neighbor who would get me the message immediately."

What would you say to whoever has Katie?

"Please bring my daughter back. I just want my daughter back." She clenched her eyes shut and a few tears rolled down her ample cheeks.

Ann Butler, Linda's mother, looked ashen as she held one trembling hand to her temple and stared down at the kitchen table, hiding watery red eyes behind thick bifocals. Her nails were adorned with ancient chipped polish, but her lips sported a fresh coat of matte bubblegum pink for the television interview.

"Katie went with Big John, who picked her up, because tomorrow's her birthday, so he picked her up to take her to Toys 'R' Us," Ann said without a breath, "and then he took her to this place over in Nesconset, and that's where everything happened. Katie likes video games and all that. She's a very happy, content little girl," she said, showing the gathered reporters who were crouching and crowding around the kitchen table a picture taken just days earlier on Saturday.

In it, Katie sported a rascally smirk with her arms wrapped around Ann's neck, and their cheeks were pressed together. In the picture, Ann beamed, a proud grand-godmother, a far cry from the visibly shaken woman now sitting before us in the kitchen.

"When she made that phone call, she was hysterical. She was crying, 'A man kidnapped me and he has a knife' and she says—'Oh my God, here he comes'—and she's hysterical crying and then the phone just went dead and that's it—that's the last anybody's heard of her."

Ann was stoic. She stared down. Her fingers did not leave her temple. Reporters asked her if Katie was a smart little girl.

"Yeah, she sure is," she said, raising her brown penciled-in eyebrows, her first sign of expression in the exchange. "John just said he went to get tokens and he just turned around and she was gone."

She bit her upper lip and pressed her fingertips deeper into her temple. "The phone rang and it was Katie on the phone and about twenty minutes later, Big John had called and he said he couldn't find her and he was crying on the phone. He said he couldn't find her and I had spoken to him a second or two. I don't know. All we want to do is know she is all right and have her come back." Ann shook her head and finally put down her trembling hand.

Do you have any indication of where she is?

"Evidently," she said, "it has to be someone she doesn't know. To say 'a *man*...'" She shook her head again, her trembling hand back on her forehead.

And then, in response to a reporter's question about what message she had for the public, Ann looked up from the overflowing ashtray filled with Basic Full Flavor cigarette butts smoked down to the tan filters and looked square into the camera lenses.

"My message would be please, please get in touch with Linda. Linda is very upset; the whole family is very upset. Linda is in a wheelchair, so she can't go running looking for her, so if anyone sees her, please call. That's all I can say," she ended, burying her head in her hand, covering the tears that dropped into the ashtray.

Police, meanwhile, told reporters they were following two trails. There were two men in Katie's life, and both of them were possible suspects.[2] They wouldn't say that publicly, but they didn't have to because attorneys for the two men eagerly informed inquiring reporters.

Facts started to come in from the assignment desk and my ever- buzzing beeper. Sal Inghilleri, the godmother's husband, was already facing first degree sexual abuse charges involving Katie after Marilyn had reported him to police. He had been arrested two months earlier and was due to appear in court in February. In fact, there was a court order forbidding him from coming in contact with Katie, which he had apparently violated just being in the Bay Shore house with Katie. With the child now missing, the cops "have an idea that it may be him," Sidney Siben, Inghilleri's lawyer, volunteered to reporters.

At the same time, Siben's law firm had also just been retained by a new client: John Esposito. The forty-three-year-old contractor had called them that morning, exhausted, saying he needed a lawyer after fielding eighteen hours[3] of police interrogation.

The case was assigned to the senior Siben's much younger nephew, Andrew. Police, the younger Siben told reporters, "tried to convince [Esposito] that he was the one who did it." The cast of characters was growing.

To the throngs of reporters now camped both inside and outside the Inghilleri's Bay Shore cape, it certainly appeared as if police believed Katie had actually been kidnapped. This was no runaway. Public information officers revealed that police operators were receiving a steady stream of Katie "sightings," and uniformed cops and canine units were searching the woods and trash bins surrounding Spaceplex. Eyes were fixed on the frozen ground, scanning for discarded clothing, or worse, a body.

The FBI, which had an agent assigned to the case almost immediately, quickly analyzed the answering machine tape and determined that the voice on the phone was, in fact, Katie's.

At this point everyone seemed cagey, and no one seemed authentically sincere. There were cigarette butts everywhere and the house air was stale and heavy, almost unbearable. Marilyn was sniffling with her eyes closed, and tears were flowing freely.

Outside, on the front stoop, a heavyset, stocky man was taking long, hard drags on his cigarette, blowing puffs of smoke high up above his head. "I'm Sal," he greeted me, raising his bushy salt and pepper eyebrows.

I stopped, got a good look at him, and tried to size him up. He smiled at me, and I thought to myself, did this guy just kill a child? Couldn't be.

What do you think happened to Katie, Sal?

A GIANT

"I don't know nothin'. Who could hurt a little girl?"

I headed to the car and gave Tony the nonverbal universal sign—the head tilt which meant to any good cameraman, *roll*. He fixed his lens on Sal and got images of him kicking a black cat out of the way, and then stamping out a butt on the front stoop.

Our final stop of the day was the nearby home of John Esposito. We shot video of his house at 1416 Saxon Avenue and could see a man with a baseball cap and dark sideburns lead detectives through a stockade fence at the end of the driveway. He scampered to close the gate quickly. As it slammed shut, I could see the sign on the outside of the fence. "Beware of Dog." The man with the baseball cap was Esposito. There was no sign of a dog.

THE HOLE

IT WAS AS THOUGH I was on a date with Big John. He let me ride in the front seat of his Nissan pickup, like a girlfriend. I didn't even have to buckle up. Sometimes he would let me sit on his lap and I would do the steering all by myself.

"Anywhere you want to go?" John asked.

"7-Eleven," I answered and minutes later I had a cola-flavored Slurpee in hand.

I didn't really get nervous until after we left the 7-Eleven. John told me that he wanted to go to Toys "R" Us to pick up a Nintendo game, too, and the Toys "R" Us is completely out of the way from Spaceplex and right around the corner from his house.

I reminded him that he had already bought me a birthday present and said that I didn't want a Nintendo game and only wanted to go to Spaceplex, but he insisted.

"We are going to Toys 'R' Us first."

"Okay," I finally gave in, but added, "then we'll go to Spaceplex afterwards?"

John knew I didn't have my own Nintendo player. I remember saying I just wanted to go to Spaceplex, and I could go play the game some other time, knowing very well that I would never be going to his house again because I wasn't even supposed to be with him in the first place.

Big John had been trying to get me alone for months. Almost every day he would call me at Aunt Linda's when she was taking a nap and ask me to sneak out so he that could buy me a new toy, take me to lunch, or buy me candy. He told me Linda was jealous of our relationship, and I would have to sneak away to play at his house. I was always scared to death to do it—scared of Linda's wrath. She would surely beat me if she found out I was with him, and not there to answer her demands. He would say, "I'll meet you at the corner at noon," and then he'd call when I didn't go and ask me why I didn't show up. I would lie to him and say that Aunt Linda hadn't taken a nap. And he would always say, "Then we'll do it tomorrow."

THE HOLE

That December day, two days before my tenth birthday, was a gray, gloomy day—but not as frigid as it had been. Big John parked his pick-up truck at the end of his driveway—behind the main house—steps from the garage that he converted into his own apartment.

The Nintendo game was upstairs in John's bedroom. I sat on the edge of the bed—pushing the controls, lost in the sounds of the new *Home Alone* game. John was busy in the walk-in games closet. I was sitting on top of the unmade covers, on a bare mattress, playing the game, and I just knew that there was something off. I had played Nintendo so many times in the same place, but there was always my brother or somebody else there. It was never just me, alone with Big John.

He spent some time in the game closet and then went downstairs. When he came back up, his Big John eyes had drained from his face and it was someone I had never seen before. Big John was gone.

And he was no longer wearing his ever-present baseball cap. I knew I was in trouble.

I remember the character in the *Home Alone* game was jumping over something—maybe over a chair or a box. The room was dark—curtains were drawn or the lights were off. The room was cold and the only sound was the repetitive arcade groan of the game.

Home alone. I was a sitting duck. I could feel my cold legs against his shiny mattress and then something even colder—his sandpaper fingertips on my white skinny thighs. I couldn't see him—he was behind me. I could smell his sour breath, warm against my ear.

"I'm not going to hurt you, Katie," he whispered.

And as he spit those seven words into my tiny ear, I knew for certain that there was something very wrong happening to me.

The uneasy feeling in my stomach came first, before his coarse hand tightened around my mouth. I couldn't see his face, but I could feel his other hand grab my waist. He was squeezing my mouth hard and lifting me up with force onto his lap. In those days, my mother used to joke that I wasn't even forty pounds, so my twists of protest barely swayed him.

His fingers made their way under my denim skirt and pushed aside my panties. My memory is hazy here. I know he penetrated me with his fingers for what in my memory was a split second. Or maybe I was so used to it with Sal that I thought, *What is the point in trying to stop him?* I was only

33

nine years old, but that was a place that had been violated many times. I was kicking, trying to get words out, but his tight grip was squeezing away my words, my breath, and my strength.

I was kicking and crying when he carried me down the stairs. I knew that unless he was going to do something bad to me, there was no reason for him to be carrying me downstairs. Nobody was home. His sister-in-law sometimes stayed on the second floor of the main house and I knew that she wasn't there now, so there was nobody that could help me. I knew whatever he wanted to do, he was going to do.

With all that had happened with Sal, a part of me knew there was no use trying to fight.

At the bottom of the stairs, he turned left into his office and dropped me on the floor and slammed the door closed. One thing that I knew about his house was that we were never allowed in his office. That was the one room that kids weren't allowed in, because he worked for himself.

That was another alarm—why the heck were we in his office? There were pillows everywhere, couch pillows scattered on the office floor. As I sat there, I shook silently, tears running out of my eyes.

John said in an icy, unrecognizable voice, "I have something I want to show you." He turned and began removing the baseball caps hanging on hooks inside a wooden bookcase. I knew he had built almost everything in the converted garage apartment himself, including this bookcase built into the office closet. It was filled with wine and travel bottles of gin and rum as well as hats and knickknacks.

John seemed to be unscrewing the silver hooks on either side of the wooden shelves, underneath where the hats had hung. Then, grasping the middle shelf, he gave a tug, and the entire unit of shelves slid on wheels out into the office. It only slid halfway out, and then he had to unlatch something to have it come all the way out, revealing a rectangular hole in the wall where the bookcase had been. I didn't understand.

I was standing there in the office, now sobbing, hyperventilating really, petrified about what he was going to show me. Then, he entered the closet, and I could see him roll up the tan rug, coil it tight, and then roll up a layer of padding, revealing a big square slab of concrete underneath. It looked like it had been cut out of the floor with a frame around it.

John then got a long metal pole from the corner in the closet, a pole with a hook on either end, and attached one end to the clothing bar and the other end to a hook in the center of the concrete slab. He dropped a dumbbell weight onto the slab and started cranking. What was he *doing?*

My heart was beating furiously and I scanned the office for the phone and found the portable on his desk. With John busy cranking inside the closet, I slipped behind the desk and crawled up in a little ball in the opening beneath the desk and held the phone in my hand and pressed the numbers: 9-1-1. And I started talking in a voice I could barely hear myself.

"I'm on Saxon Avenue," I whispered.

I didn't know what town I was in. I didn't know the house number. I didn't really know anything. I was crying. Somebody came on the line.

I must have said it too loud. The feet and blue-jean-clad legs in front of my wildly shaking body made that clear. John reached down and he took his big carpenter hand and yanked the phone away from my ear and slammed the phone into its cradle.

I never saw him coming—I had my eyes closed tight—I could only feel the phone snatched out of my hand. Then, he picked me up and threw me like a rag doll into the closet and raged, "Don't touch that phone again!"

Sharp sticks of pain instantly shot through my shirt and into my back as I realized that I had landed on a wall of exposed nails. Inside the closet was the back of something he had built in his kitchen. He threw me up against it with such force, I was certain that I was bleeding. I was crying hysterically. John went back to work as blood dripped down my back. He finished cranking up the concrete slab, revealing a hole in the floor. It was dark in there. He worked and said nothing. The only sounds were my uncontrollable sobs.

I still don't think he said anything. And if he did, I might have been crying so loud that I didn't hear him. I remember he was crouching in the closet. The closet was built under a staircase, so it had a high ceiling on one side and then it came down on a slant. He stooped over and held me at the edge of the hole.

The concrete slab was now dangling above the opening in the floor, and John moved it to the side and ordered, "Get down the fuckin' hole."

"No, I don't want to. What is it?"

"A bomb shelter," he barked and scooped up my shuddering body, dropping me feet first into the black hole.

"Start crawling," he yelled after me.

It was straight down, too dark to make out a bottom. There were wooden planks for makeshift steps, but they did me no good. I was dropped too hard to make use of them and landed on the cold plywood in a cramped tunnel.

I was in a dark hole. It seemed almost like Alice going down the rabbit hole. I remember when she was falling, it was a cartoon fall, and it took forever. That's how it felt, being dropped down that hole. Just like that.

He was still up in the office, getting ready to climb down, when he shouted again to me to crawl—to where, I had no idea. But I started crawling.

First, John was behind me, and then he maneuvered himself in front of me. Next, I heard drilling, something very noisy and shrill. The drilling went on for a minute or so, and then there was an opening. There was a small room at the end of the tunnel. I could tell right away there was no way out, and I knew that I wasn't going to get out unless he wanted me out.

John made me go in first, and I plopped myself down into the stifling chamber. Then he followed.

I quickly sized up the landscape. It was bleak. There was one square area no bigger than the closet in Mastic Beach, and then elevated off the floor what looked like an enclosed cabinet, not much more than a coffin-sized box, outfitted with a door padlocked shut. The outer room had a toilet in the corner—not hooked up to anything—but with a black plastic garbage bag in the hole. There were two wooden shelves attached to the wall. I could see what looked like a security monitor on one of the shelves.

The room felt like an animal cage. There was yellow soundproofing and cork covering the walls. John opened the padlock hanging on the small door leading to the enclosed box.

"Get in."

Terrified, I reached up and climbed in. There was a thin, blue-striped camping mattress and a pillow, blankets and a television sitting on a shelf on the narrow wall. I noticed that there was a *101 Dalmatians* nightgown on the bedding. I asked Big John if it was for me, and he said yes. I then asked him if he had been planning to kidnap me, and he answered, "Yes, for a while now."

"When am I going to go home?" I pleaded.

THE HOLE

"This is your new home now," he stated. "You are going to live here."

John said he was going back upstairs to get me more blankets and left me alone for a few minutes. In that box alone, I was scared to death. He closed the door, but didn't lock it. He came back in minutes with the blankets, a can of soda and some candy bars and told me that I was going to make a recording. He pulled me down from the coffin-box and took a small tape recorder out of his back pocket and recited exactly what he wanted me to say: "I have been kidnapped by a man with a knife, and here he comes now."

I had to practice it several times and then he said he was going upstairs and he wanted me to record it without him in the room. I did what he asked, crouching down as I spoke. And then, at the end, in a very soft voice, after a long pause, I whispered into the recorder, "Big John took me! He has me at his house!"

I was afraid he was in the tunnel listening, but when he came back he didn't let on that he had heard a thing. I thought it had worked. But then, he grabbed the tape recorder and hit Play. When he got to the end, he looked at me for a moment, and without a beat, smacked me in the face. I was stunned. He had never before struck me. This was a completely different John than I had ever known. This time he stood directly over me and ordered me to record it again.

"I've been kidnapped by a man with a knife, and oh God, here he comes."

Seeming satisfied with my acting skills this time, John then ordered me up into the small box with the wafer-thin mattress, a pillow and blankets. He told me he was going to play the tape for Aunt Linda, and I asked him why.

"Because you're going to be staying here for a while."

"How long are you going to keep me, John?"

"Forever."

His next request scared me more than I had been all day. Big John told me to pose for a picture and make it look like I was sleeping. I asked him why in the world he wanted to take a picture like that.

"So that the police will not look for you because they will think that you are dead."

I refused. He again ordered me into the box.

The TV inside the box was on, flickering shadows on the egg-crated walls. He slammed the small door closed and I could hear him securing the door, but wasn't sure with what. Then I could hear the churning of the drill again.

When I heard the drill stop squealing, I knew he had gone back upstairs. The sobs had subsided now and I was focused solely on getting out. I positioned myself with my feet on the door, bracing my back, kicking at the wall in front of me, not knowing what was holding me in.

I kicked and pushed and punched and kicked some more in the flickering light of silent TV newscasts. I kicked for what seemed like forever, with my back pressed as hard as I could to the back wall of the box I was locked in. It may have been hours. It may have been a whole night. Or a day. I have no idea. There was no light in my cage, just the flickering television.

The door finally broke open. When I fell out into the bigger room, I could see that John had used a two-by-four piece of lumber to wedge the door closed. I had snapped it in half.

I was in survival mode. I knew that I needed to somehow survive and get out of there. Trying to figure out my surroundings, I scanned the room for what I could use for my escape, but there wasn't anything. I hid in the shadows underneath the little box, hoping that when John came back, I could run out and overtake him.

Funny, now that I think of it. My plan was short lived. As soon as John stepped back into the chamber, his eyes landed on the broken two by four—and then me, quaking in the shadows.

"I see you," he said apologetically.

He was not angry now. He was the Big John I knew again and Sadistic John was gone. He seemed nervous, preoccupied. I asked him what had taken him so long and he told me that he went to Spaceplex to "look for me." While there, he asked the manager to call the police. He then used the tape that we had made to call Aunt Linda and leave her a message.

I told Big John that I wanted to go to sleep, so he left me for the night—if it were night. I didn't sleep of course. I only said that to get rid of him.

I remember everything, but in no particular order. Like the television images flickering on the soundproofed walls in the box where I lay. I can still see flashes of what happened in that dungeon, but have no idea which day they occurred. With no windows, no light, no meals, no hope, it was one endless, sickening day.

Big John's bed. I knew for certain that there was something really very wrong happening to me. (Suffolk County Crime Lab)

Above:

Big John removed the hats and unscrewed the silver hooks on either side of the wooden shelves then slid the cabinet on wheels out into the office. I didn't understand. (Suffolk County Crime Lab)

Right:

*Big John got a long metal pole and attached one end to the clothing bar and the other end to a hook. He dropped a dumbbell weight on the slab and started cranking. What was he **doing**? (Suffolk County Crime Lab)*

THE HOLE

The opening to the hole in Big John's closet that led to the cell where he locked me for 17 days. (Suffolk County Crime Lab)

UNUSUAL SUSPECTS

M Y TELEVISION REPORTING DAYS were often punctuated by reporting to my parents' house at day's end, where Dad sat on the other side of the television, a chunk of the left hemisphere of his brain missing after neurosurgery. Having looked up "astrocytoma" in my husband's *Harrison's Principles of Internal Medicine*, I found a survival rate of thirty percent for his sort of brain tumor. It was a devastating number. Dad turned to me one day and said, "Shorty, you better hurry up and have children." I didn't comply fast enough. My first child was named in my father's memory.

Dad was the original news hound, and he never lost that faculty. He always had his face buried behind *The New York Times,* sections scattered all over the den's red shag carpet, his fingers smudged with newsprint. If news junkie is an inherited trait, my addiction surely came from him. He wanted to know every detail of the stories I was covering, and he couldn't get enough of the Katie Beers case. He and everyone else.

A swarm of Suffolk police officers camped outside Spaceplex in Nesconset, a stucco behemoth of a building that blended into the rainy winter landscape. Inside, the cavernous play space glowed with disco lights. Co-owner and general manager Gary Tuzzalo was granting interviews one at a time. He was practiced, but his curt answers and focused gray eyes couldn't hide the tell-tale look of panic over the thought of a missing child in his arcade.

"It's hard; we see hundreds of families in here a day. It's hard to pick out one face."

Did anyone see a child taken from here with a stranger?

"We have private security, we have staff, and nothing strange seemed to happen."

Did you see John Esposito?

"He went to one of the mangers and said 'I can't find a little girl,' so we began paging her, and when she didn't answer the page, the police were called."

Spaceplex was a very noisy place. Maddeningly noisy. Midnight blue walls were painted with tempera cartoon characters, and in the vast space below them, kids held tight to their daddies' hands, nibbled on salted pretzels, took aim into skee-ball machines, and crashed blinking bumper cars into one another. It was business as usual in the frenetic space, except for the reporters talking to tuxedo-shirted employees, scribbling down notes on spiral steno pads.

Outside, what looked like a class of police cadets searched in and under big blue dumpsters and walked through the leafless forest around the building, eyes fixed downward, scouring the ground for clues.

Randy Jaret, a spokesman for the Suffolk Police Department, agreed to an on-camera interview. He wore plainclothes and spoke in plain English.

Is John Esposito cooperating?

"We have been talking to Mr. Esposito—of course we would want to talk with the last person she was with—and yes, he's cooperating."

What has he told you?

"He has told us they had been to Spaceplex, they became separated when she went to get some coins, he couldn't find her, he searched the premises for her, and when he couldn't find her, he had her paged and then they called police."

You have to admit, the phone call, 'a man has me and is coming at me with a knife.' Kinda strange?

"We are in possession of the tape from the godmother and we are verifying its authenticity."

Sound as if she is being put up to making that call?

"Can't comment at this point."

The next interview was less predictable. Sal was sweating profusely, even before cameras started rolling. It was the regular cast of characters crowded into Siben & Siben's conference room. The Long Island press corps was a tight group—the same faces for years, and we all knew the pecking order: who would get the first question in, who would dwell on the obvious, who would ask the uncomfortable but necessary question, and who would have the last word.

Even the attorneys in the room were familiar faces. Andrew Siben and his uncle Sidney seemed to have cornered the market on odd-ball Long Island stories that were television news magnets. In fact, Sidney Siben made no apologies as a self-proclaimed publicity hound.[4]

Salvatore Inghilleri was the only unknown entity in the room, but was perfectly cast in the part of the "dirty Uncle Albert." Life's wardrobe department certainly didn't have to struggle to outfit him. Wearing a fake leather "Member's Only" jacket, complete with the requisite aviator sunglasses hanging precariously from the front pocket, he squirmed uneasily while folding his black finger-nailed hands in front of his huge frame. His neck hung heavily from his indistinguishable chin, and his wiry, wavy hair was full of improbable gray for his thirty-nine years.

Do you have any doubts about the sincerity of Katie's mother, Marilyn?

"Yeah. She's a phony, anyone can see past those tears."

You don't think she's distraught?

"I know this girl a very long time. I know her inside out like a book, and those are phony tears."

Why?

"Why? Maybe she has a sick mind. I don't know."

Sal had told a parade of reporters that Marilyn had abandoned "the kid" when she was two months "to, you know, my wife because she didn't want to raise the kid, then her mother decided to come back into the picture."

The two women, Sal said, were now bitterly feuding over custody, and Marilyn was on the warpath. The battle also seemed to cost Katie any semblance of a normal education. Her attendance in school was spotty as she was moved from one school district to the other, and it was unclear to school officials in both Bay Shore and Mastic Beach where Katie was permanently residing.

The tensions between the families also muddied the apparent sex abuse case against Sal. It was Marilyn who had filed charges against Sal, alleging he molested Katie.

Have you been served with an order of protection?

It had not taken reporters long to dig up public documents that showed the order of protection and felony sex abuse charges against Sal. Sources said he confessed to molesting the now-missing girl, and while awaiting trial, he was barred from being anywhere near Katie.

Andrew Siben quickly jumped in before Sal could answer, and interjected, "It's on file. In the normal course, whenever there is a complaint by an infant, Child Protective Services has a duty to investigate."

"We are not going to comment on an order of protection," added the elder Siben.

Sal, can you go over again why you think the mother's tears are false tears?

"I don't truly believe that she don't really have no love for that child," Sal responded, completely unaware he just made no sense.

If you were Katie, would you want to run away from the situation?

Sal didn't answer that one, but chimed in again when someone asked what his dispute was about with Marilyn. "It wasn't a domestic situation. It's financial. I will say that."

A reporter then asked the Sibens about their simultaneous representation of both John Esposito and Sal Inghilleri. It wasn't lost on the press corps that both men were suspects in the disappearance of Katie Beers, with possible conflicting interests.

Sidney was dressed in a pin-striped suit, contrasting striped shirt and impossibly patterned tie. From behind his enormous black square-framed glasses, he answered authoritatively, "I can tell you they are free to go; they are suspects like everyone else.

"I think it's fair to say that until they find the girl, dead or alive, they will never be able to prove our clients did it, John or Sal."

Andrew, clad in a different variation of pin stripes upon pin stripes, added with conviction, "John and Sal both are concerned about the well-being of the child. They both want to see her safely returned." He nodded his head for emphasis.

Then, Sal seemed to speak out of turn. Andrew was too late to reel in his client this time. The words were coming out of Sal's sweat-beaded lips. "Let me say this again—and let me say this *explicively*. The man, John Esposito, is," he paused, "I have no problem with him and I don't think he is capable of doing any horrendous act like this. Yous may want to press him in the papers, but that's my opinion."

He couldn't be stopped.

"Never heard of him doing anything to a twelve-year-old child. Never heard that till yesterday on the news."

Someone, a reporter this time, changed the subject back to Marilyn.

"The only reason I ever tolerated her is because of my wife. I never really cared for Marilyn—I had her number from years ago and I always told my wife, 'You be careful of that woman because one of these days, she's gonna turn around and backstab ya.' Howeva yous fellas wanna write it up in the papers fine, I have nothing to hide."

Sensing his client's bravado beginning to swirl anew, the senior Siben then announced with a booming voice, "Let's bring this to a close. Two questions: Do you know where Katie is now?" he asked, playing journalist.

"No, I have no idea," Sal said innocently.

"Did you have anything to do directly or indirectly with her kidnapping?"

"No, sir."

The press, though, wasn't taking their direction.

What do you think happened to her?

"It's a mystery. It's a mystery."

So you think any of this has anything to do with her disappearance—this conflict between you and Ms. Beers?

He stammered, "N...no, it don't have nothing to do with her dissapperance."

John Esposito's house on Saxon Avenue was next on the list of venues to shoot for the evening newscast. The house was peculiar, as its design was a patchwork of brick, split cedar, and partially painted shingles. The apparent work of an indecisive builder, it was a collage of mismatched architectural features such as columns and port windows. The builder's work was only further muddled by the homeowners, who had added in the front yard a small statue of Saint Francis, inexplicably paired with a plastic flamingo and stone lions. If these were intended to convey class, they failed miserably.

Is Mr. Esposito here?

Surprisingly, a plainclothes cop at the door spoke without hesitation, even though he seemed aware the camera was rolling.

"Mr. Esposito is here, but he wishes no contact with the press." From the front door, dead ferns were visible on the sills inside the picture windows. Tony and I noticed a brown shingled two-story garage in the back, behind the main house and shot video of it, but didn't pay it much attention.

Neighbors back at the Inghilleri house, however, were offering a view of the missing girl's life that was more difficult to ignore. Mike Bergo, a heavyset young man in a Georgetown University sweatshirt, was one of the first to give reporters reason to believe that all was not well in Katie's world—even before she disappeared.

"Katie's a great kid, a really good kid. The family, though, I do *not* like them," he said, gesturing to the Inghilleri house.

"Screaming, yelling all hours of the night. It's like constant; cops are here *all* the time." Such bluntness is rare on camera. People usually don't like to offend their neighbors, but rules of civility did not seem to apply in this neighborhood.

What do you think happened to Katie?

"I don't know—I thought she had run away at first, too, but I heard about the phone call, so I have doubts. Katie," he added, gazing directly into the camera lens, "I hope you are alright."

You think she'd want to run away from this family?

He didn't hesitate: "*I* would."

Did Sal abuse her?

"She's real quiet when we discuss Sal. I just hope they find Katie—I really do."

The still images of Katie provided by Linda defied the picture that was being painted by those who knew her. In the photographs, Katie looked neat, clean, happy. In one, she wore a black dress with a floral patterned collar. The smile looked authentic. Where in the world could this little girl be? I felt it gnawing at me like few stories ever had. Each day that passed without a sign of a missing child was another day closer to an anguished ending I didn't want to have to write.

Sal Inghilleri, the husband of Katie's godmother Linda. He is holding a picture of Katie in the "Blossom" hat. (AP Wide World Photos/Mike Alexander)

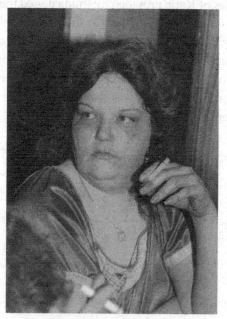

Right: Linda Inghilleri, Katie's godmother. (Courtesy Newsday)

SUBMISSION

BIG JOHN CAME DOWN to my cage regularly to see how I was doing. It seemed like once a day. But without a window, without a clock, without sleep, I just couldn't keep track of time.

"Is there anything I can do to make you more comfortable?"

At these moments, he was the gentleman I had known my whole life. I asked him for another blanket. I was shivering.

"You are going to have to get back up in here," he said sheepishly, tapping his dirty nails on the coffin-sized box on the wall.

"Pleeezzee Big John," I begged, "let me stay in here so I can move!" I could just barely sit up in the coffin-box, and I couldn't stand up without crouching over.

When I was in there earlier, I noticed that there was a chain attached to the wall with a padlock on it. There was also some sort of contraption in the area my head would go. It seemed to me that it might be some sort of soundproofing box with a hole on one side for a neck. It was terrifying. What could that possibly be for?

There were also handcuffs attached to the walls where my hands would lay. When Big John was gone, and I was certain he was gone, I scanned my surroundings for any way out. A television monitor in the corner of the room showed video of the outside of John's house; it was aimed at the driveway. Some keys sat on the shelf to the right of the monitor. I stood on a milk crate and reached for the key, then climbed up into the coffin-box and hid the key under my pillow. That's when I heard the drill again. I knew I had seconds to jump down out of the box and appear as if I hadn't moved. He dropped a blanket along with a change of clothes in the box.

"Ever have sex before?" he blurted out.

I tried to hide my concern about why he wanted to know, but told him a little of what happened with Sal. I had never told him before.

"Oh, so you are experienced!" He seemed excited by the notion.

At first, I didn't know if I had said the wrong thing, and then, I was sure I had. Big John told me to undress and change into the clothes he bought for me—a nightgown with boy's underwear.

"I'll change later," I said.

Big John didn't like that, and he wasn't about to argue. He grabbed me by the arm and took my clothes off for me, telling me he was going to "pleasure" me.

He ordered me to stand up on the milk crate. I don't know why. Maybe he wanted to elevate me. He pulled down my underwear and I remember feeling pain when his finger nail scraped inside of me. I remember thinking how disgusting he was for then putting his finger in his mouth with a very happy look on his face. After a few minutes of John "pleasuring" me, he announced, as if he had suddenly remembered something, that I should lie still on the floor naked, making it look as if I were dead. He said he would take a picture and leave it for the cops anonymously, and that way they would stop looking for me.

This meant one thing to me: John was trying to kill me.

"No way," I snapped back.

Big John backed off. "Okay, Katie, we'll do it another day."

After this, I rarely slept. Adrenaline. I was sure that if I slept, he could come down one time, and that one time that I didn't hear the drill, he would kill me.

He also saved the worst for another day. I'm not sure which day it was. My sense of time was off. It must have been a few days in. But my sense *is* quite clear that it happened more than once. The memories, though, are together as one.

John would arrive in the chamber with a blank look on his face. His eyes would never meet mine. Nice John was gone and in his place, Sadistic John. That's when my breathing would begin to quicken and my stomach turn. He made me lay down on the floor in the bigger room. As I stared at the cork-covered ceiling, I think my arms were up, and I thought about how gross it was to be lying on that dirty floor and how I just wanted to get it over with. Get it done. Whatever I needed to get it done quickly, I would do.

Fighting, I figured, would only make it take longer. Fighting with him might arouse him more, he might like it better. Maybe if he realized I would just submit, maybe he wouldn't want to do it anymore.

That made no difference. Big John had come with a purpose and would proceed to use my tiny body until he was finished and drained and I was covered in his putrid sweat and fluids. He undressed me and laid me on the floor. He got on top of me. He was a super skinny man. I was going from one extreme to another. From Sal a fat slob, to this, skin and bones. It disgusted me.

I didn't look at him. I kept my eyes open to be aware of what was happening around me. I focused on the ceiling. I just wanted to know when he was done and I was off the hook.

It seemed to take a long time, and then there was silence. Big John got himself dressed, locked me back in the little box, chaining me around the neck. He tried to use the handcuffs, too, but my skinny hands slipped through the cuffs. He left with a few words about how he'd be back soon with more food or anything else I needed.

There were times he would come and rape me and other times he would bring me a toy from his toy closet and food. Looking back, I would describe it as a split personality. Sometimes he would transform while he was there, in front of me. He would come bring me a toy or juice and then he would rape me.

I couldn't believe it. I couldn't believe Big John was doing this to me.

BIG BROTHER JOHN

I N THE DAYS THAT FOLLOWED, there was no morning debate surrounding my assignment. The child's disappearance was front page news, a "must cover." Wednesday, December 30, was a particularly poignant day. Katie would be turning ten years old, *if* she were still alive.

I knocked on the Inghilleris' wooden front door again. The Mylar sign was still hanging, as were Christmas lights. An inflatable snow man stood on the front stoop. Yellow ribbons were now tied and strewn haphazardly on the bare branches of trees and shrubs around the front of the house.

Sal was getting out of a beaten-up sedan with his aviator glasses dangling from his mouth. Before I could even ask for Linda, he garbled something about her being in the bathroom. I knocked anyway, and a young woman with a Russian accent and cigarette smoke billowing out from behind her opened the door only wide enough to say bluntly, "We don't want to talk to anyone." She then shut the door with a creak.

I pressed the issue, literally pressing my cheek against the door. "Well, maybe Linda would want to know what we know—that there are reports of sightings upstate."

I had no idea if the reports were true, but I had a New York State Police report in my hand indicating that a girl fitting Katie's description had been seen in the Hyde Park vicinity one hundred miles from the arcade. The girl was seen "in the company of two men." The door remained closed, but I remained determined.

"Linda?" I spoke into the door. I could hear a slide lock engage on the other side.

Undeterred, Tony and I headed to West Islip, where Katie was born and spent most of her life. We videotaped the outside of the house on Higbie Drive and walked across the street to a strip mall. The Q.T. Laundromat advertised free coffee and tea in the window alongside a "Missing Child" flyer with Katie's picture on it. Inside, I found a long row of industrial-sized washers and dryers lining the walls, and Trudy, a woman of a certain age wearing a royal blue sweat suit and an abundance of thick gold chains around her neck.

BIG BROTHER JOHN

Trudy also had thick black eyeliner and wiry strands of gray peeking out amongst her long auburn hair. She was a colorful sight who gladly answered reporters' questions. We were not the only crew there, and microphones were propped before her weathered, but pleasant face.

"She came in here for a number of years and did all the house chores for her family." Trudy said.

She painted a bleak picture of little Katie's life. "She would get up early and do the chores for her family, get them breakfast. She didn't have any time for herself. She was a little girl growing up too soon—didn't have any friends of her own."

Trudy had some good grains of information for reporters desperate for details. She didn't know Katie's parents well. No, actually she didn't know them at all. She understood the people who lived opposite them were elderly folks who always wondered why Katie looked so shabby—and so terribly skinny.

"She'd come in with a little handbag with her change. And sit right there. I'd help her with the wash. She'd always have a big load—first for her mother and then her grandmother. I felt sorry for her.

"She used to drink coffee. I'd ask, 'Katie, why aren't you playing with your friends?' She would say, 'I don't have any friends.' Probably 'cause the house was filthy."

The strip mall housed an eclectic assortment of Suffolk county essentials: a beauty salon, a delicatessen, a stationery store, pizza parlor, porcelain doll store, a dry cleaner, a florist, and a paintball supply store.

I went door-to-door with cameraman in tow. Tony didn't have an impatient bone in his body. A perfectionist for just the right lighting and camera angle, he was tireless. He and I were young and eager and knew we needed a scoop in the story that was putting our Long Island beat on the national map.

One by one, merchants told us of a lonely little unkempt girl with no shoes or coat and yellow teeth, a little girl the neighborhood kids called "Dirty Katie."

J&B Stationery Store also had a missing child poster in the window, offering a ten thousand dollar reward for information about Katie's whereabouts. The owner, Bob, readily spoke to reporters from behind a counter boxed in with cigarette cartons and lottery tickets.

"She was probably six, maybe seven years old," Bob said with a shrug. "She would come in to buy essentials for her family at six in the morning, like newspapers and birthday cards."

Doesn't that strike you as odd?

"Of course, that's just the way the family was. There was one time my daughter had a confrontation with Linda. She told us to mind our own business. Katie was in here buying birthday cards and was too young to read them. So she would go home and show them to Linda and Linda didn't like them. So Katie would bring them back, and we'd have to exchange them. So my daughter said something."

So you mean she spoke to Linda about Katie's care and welfare?

"Yeah! And she was told to mind her own business…so what can you do from there?" There was an awkward pause. "I mean, my daughter, Dawn, was very concerned about Katie. Katie would come in here all the time and stay sometimes for hours. She was dirty, had knots in her hair. Dawn would try to get the knots out. It was a bad situation. Her brother, too, he'd stay here. Help out, for hours."

The stories got worse with each store owner. Mary Ann, with big red hair and matching nails, said Katie would always wander in to Beauty Corner, her hair salon, like a lost dog.

"She was always underdressed, never had the right clothes on, no shoes, no hat, never right for the weather. It could be freezing cold, it could be pouring rain, she'd come in, she'd look like a little shaggy dog," she said, raising her hands for emphasis. "She was a child who you'd say, how can she be out like this? I would go to the door, watch her go across the street—tell her, 'Make sure you go right home,' that nobody picks her up. You wouldn't have a little child walk around like this. She was only three, four years old like this!"

How would you describe her hygiene?

"She wasn't a clean child. We wanted to take her home to clean her, to give her a bath. I just hope that she is all right wherever she is," she said with a glazed look. "My husband said to me, 'You know how the child was—how come you never said anything?' I said, I don't know. I mean, I have children, I have grandchildren. I really feel very bad."

For a dog, someone would have called the pound. For Katie, no one knew what to do. The story was beginning to sound like Little Orphan Annie and Miss Hannigan, but *gee whiskers*, there was no Daddy Warbucks coming to the rescue. The utter lack of response to what seemed like an obviously neglected child was mind-boggling.

We were on a roll, but we knew that we had more essential ground to cover. Katie's mother lived twenty-seven miles east in Mastic Beach, and we had to make a quick pass to see if anyone was talking.

The house on the corner of Mill Drive and Pineway Avenue looked like a sorry place to call home. It was a typical one-story Suffolk ranch, except this one was falling apart. Tan, peeling shingles and some patched-up elevated windows made it an eyesore, even in a stretch of slightly less dilapidated homes. There were none of the ornamental plantings that adorn the front of even the most modest suburban residences. The white garage door had gaping holes in it, as if someone had taken a baseball bat to the wooden panels, or perhaps had used it as target practice with a BB gun. The front stoop was cement, with no effort to dress up the undeniable fact that this place was a dump.

But dressed up like a Metallica band member was Katie's sixteen-year-old half-brother, John Beers, who was speaking to reporters next to an overturned wheelbarrow and ladder on the cracked asphalt driveway.

When Tony and I pulled up, the adrenaline kicked in. Little John, as his family called him, was already busy fielding questions from a small pack of reporters in the driveway. We sped up and squeezed ourselves into the tight semicircle of press to catch up. Little John sported all black—a black studded leather jacket, black sneakers and black jeans. The requisite mullet stuck out under his black KISS baseball cap with a black cat iron-on in the back. As he spoke, he exposed chipped front teeth.

By the time I managed to get the microphone in front of his mouth, all that came out was, "I'm outta here." He stepped on a cigarette butt and strutted away.

What? I called after him, introducing myself.

"Get it from them," he said with his back to me, gesturing to the crowd of media that was packing away tape recorders and coiling up cables. It happens to all of us eventually. But missing a big "get" like this, the brother of a kidnap victim, stung badly.

"Don't worry," said one of my competitors snidely. "You didn't miss much. He just admitted he's been molested by Esposito."

———————

The conference room was cramped and cameramen were jockeying for positions in the center for a head-on shot, rather than a profile. But it was futile in such tight quarters. Any position was better than nothing. More than a dozen microphones created a tangle of wires and station logos in front of an obviously uncomfortable and quivering John Esposito, who was flanked by the two Siben attorneys. Andrew decisively slid the collection of mics his way.

"He has fully cooperated with the investigation. His sole concern is that the child is returned safely," he said, impassively.

It was their idea to have John Esposito face the media, and they had called the news conference, even though police had been telling reporters, on background, that the mild-mannered home improvement contractor had a criminal record.

John had been arrested back in 1977, fifteen years earlier, accused of trying to pull a twelve-year-old boy he knew into a car at a local shopping mall. He copped a plea to the lesser charge of misdemeanor, and details of the case were sealed.

There were other troubling allegations. The previous December, Marilyn Beers had called the Big Brothers/Big Sisters Organization of Suffolk County, worried that John, who was spending weekends with her son for years, might be molesting him.[5]

John Esposito, the organization's director told reporters, was never a member, but withdrew an application four years earlier during the rigorous screening phase, after trying to pin the attempted abduction of the twelve-year-old on his twin brother, Ronald. John Esposito, the director said, tried to make it look as if it were a mix–up, and that it had been his twin brother who was arrested.

The director was concerned enough to contact Suffolk police, he said, because John might have been posting ads on local supermarket bulletin boards and in the *Pennysaver*, trying to pass himself off as an official "Big Brother."

I am a Long Island Big Brother. I am doing it on the side. If you have a son who you think needs a man's influence, I may

*be able to volunteer my time. Every boy needs a man in his
life. A person of good character who he can trust and respect.
I have been a big brother for over ten years. I have character
references.*

The bulletin board ads were neatly handwritten and signed "J.E.,"
offering a phone number for contact purposes. John denied posting the
cards and the police investigation into allegations he had molested "Little"
John went nowhere.

Why then, after Suffolk police had been flagged that John was a
potential threat to children, were his attorneys serving him up for grilling
by the media in a missing child case?

None of this seemed to shake the Sibens. They invited news coverage
and counted on a huge turnout. We didn't disappoint.

What they may not have counted on was John Esposito breaking down
in sloppy tears as the cameras were rolling. He told reporters that he had
known Katie since she was a baby, met her through his sister-in-law, Joan.
He had been to the Spaceplex arcade three previous times and he and Katie
always spent time together. She would run and hug him whenever he came
to pick her up. She called him "Big John."

Reporters, keenly aware of the golden opportunity to question a
"person of interest," dug in. A cacophony of questions was hurled at the
pallid John.

When did you see Katie last?

Why would you leave her alone at the arcade?

Were you ever accused of sexual abuse?

John, wearing a blue sweater, black vest and a pained look on his
face, stared down at the table as he spoke. He said Katie had called him
on Sunday, saying she'd saved a piece of birthday cake for him from her
party. Then, he said, she begged him to visit her on Monday.

"Can you pick me up today? Can we do anything?" John said he
remembered Katie pleading.

He said he picked her up at one o'clock in the afternoon, took her to
a toy store, where he bought her a troll doll for her birthday and a *Home
Alone* video game, then to a 7-Eleven because Katie wanted a Slurpee, and
stopped by his house for a little while to try out the video game. He said

they didn't like it, so they decided to go to Spaceplex.

There, he said, he didn't hesitate to send Katie off by herself to get tokens with a five dollar bill while he played pinball. After a few minutes, he added, as if he had already explained it *ad nauseum*, he couldn't find her.

"The last time I seen her, I gave her five dollars and she was walking toward the machine. Then after a while, I started gettin' scared, where is she?"

If he was lying, it was impressive. His horseshoe-shaped dark hair and gray-tipped wisps of sideburns framed an anguished look on his face, which appeared to be one question away from actual tears. So reporters pressed on.

"I was gettin' scared. I couldn't find her. It's a big place. I'm going crazy looking all over. Then I went to security. 'Could you page Katie Beers?' They did it about three times." The tears were flowing now.

He said he started frantically searching and was then paged to the arcade office, where he was put on the phone with Linda Inghilleri and told that Katie had left a message saying she was kidnapped.

"I just want to do everything I can to find her," he said, his forehead etched with deep lines of despair.

"If you heard the tape," he said through sobs, "you'd know it was her. She said, 'Somebody kidnapped me, a man, a man with a knife kidnapped me.'"

Sidney Siben chimed in. "If it was him," he said, pointing to his now trembling client, "she'd say, '*John* kidnapped me.'"

Police had confirmed that Esposito had indeed been to Spaceplex, but no one in the cavernous arcade recalled ever seeing Katie.

COURTSHIP

JOHN TRIED TO MAKE me his partner in crime. He politely requested that I make as much noise as possible while he listened for me upstairs. He said he wanted to make sure the cops wouldn't hear me if they should come. While he made his way upstairs, I was trying to figure out how I could trick him into thinking that I was making noise, but not actually do it. A Playschool baby monitor sat on the wooden shelf in the outer room—below the video monitor. It was always on and I knew it was connected to the upstairs, but because I couldn't hear John, I assumed he could hear me. If he could hear what I was doing when he got upstairs, I figured I better make some noise.

I turned the baby monitor all the way down on my end and yelled directly into it. I made sure that I didn't make enough noise for him to hear me upstairs without the monitor. I held back. After a few minutes of this controlled, pseudo-yelling, the drill groaned and the door crashed open.

"Did you do it, did you make noise?" he anxiously asked.

"Top of my lungs."

"Good."

He believed me. I was hoping the sound test would pay off, if police ever came.

They finally did.

Maybe it was day two or three, I can't be sure. But suddenly, the cops showed up at Big John's house. I was in the outer room, having let myself out of the cage above with the secret key I had hidden under the pillow. Big John had chained my neck to the wall before he last left, pointless, I thought, because I wasn't going anywhere. But I snuck out and suddenly, I saw the cops walking up the driveway on the closed-circuit monitor. Finally, police!

As soon as I saw the cops on the monitor, I just started screaming—this time truly at the top of my lungs. Maybe the dungeon was not soundproof. I could hear the cops upstairs talking to Big John—so maybe, just maybe, they could hear me. I yelled and banged. Then, I remembered the baby monitor! I yelled as loud as my vocal chords could stand—screaming that made my hands shake and my head ache.

One voice asked Big John if he remembered anyone talking or looking at me at Spaceplex. I could hear their conversation in muffled tones. How was that possible? Why can't they hear me?

Then I realized, and I went limp. It must have been when I was chained up in the box. John had reversed the baby monitor. Now the sounds upstairs could be heard in the dungeon and nothing could be heard of my voice beyond the egg-crated walls. I don't know when he made the switch, but the realization was shattering.

Big John told the cop that he remembered a man watching me at the arcade, but didn't think anything of it until just then. And as they talked upstairs in the house just above me, downstairs I continued to scream my lungs out.

"I'm downstairs. Go into the office. I am down here."

Over and over again, until my voice was lost.

I screamed, "Help me!!!!"

I screamed, "I'm HEEERE!"

I yelled and screamed and begged and hit the monitor, "Pleeeaaaseee! I'm hhhheeeere!!"

I collapsed in exhaustion as I watched the cops walk away, down the long driveway, get into their cruisers, and drive away. No one heard me. Grave disappointment came over me. It was fear to my core. I knew, at this moment, that I wouldn't be found.

When Big John returned, I cried.

"No!" I sobbed. "How will I go to school? How will I learn things?"

"I'm gonna keep you down here forever until people forget about you. They'll forget."

"What about MY life? MY future," I demanded. "Like going to college and getting married and having children and having a normal adult life? WHAT ABOUT THAT?"

"You'll marry me. You'll have children with me. You won't have to go to college 'cuz I'll take care of you, Katie, forever."

He would try to muster a smile at these times. His transparent attempts at courtship made me even sicker.

I told Big John that if he kept me in the dungeon forever, I would not be a normal child. I told him that if he let me go, I would protect him; no one would ever have to know what happened to me. I would tell the cops and my family that I had run away because of Sal.

I told Big John that he could let me out of his house in the middle of the night, and I would run through the woods to the highway and no one would ever know that he kidnapped me. After he let me go, I would stay in his life. I would come visit him all of the time.

Hundreds of times, I told John I loved him, that I cared about him, but only if he released me. I thought it would soften him, make him pity me and let me go.

"I love you, too, Katie. That's why you're here. I took you to protect you," he said.

"To protect me? How am I ever gonna grow up living down here, locked away in this box?" I asked so many times, I lost count.

"I'll teach you everything you need to know. You don't need anyone else. I'm the only friend you'll ever need, Katie," he said.

"You can let me out the back door! I'll run far away from the house and I won't stop until I'm miles away and then I'll call for help. Big John pleeeaaase—I wanna go home!"

"You're not going anywhere, Katie—you're staying here with me forever. Maybe when the cops stop looking for you, you can live upstairs with me."

"But I want to have kids. What am I gonna do about having children?"

"You'll have kids with me."

This thought repulsed me, and this conversation was repeated over and over.

I had been held captive my whole life. I wanted to be free. I was a maid to Linda, a sex slave to Sal, and now a prisoner of Big John. I had never felt sorry for myself until that moment.

No attempts at reasoning or psychology with Big John seemed to make a bit of difference. I tried every personality, every attitude I could think of. I tried being nice, devil's advocate, mean. Maybe if I were mean, he wouldn't like me anymore and would let me go. I even kicked him once, and he hit me across the face. The questions that I posed seemed to make no impression on him. He had an answer for everything, and he was very focused on one thing. During this entire time, I remember Big John "pleasing" me regularly. Maybe it was every day.

Day three, or so it seemed, I may have dozed off for a minute or two. I woke up to the sound of a news anchor and a sad realization.

"Good morning. It's Wednesday, December thirtieth, nineteen ninety-two," the newscaster said in a perky voice. I'd missed my birthday. I'd missed my tenth birthday. I cried over and over again.

My picture was on every newscast, every hour. So was Marilyn's, lying on what looked like a child's bed, decorated in *101 Dalmatians* bedding, holding a pillow and crying. The news report said that the room was in Aunt Linda's house, and that it was my room.

My room at Aunt Linda's consisted of one of those little chairs that flips out into a really small bed with a hamper. I don't remember having toys in the room—I didn't have many toys at all. This new room looked like the Disney catalogue. It had a beautiful day bed with a Dalmatians comforter, shaped pillows, curtains, an area rug, and lots of toys.

This room was not mine. It was a fabrication. And yet on the news report, Aunt Linda was telling the reporter how sad she was that I was missing and she wanted me home.

On this birthday, Big John told me that when I turned eighteen, he would give me his red and black Camaro. And he would give me one hundred dollars for every day that he kept me. I would be rich by the time I was all grown up.

Big John's main house and the converted garage behind it. I was hidden in a bunker beneath the garage and had no idea police were located in the front house for surveillance. (Suffolk County Crime Lab)

The coffin-sized box where John chained me within the bunker. "This is your new home," John told me. "You are going to live here." (Suffolk County Crime Lab)

Located in the "outer" box was a video monitor for John to watch the driveway and a mini-tape recorder. I didn't know then that he was making audio tapes of my captivity. (Suffolk County Crime Lab)

Inside the bunker, a commode was hooked up to nothing. John used it as an excuse to take me out of the small box and touch me.
(Suffolk County Crime Lab)

HARM'S WAY

NEIGHBORS DIDN'T HESITATE TO come out of their homes to bask in their fifteen minutes of fame. They added obscure pieces to a puzzle that was taking shape as a grotesquely distorted image behind the veil of normal suburban family life. On Marilyn Beers' block, yellow ribbons hung, or rather flapped, from tree limbs, as if they had been randomly scattered by the gusts of a nor'easter. On one home, the words "Prayin' for Katie" were scribbled in crayon on cracking window trim.

A young mother with a big-hair perm seemed to mean well. Standing on her driveway in a gray sweatshirt, she had no trouble fielding questions about her little neighbor, Katie.

"I was standing by my sliding glass doors and Katie had axed my daughter why don't you see your Daddy and she just said because I don't. And Katie axed, 'Does he touch you in any sorta way?' And my daughter said, 'No.' Katie just turned around and said, 'Don't ever let a man hurt you, 'cuz they hurt you a lot.' So I went over to the pool and I said, 'Ya know, Katie, if yous ever have a problem, ya know, I'm a Mom, ya know, you can tawk to me,'…and she just axed me not to say nothin' to no one and I couldn't go tell the mom 'cuz, ya know, there's an ongoing problem." She shook her head. "So there wasn't nothin' I could do."

How about calling the police—did you ever think to do that?

"Yeah, I thought about that but, ya know, I had a problem with the court system myself with my daughter's father so, ya know, …as far as I knew with the schools and all…" Her voice trailed off as she changed the subject. "Katie was a well-kept child—a well-kept child." She emphasized the word "well," as if to convince herself and reporters she hadn't overlooked blatant clues.

It was quite obvious that Katie had fallen through so many walloping cracks, it was hard to keep all the gaping crevices straight and pack the disturbing details of the unfolding travesty into the limited time we could devote each night to the story on the evening news. Neighbors suspected the little girl had been sexually abused; schools were aware she was chronically absent and had dropped out altogether soon after starting fourth grade; merchants were troubled for years by her abominable hygiene and lack of supervision; Suffolk County's Child Protective Services had been to Katie's house at least twice and in one visit claimed Linda hollered and chased the caseworker out;[6] police not only had a confession from Sal Inghilleri, her godmother's husband, that he had molested Katie, but also had a sex abuse allegation against John Esposito, a close family friend. Astonishingly though, Katie continued to live as a ward of the same adults who seemed to have undeniably placed her in harm's way. It was as if an entire community had witnessed a hit and run, turned its collective head, and kept driving.

With a virtual rogues' gallery of misfits and accused perverts in her life, it also seemed inconceivable that Katie could have the uncanny bad luck of having been abducted by a complete stranger. But this was Long Island...

Allan Binder, a Suffolk County legislator who headed the Committee for Health and Human Services, called for hearings into the apparent missteps by public agencies and schools.[7] Binder could be counted on for an on-camera interview even now, when he knew he'd be on the defensive.

"The question is whether our Child Protective Services is following up and doing the job it should. We will be looking at this case and looking at other cases. We've been getting a flood of calls from people who have had similar problems."

A flood of calls? What are "people" saying?

"They are saying they had instances where they have let CPS know about something and there wasn't any follow-up, and if there was an initial follow up, it ended there. That maybe a child died or was hurt. We are hearing these kinds of stories. They haven't been confirmed. Obviously we have to investigate."

Obviously.

More than a week into a criminal mystery, a journalist's job is not entirely unlike that of police. One runs at every lead, hoping it will be a big break in the case. To cover a story is one thing. To have an exclusive, that's pay dirt. So when a promising call from one of Katie's neighbors came into the newsroom, I ran.

A man with an Indian accent and a thick, bushy mustache welcomed reporters and camera crews into his small kitchen. This was apparently no exclusive, but he said he had a valuable clue and was willing to share it.

He gestured to an answering machine on the counter and waited until the crews indicated they were ready to roll. Then, he hit play.

It was almost too quick to decipher, so he played it again. And again. It sounded like a gasp.

The problem was, lasting only one second, it could not definitively be characterized as a human gasp. Maybe it was that of a child. Or a dog. I couldn't be sure. The man said the gasp came into his answering machine between nine and eleven-thirty that morning. His niece, he explained, was a school friend of Katie's.

Why do you think Katie would call here?

"I think maybe because my niece is her friend."

Has Katie ever been here?

"No...um, no."

Did Katie have your number?

"Maybe my niece gave it to her."

Reporters huddled around the answering machine with microphones and gave each other disheartened glances that said, without words, this was a total waste of time, a vital commodity that was in short supply if Katie were to be found alive.

John Beers, surrounded by a group of a dozen friends, took deep, long drags of a cigarette. His jet black hair, styled into a nineties mullet, was tinged with scattered pink highlights slicked with hair gel. He had shed his KISS hat and now wore silver chains around his neck, several of them, and a leather motorcycle jacket. Reporters gestured subtly to their cameramen to come quickly. Run!

It's an essential skill in television journalism that takes some practice. Request that the photographer pick up the camera immediately, aim and shoot, without interrupting the focus and flow of a productive conversation with a news subject.

Thankfully, John kept talking. "That's all lies, really."

I came in mid-interview with a radio reporter.

"We don't know anything about what happened to Katie."

He took a hard drag of his cigarette.

You told me last week John Esposito had abused you. Now you're being more specific. How old were you?

"About seven years."

How long did it go on?

"Years."

Did you ever tell an adult about it?

"No." He took another hard drag of the cigarette, holding it with his thumb and middle finger.

Why didn't you ever tell anyone? You were ashamed...?

The question went on circuitously while John dragged hard on the butt. You could see smoke curl up out of his mouth and into his nostrils. He exhaled and responded obliquely, "I just didn't want to."

What do you want to happen to John Esposito now? Do you want to see him punished for what he did to you?

"Yes and no. I do and I don't because...he's a friend."

You still consider him a friend despite what you say happened?

"Yes."

Is that because he bought you gifts and did things for you?

John shook his head.

So why would you call him a good friend if he did those things to you? Did you talk to police?

"I talked to police," he said, exhaling smoke.

At sixteen years old, John had movie star looks. High cheekbones and big blue eyes, cupid bow lips, and a slightly oversized nose too large for his sculpted face. But he lived in Mastic Beach, dubbed "Appalachia without the mountains"[8] by one late-night TV comic, and all of his beautiful looks were packaged in a coat of street grime and dime-store "pleather."

Did they do anything? Did they investigate?

"Not really, I didn't tell them what he did."

Do you think John Esposito would want to hurt Katie?

"I don't think so, no."

Do you think Sal Inghilleri would hurt Katie?

"I'm not sure about him. I don't like him."

Why not?

"He's a liar, a two-faced fat slob."

One of John's friends giggled loudly and John revealed a smile of chipped, broken front teeth, quickly chiseling away at the movie star charm.

Well, he's suggesting that the family here in Mastic was involved in rituals.

"No, we were not involved in rituals or Satanism."

Why pick now to say something about what John Esposito did to you?

"I think it's the right time to say something."

Help me understand more on that.

"That's all I'm saying."

Another reporter pushed him beyond his comfort zone.

You realize by saying these things about John Esposito in Bay Shore, you are taking the focus off you and your family here in Mastic? You know this is an extensive investigation into where your sister is. People are confused; they want to know if something happened to her here, instead of with John Esposito, who was the last person to see her?

Now John was glaring at the reporter. "I don't know if anything happened to her out here. All I know is she said Sal did something to her."

No one told her to say that because there was a custody dispute?

"No."

You say John Esposito molested you. Do you think he would have done that to Katie?

"I don't know."

Is it possible?

He blinked. "Yeah, it's probably possible."

Why do you say that?

"I don't know. It's just my gut feeling. I don't know why. Strange feeling I have."

LOW NOTE

ALMOST TEN DAYS AFTER Katie's disappearance, the press, the public, and, most significantly, the police were truly baffled. Privately, they were telling reporters they were split as to whether she was kidnapped or killed.[9] It couldn't be established if Katie was ever at Spaceplex. No one saw her there. What's more, no one had seen John Esposito in Spaceplex, either, until he claimed she went missing.

The infamous "man with a knife" phone call was made, it was determined by police, at 5:06 p.m. from a phone booth across the street from Spaceplex in Nesconset. Eight minutes later, John was imploring the arcade manager to please page Katie. Eight minutes. Those crucial eight minutes haunted detectives, their instincts relentlessly reminding them that there was no accounting for John Esposito's whereabouts at the time Katie's voice was being left on Linda's answering machine.

They had traced the mysterious phone call to a phone booth at an Amoco Gas Station. A New York Telephone worker was installing a new phone when I got there. The coins, he said, had already been removed by police. The original phone, he said, was part of the police investigation, now removed to check for fingerprints. Icy rain fell on the camera lens as he hard-wired the replacement.

Katie's "unconventional" family dynamics had police openly admitting they were frustrated and running into dead ends at every turn. Police Commissioner Peter Cosgrove told reporters that the two families quarrelling over Katie "complicated an already difficult case."[10]

"We have a girl who was torn between two apparently dysfunctional family groups. That situation produces so many leads to track down, and it's what makes this one more unique than most."

"Unique" was a generous word, police-speak for "hopeless." The greater the frustrations, the more bizarre the characters entering the spotlight. The story had become the textbook definition of "media circus."

Ten days in, as the reporter parade at the Inghilleri home was beginning to thin, Linda Inghilleri produced, for police and the media, a folded note made out of construction paper. In black marker, the words were scrawled in juvenile handwriting:

> To Aunt Linda,
> I love you. You are my favorite person in the world. But I am stuck in the middle of You and Marylin. I love you both but I love you more than Marylin. You and I have a lot of good mermies to share. But you got to understand I am only ten years old so it is very hard for me to decied who I want to live with Becaus I have lived with yo both.
> Love Always, Katherine
> p.s. I love you

On the left side of the card, a red heart was drawn in felt marker, and inside the outlined heart, the words "I love you," six times, with big red oversized lips scribbled below.

Police had searched the house from top to bottom several times, but the note, Linda claimed, was found the night before, lodged within the pages of a book in Katie's desk drawer, by a psychic, one of four who had donated time to help find the missing child.

The next day, Marilyn plopped down on a floral, mustard-colored couch below a velvet Kung Fu picture hanging from prefab panel walls. She sat ready to answer questions posed by a cohort of news media gathered for a hastily called news conference at the home of Teddy Rodriguez, Little John's father. A man in a tweed jacket squeezed in next to Marilyn in what scant space remained on the couch. He introduced himself as John Monti, Marilyn's spokesman and her own "psychic."

Marilyn smiled and uttered some sounds, revealing both the fact that she was missing several teeth on top, and that she had a horrendous case of laryngitis. An impossible number of cameras and reporters jammed into the cramped living room, struggling to hear Marilyn's words.

I got us started.

You've asked us all to be here—what is it you want to share with us?

"Just to…" she coughed. With the loudest whisper she could muster, Marilyn said, "Just to straighten some things out that have been written in the papers."

Do you believe your daughter wrote that letter?

"I believe that letter is a fake," she said flatly, then coughed.

Why? Was that your daughter's handwriting, Ms. Beers?

Cough, cough. "I don't know. I didn't see it."

You didn't see it? But you think it's a fake?

Someone showed Marilyn the *Newsday* article with a picture of the note.

Would your daughter have referred to you as "Marilyn?"

"No."

How would she refer to you?

"Mommy."

In the letter, she referred to herself as ten years old, but it was supposedly written before her birthday. Does that make you suspicious?

"No, because we always rounded her age off."

Sal has said that the answer to what happened to Katie "lies in Mastic"—that you know what happened to Katie or your son knows. How do you answer that?

"He's talking out of his hat. If I knew where she was, don't you think I'd have her?"

He was saying today that there were all kinds of rituals, voodoo that went on at your house.

Marilyn's laugh, at this point, was just a barking cough.

"Ya right. I'm not into witchcraft…or the occult. I have nothing to do with my daughter's disappearance. I want her back. She is my daughter, I love her, and I want her back."

If she is listening—what would you tell her?

"Katie, please come home. Mommy loves you. We love you and we want you back."

Why do you think the letter is a fake?

"Because the psychic found it. Why didn't the psychic find it sooner? Why didn't the detectives find it when they were searching her room?"

The letter suggests that Katie preferred Linda. Does that sound like her?

"No," she paused. "No!"

Does she prefer you?

"She loves us," she answered cryptically.

LOW NOTE

Marilyn kept her eyes on the newspaper and picked at her thumb cuticle, as reporters kept firing questions.

Is there anything familiar about that note? Does that look like Katie's handwriting?

"No, it does not," said Marilyn, still looking down.

Would she ever sign her name Katherine instead of Katie?

"No."

Marilyn's one word answers frustrated me and the other journalists, who simply needed one or two coherent sentences to use for quotes. The goal is to generate answers that can stand alone, without putting words in anyone's mouth. But here, even with coaxing, nothing was working.

I guess what this boils down to, Marilyn, since you're saying you don't believe that note, is that someone had to put it there—that equals what?

"It equals deception…or a joke," she hedged. "I don't know. I don't believe this letter is Katie's."

What do you think has happened to Katie, specifically?

"Someone took her, I want her back."

Do you think the Inghilleris have anything to do with it?

Marilyn paused, and then coughed, "I know she is being held against her will. All I know is I want my daughter back."

The next question was asked inevitably, but meekly.

Ms. Beers, I wouldn't ask this but, um, your son brought this up himself. He said over a period of years, he was molested by John Esposito. Do you believe your son?

"I believe my son."

Are you going to file charges against John Esposito?

"I thought this was about Katie."

For reasons I still don't understand, that shut up the reporter.

Did Katie ever say anything about abuse by John Esposito against her?

"No comment." It was answers like that one that made many in the room wonder who was hiding what. Why would a mother cover for a man she believed abused her child? We were not getting straight answers.

Linda Inghilleri has said she is convinced Katie is still alive.

"So am I!"

What makes you so sure?

"In my heart, I feel it. I feel in my heart that she is alive."

Ms. Beers, you are probably aware of the stories that have come out over the past eleven days, about Katie's past three or four years. People have written long stories. Was Katie getting the proper schooling?

"She had missed a lot of school, but her grades are very good."

Why did she miss school?

"Here is a copy of her grades, if anyone wants to see." The question went unanswered, and no one pressed further.

What kind of grades did she get?

Marilyn looked at the yellow crumpled report card. "All S's, which is satisfactory."

The subject was changed by the next reporter, and no one ever got an answer as to why Katie had not been attending school. Instead, the camera lens zoomed in on her left eye, revealing a slash at the brow line and a yellow, black, and blue bruise below it. Marilyn had the beginnings of a shiner behind her large wire rimmed glasses. She had explained to those of us who asked the day before that Little John had punched her in "a fit of nerves."

"We're all on edge," she told reporters while sitting on her stoop, smoking. "He never hit me before. I guess this thing is getting to us." [11]

Are you satisfied police are doing enough to find your daughter?

"I believe they are doing all they can."

At this point, Mr. Esposito seems to be the prime suspect. You have your suspicions on him?

"He was the last one to have seen Katie," she coughed.

So why would this note turn up in the Inghilleri's house?

"Why would it turn up after nine days? And not when police were there? It's gotta be a fake. Otherwise it would have turned up sooner."

So "Katherine" seems a bit odd?

"Yeah." The cameras zoomed in on Katie's birth certificate, which Marilyn held up. Katherine Marie Beers, born South Side Hospital. December 30, 1982, 4:40am. Born to Marilyn Beers.

Side conversations started up and there were some chuckles as reporters asked Marilyn how Katie came to be spelled *Kattie* with two t's in the initial police release, and consequently some news reports. She had no idea. Others were videotaping a note that Marilyn provided with

Katie's handwriting, as a means of comparison. On it, a red heart and the words, "To mommy—I love you" in bubble letters, then "love Katie."

This had become a battle of love notes. I'm not a handwriting expert, but they did appear to be the work of one author.

Off camera, Monti was conversing with a subgroup saying, "I have information that I can't reveal right now."

Why not? asked incredulous reporters.

"I just can't."

It is never wise to suggest to news reporters, when someone's life is on the line, that you have a critical nugget of information, but just can't reveal it yet. We were growing visibly impatient, many of us removing microphones and packing up tripods and lights. Monti directed his next comments to the assembled group, revealing a New England accent and the fact that he, too, had laryngitis.

"That's not her handwriting, that's not something she would write. She didn't run away. This is just another means of distorting the facts. It's an attempt to discredit Marilyn. And I believe the Suffolk police thoroughly searched that house. If there was a hair left on the floor, they would have found it."

Did you throw a radio and yell a racial slur because you weren't allowed to register your daughter in the school district where she was living with Linda?

"I did not throw a radio," said Marilyn, refocused now on the remaining cameras. "I didn't have a radio with me."

"There may have been a few words exchanged," admitted Monti, "a bunch of mumbo jumbo. But over at that other house," he said, referring to the Inghilleri's, "there have been signed confessions of things that someone did to this little girl. One thing is clear," he said, "this is the child's natural mother and this mother wants her child back."

No one knew if Katie was alive or dead, but this was the opening salvo of a custody war.

The phone call to Linda's answering machine had police perplexed. "I don't think we will ever know, quite frankly, how that call was made," Commissioner Cosgrove conceded to reporters on the morning of the fourteenth day.

"If we don't know by now, it may not be possible to determine, because we may be dealing with a tape of a tape, so to speak. We have a tape machine used and the tape has been taped over many, many times, the way telephone answering machines are, and it's very hard for analysts to make a determination. We haven't gotten a determination yet, and I'm wondering," he paused, "if we ever will."

The Commissioner was disavowing what sources were telling us, that the FBI had concluded the phone call to Linda's answering machine was actually a tape recording, played into the mouthpiece of the Nesconset gas station phone booth. The FBI's conclusion was based on the lack of background noise on the tape. If a live call had actually been made from that phone booth on Nesconset Highway, there would have been a hum of ever-present cars zipping past. Instead, Katie's call sounded as if she had been inside a soundproof booth.

"We don't know that, definitely. We don't have conclusive evidence, and again, I don't know if we ever will."

Well, don't you have a gut feeling?

"Everyone has gut feelings but we really can't work on gut feelings at this point."

How could this girl just vanish?

Cosgrove stood patiently answering questions now delving into the realm of speculation. Reporters had little to fill a minute and a half hole in the newscast, and fishing expeditions like this one were inevitable.

"Obviously, it is frustrating. Even the officers assigned to the case get frustrated when a lead they are following ends up being a dead end. We've had the Nesconset Fire Department search the entire area. We had cadets in the police academy search, and we had a roadblock by the phone booth stopping motorists asking if they had seen anything. We think we have covered every lead we can. That is what makes it so frustrating."

Police had also searched John's garage apartment three times and were camped out in the front house, monitoring the phones.

Is the terrible truth that we may never know what happened to her?

It had been two weeks, but police were not ready to give up. "It's always a possibility—we don't like to think that way. There are some cases that don't get solved, but I would like to think this is not one of them."

LOW NOTE

Reporters sullenly realized there would be no scoop from this interview and retreated to the wide-shot position, where cameras continued to roll. It was during this wide-shot that the conversation became hushed, and the top cop acknowledged that police had no firm suspects in the disappearance of Katie Beers.

Katie's brother John Beers (Right) and his father Teddy Rodriguez (left). (Courtesy Newsday*)*

CATNAPS

THERE WAS NO SLEEP. Just catnaps when my eyelids would become so heavy, I could no longer fight off the urgent need to close them. And I would fitfully open them when I realized my terrible mistake. I was terrified that if I fell into a deep sleep, Big John would get that picture he wanted of me looking dead, and then cops would call off the search for me. And I would be his, forever. So I stayed awake, the whole time.

Relieving myself and trying to clean myself was a disgusting and humiliating ordeal. Of all the painful memories, this one hurts most. And it's strange because, looking back, I know I was subjected to far worse. And yet this turns my stomach still. Of course, I had no bathroom or shower. John had left a commode in the bigger room of the dungeon with a black plastic bag in it, but it was attached to nothing. I had no access to it, being chained at the neck, or so Big John thought. Each time he left, he locked me inside the smaller box. Big John thought that I couldn't get out, so I couldn't sneak out to use the commode, leaving him a putrid sign of my escape. So I did what I had to do so as not to rouse his suspicions.

In the little box, there was the thin mattress, handcuffs on the side walls, the neck chain, that horrible wooden head box and a television. Under the TV, there was an area that the mattress was not covering—this is where I would go. And the bottom part of the blanket was all I had to clean myself. To this day, I must have a bathroom close at hand so as never to be reminded of the shame of a pile of one's own excrement at the foot of one's own bed. I am actually quite embarrassed sharing this, even though, for the first ten years of my life, I had become almost immune to humiliation and neglect.

One of my earliest childhood memories is of a snowy winter day when I was really young. I must have been only two or three years old.

Aunt Linda had just bathed me and Marilyn was coming to pick me up at the Inghilleris'. Aunt Linda instructed me that when Marilyn came, I was to say to her that I wanted to stay over. I did as directed. But Marilyn wasn't about to follow Linda's orders. Marilyn announced that I could not spend the night and that she was going to take me home. That's when voices got loud and pots started flying.

The story Linda later drilled into my head was that Marilyn had a headache and dropped me off one day when I was two months old and didn't come back for me for weeks. Marilyn's version was that, yes, she'd had a headache, but that when she tried to pick me up, Linda put up a fight. At this point, it was all-out war.

Aunt Linda screamed at Marilyn, "She is not going home with you, she is my daughter! I am not allowing her to go with you."

Marilyn yelled back that she was going to get the police. I was crying, begging Aunt Linda to let me go home with Marilyn. Aunt Linda then ordered Sal to get me out of the room, adding, "If I have anything to do with it, you'll never see Marilyn again!"

Sal shut me in Aunt Linda's bedroom, but I didn't stay put. I pried the door open and watched as Aunt Linda threw pots and pans at Marilyn and anything else that she could fling. Sal joined in hurling chairs and a lamp at Marilyn, trying to kick her down the apartment stairs. I was screaming to stop hurting Marilyn. Marilyn's glasses fell off. She screeched that she couldn't see, but Sal yelled back he didn't give a crap; she was not going to take me away from Linda.

When Marilyn finally found her glasses, they were shattered—she couldn't see. Marilyn left me inside and stormed out the door. She ran to the next door neighbor's house and called the cops. The neighbors allowed her to stay there until police arrived, but when they did, the Inghilleri house was dark. Aunt Linda had locked the doors and turned off all of the lights.

The cops had to break through the front door. Aunt Linda was holding me, hostage-style, with her arms wrapped around my arms shouting, "Marilyn cannot have *my* daughter."

Marilyn told the cops that I was actually *her* daughter and that she was going to take me home. She did. I don't have any memory of how Linda and Marilyn made peace after that battle, but I bear the battle scars: fear and skepticism of the people who say they are protecting me.

It was also the first time I knew Sal was really bad news.

The story of the Inghilleris in my life begins with a five-dollar cab ride. I have always been told that Aunt Linda was one of Marilyn's customers. Marilyn gave Aunt Linda a ride home, but Linda couldn't scrounge up the few dollars to pay. Payback was simple: a phone number scribbled on the back of a match book and an I.O.U.

By the time I was three, Aunt Linda was around as much as Marilyn, and I didn't call either one "Mom." That title was reserved for Linda's mother, Ann Butler. I was at "Mom's" house in Bay Shore when I almost drowned. "Mom" had an above-ground swimming pool. Aunt Linda knew that I was not able to swim—everyone knew that I couldn't swim—and no one cared. Aunt Linda left me alone in "Mom's" pool on a raft without any sort of flotation device—and warned me that I'd drown if I fell in.

Of course, I fell in. I was clinging to the raft, trying to make as much noise as I could so that maybe "Mom" or Aunt Linda would hear me and run over to save me. Finally, they came down the stairs. There did not appear to be any rush as I bobbed up and down, swallowing pool water and frantically struggling to hold on. I was sure I was going to die—that I wasn't going to make it out. Aunt Linda leaned in the pool, reached for the raft, pulled it to the edge and lifted me out. It seemed to me she didn't want to get wet.

I almost drowned at the beach, also. Linda's sister had me at Jones Beach, on the south shore. She was holding my hand, but a gigantic wave came and knocked me over. I was under water, struggling to get up for long enough to think it was the end for me. Looking back, I realize the constant message was, I was on my own—sink or swim—literally.

The word "careless" comes to mind. There was no care for me by anyone in my life.

When I was around five years old, the Inghilleris had Aunt Linda's brother, Charlie, over with his girlfriend, Michelle. I don't know what I was doing to annoy them, but I did something that they didn't like, so Sal and Linda threw me in the pantry closet and locked the door. As I was being tugged by the shirt and pushed into the closet, I pleaded to first let me use the bathroom. The answer was "no." The closet door slammed shut. I was in the closet for hours, banging on the door, crying hysterically.

"If you don't knock it off, Katie—we're leaving the house. You'll stay in there till you calm the hell down!" Sal pressed his fat cheek against the door to bellow.

I sat in there in the pitch black, curled up in a ball, trying to hold in my bladder, crying. They left the house and headed to a movie theater, keeping me locked in the pantry closet. When Sal and Aunt Linda returned from the movie hours later, they unlocked the door and found me on the closet floor covered in pee. Aunt Linda beat me until I was purple.

It was there, in that rented mustard yellow house on Belmont Avenue in West Babylon, that Sal first showed me his true colors. I was sick with a bad cold. Linda left the house to buy me cough medicine at the drug store. I remember I was playing with my Barbie dolls, and Sal sat down on the floor next to me. I was barely old enough to speak in sentences, and yet I could formulate the thought that it was strange, because Sal had never ever taken any interest in me or Barbie dolls before.

I don't remember his words, but I remember what he did. He touched me under my underwear. I was maybe two or three years old. I don't remember how it started, but I do know when he was finished, I felt really ashamed and embarrassed, like I had done a bad thing. Linda came home with cough medicine and the cough, I assume, cleared up quickly.

But the abuse would escalate for years.

Everyone was scared of Sal. My grandmother, my mother, Linda, and my brother John—he smacked them all around. But it was my brother, who is a bit more than six years older than I am, who took a big share of Sal's wrath. One day, Sal shouted to John to mow the lawn, to which John replied that he was busy and would take care of it later. Sal yelled at him and told him to get his ass outside, and to get the lawn mowed. John yelled back that Sal was not his father and had no right to tell him what to do. The shouting went back and forth, and John threatened to leave—that he'd had enough of Sal's bullshit.

Sal ended it definitively. He grabbed John, threw him to the ground, and kicked him square in his gut with such force, it knocked the wind out of John. My big brother was as helpless as I was against Sal's terror.

When Sal wasn't getting what he wanted, he would also grab me by the shirt near the collar and "jack" me against the wall, holding me there with my feet dangling below me like a ragdoll, pointing in my face with his other hand, spitting curses inches from my eyes. When his arms got tired, he would drop me and wrap his hands around my neck.

There was no escape from Sal. My grandmother, Helen Beers, owned a house at 12 Higbie Drive in West Islip. She and her husband, Stewart, had built the house and raised Marilyn and my uncle Bob there. My mother, brother, and I all lived there with her. We each had our own bedroom. My grandmother and I each had a room on the bottom floor; John and Marilyn's rooms were upstairs.

One day, Sal and Aunt Linda came over and told us that they had been evicted from their house. Marilyn offered for them to stay with us for as long as they needed to. When Sal and Aunt Linda moved in, Grandma kept her downstairs bedroom, John and Sal shared my old room, Marilyn kept her room, and Aunt Linda took over John's room upstairs.

I was left to share Linda's bed, but when I missed her curfew and didn't arrive in her room at her designated time, there was hell to pay. Being late meant being locked out—and becoming Sal's prey.

Aunt Linda's rule was firm. If I was not upstairs by nine at night, I was not allowed to sleep in the bed. If I did not make it upstairs in time, I had to sleep on the couch in the living room and Sal would have his way with me. I would often awake to Sal hanging over me, taking off my underwear. He would lie next to me, masturbating and touching me. He would rub up against me and touch me, and then it became me touching him. He would tell me what to do, sometimes holding my hand to show me. It went on like this for a while.

Later, if I didn't make it up to bed with Aunt Linda, Sal would come hunting for me in the house. When he found me, he would turn me over and lay me on my stomach. He would take off my underwear and start to rub his dick in my buttocks, never penetrating me this way. I guess he just used it to get off. It went on for years like this—at first once a week and then every day. Eventually—when it was clear he wouldn't get caught—he began to rape me.

Marilyn was never there at night. She spent the nightshift caring for an old woman. She needed to work more than one job because she was the only one in the house earning a dime, so there was no one I could turn to.

Sal knew the nine o'clock rule and would deliberately delay me.

When he was finished, Sal would pull my underwear up and tell me to clean myself up. He would always escort me to the bathroom and watch me while I cleaned up. He would do the same, then walk out and return to his La-Z Boy chair in the living-room, lean back and crack open a can of beer.

Aunt Linda's rule got even stiffer. If I went upstairs too late, even if she were awake, she would send me back downstairs saying, "You didn't listen; you were supposed to be up here ten minutes ago."

There were times that I would sleep on the floor behind the couch, hoping that Sal wouldn't be able to find me. There were times that I would accidentally fall asleep on the couch, and I would awaken to Sal grunting at me to roll over or giving me some other command, not to move, to keep quiet, no talking, hold still while he penetrated me. Grandma Helen was right down the hall on the same floor, but never heard a thing. I'd pretend to be asleep while he raped me, night after night. I thought if I would pretend to be sleeping, Sal would leave me alone.

It didn't happen that way. When he would finish, he would shake me and tell me to go clean myself up. I have memories of waking with my underwear soaked, and I hadn't peed myself. Sal was using my body as I slept.

I started to beg my grandmother to allow me to sleep in bed with her. Sometimes she let me. I felt safe there. But it was short lived. Sal then realized where I was sleeping and would come wake me up and make me come out and "play" with him. It was always in whispers—whispered threats.

As Sal started to feel more comfortable with abusing me, he started to do it during the day. I would try to avoid coming home from school because I knew what was going to happen as soon as I arrived. Sal would ask me to come to his bedroom. As I slowly took steps across the linoleum tile floor, he would gesture to me to come closer, over to his bed. There, with his enormous pot belly and erection sticking up, he would lay with no pants on. Then he would tell me to play with him. I was seven years old and this was my daily routine.

As his confidence that he wouldn't get caught increased, so did the abuse. He raped me on a regular basis. I don't recall anymore how often it was, but it seemed like it was more than once a week, for years. When he raped me, I always had to be on top because he was an obese man and would have probably crushed me. Sal would make me use lotion when he would make me play with him—he kept the lotion right next to his bed or in the closet in the bedroom. Lubriderm. I would sneak into Sal's room when he was not home and steal the lotion, hoping that if he didn't have the lotion, then he wouldn't make me play with him. It didn't work. I would throw it in the dumpster in the strip mall, but a new bottle would always appear. When I saw it there, I would cry my eyes out.

Aunt Linda, who never left the house, rarely left her upstairs bedroom. There, she spent hours on the phone. She ran up my grandmother's phone bill over one thousand dollars. She was calling the "900" numbers that you see on late night TV. Aunt Linda and Sal never slept in the same room, or even associated with each other. Aunt Linda would call the "900" numbers and talk "dirty" on the phone. I would hear her talking, saying what she was wearing, talking about her body, and of course, lying about how sexy she looked. In fact, she looked like a bulldog, with massive rolls of fat. She would spend her days and nights on the phone talking to anonymous voices on three-dollars-per-minute hotlines. "I'm sleeping next to a little girl," she told one of the men, trying to sound sexy. It was four in the morning and I was pretending to sleep. Aunt Linda shook my shoulder and ordered me up to speak to the man.

"He wants YOU," she barked.

"I don't WANT to talk to him," I whimpered. I just wanted to go back to bed because I had to wake up for school the next day. I vividly remember Aunt Linda telling me that if I didn't talk to the man that wanted to speak to me, I would not be allowed to go to school the next day and she "would make me sorry." I really wanted to go to school the next day, so I got on the phone.

Aunt Linda fed me the words. I was to say, "Hi, this is Tinkerbelle," so I did. The man asked me what I was wearing and if there was "anything I wanted to do" to him. I started crying, and Aunt Linda grabbed the phone from me screaming that I was "embarrassing" her. She slapped me across the face and ordered me to go to sleep.

CATNAPS

Both Sal and Aunt Linda made me watch porn—for different reasons. Sal made me watch while he made me play with him. This was an almost daily occurrence. Sal had quite the porn collection; he had over fifty porn VHS tapes—John and I counted one day. Linda made me watch porn with her and would play with herself while I watched the video. There was one video with a woman named "Angel." I couldn't believe that a woman with such a beautiful name could be so dirty.

Sal also liked to abuse me in his Firebird. He'd tell me to get in the car to visit his mother, to run an errand for Aunt Linda, or to bring me to school. He would park the car somewhere—usually a vacant lot, the parking lot of the mall in a secluded area, at the school after hours, or the park—basically anywhere he could find that was infrequently used.

The nursery around the corner from our house was a favorite of his. In the off-peak season, the parking lot would be deserted and Sal would drive us there so we could "be alone." He'd park in a spot that couldn't be seen from the road. Sal would take lotion out of the glove box, recline his seat and order me to "play" with him. I would have to play with him until he was satisfied, which usually took anywhere from a few minutes to a half hour.

Another favorite spot of his was behind a strip mall off of Sunrise Highway. The stores were closed on Sunday afternoons; this is when Sal would take me there, because there was little chance of getting caught. He would go through the same routine as in the strip mall parking lot—lotion and brief instructions to "get busy."

I hated getting in that Firebird. In fact, I hate getting into any car with a man now. There are still some people who make me skittish—I size people up quickly. I don't want to say I'm judgmental, but I'm very aware of people and how they make me feel. I mistakenly trusted everyone when I was younger. Now I have a sixth sense. I can tell what people's intentions are and know when to retreat. I will never be used again.

The drill. I could hear the snarl of the drill again, and pulled myself up into the coffin-box, locking the neck chain as if I had been there all along. I was proud of myself; I had not fallen asleep. I had just drifted into an even uglier place.

ALIVE

I MADE THE ROUNDS each day, green spiral steno pad and mini-recorder in hand, knocking firmly on dented doors and tin thresholds in the absence of working doorbells. The competition had become acute. Katie stories were dominating the headlines of the city tabloids, a new genre of tabloid TV was devoting entire shows to the saga. Each astonishing revelation about Katie's Cinderella existence was intently followed by a mesmerized national audience. The little missing waif had won the nation's collective heart and each day the pressure was enormous to dig up new dirt on those who'd failed her.

News 12 Long Island, the first regional twenty-four-hour news channel, was considered a training ground by the people at Cablevision, who owned and operated the place. There were, though, plenty of folks who worked there who were already "trained," and for us, it was a tough spot to be in, competing with the likes of the CBS, NBC, and ABC flagship stations, *The New York Times*, *New York Post*, and *New York Daily News*. Turning on News 12 had become a fixture in the daily routine of many across the island.

Nonetheless, calculating newsmakers still considered the city stations and newspapers the gold standard. Each of us within the press corps was jockeying for scoops in this story, and they were awarded, most often, to those with big city links. Attorneys and law enforcement sources took my calls and answered my questions, but at times it was a skittish game of catch-up. I tried to remind myself often of the bigger picture and why we did what we did. A little girl's fate was more important than who revealed the next dreadful detail about her miserable existence.

I didn't need to sharpen my news fangs on the likes of a missing child. Yet, a competitive streak is innate in most red-blooded reporters, and at times blinding. So there were nights I would go to sleep fearing the morning headlines.

The Suffolk Police Department felt the heat, too, and in an effort to shut off the rushing current of leaks, issued this unprecedented statement on January 12, 1993:

ALIVE

It is now sixteen days since the sudden unexplained disappearance of Katie Beers. No effort has been spared by the Suffolk County law enforcement community to follow every lead in an attempt to locate her and identify those responsible for her disappearance. Understandably, the human drama presented by the plight of this ten-year-old girl has sparked enormous media interest, as witnessed by the daily intense coverage both in newspapers and on radio and television. Unfortunately, as day follows day, the media's efforts to report further developments has at times hindered police investigators who are primarily responsible for bringing this case to a definitive conclusion. While we are mindful that ofttimes media attention is case-beneficial, nonetheless, there are occasions when law enforcement activities may actually be thwarted and/or short-circuited by undue exposure or discussion of circumstances and hitherto unpublished "facts." Accordingly, until further notice, Suffolk County law enforcement officials and personnel will decline to respond to media inquiries concerning any aspect of this investigation. We request the media's understanding and cooperation in this information embargo.

The pipeline of leads, though, remained free flowing. The television show, *America's Most Wanted,* aired an episode about Katie's disappearance and more than fifty tips were phoned in from around the country. In the Hudson Valley, two people were certain they saw a young girl, the spitting image of Katie, outside a Grand Union supermarket trying to make a call at a pay phone, then pushed into a waiting car. I was dispatched to file a live report.

In another call, a Bay Shore mechanic told police he was certain he had given Katie a ride earlier that day.

With police maintaining their silence, we worked around them, covering a circular rotation—the Inghilleris in Bay Shore, John Esposito's house a mile away, and Marilyn's place in Mastic Beach—in an unnerving race to lead the news. The players in this story had become caricatures in a twisted modern version of Cinderella. But the macabre characters, drawn on tabloid TV in stark black and white, were in reality shaded in hues of gray.

Even the wicked godmother had redeeming qualities. Linda never struck me as a threatening woman. She seemed broken, genuinely crushed by Katie's disappearance, often lost in thought and a cloud of smoke, attached to her wheelchair and the plausible notion that Katie had run away to find a "Whole New World," just like the song she said Katie adored.

Whenever I would sit with her, choking as she chain-smoked, she'd well up as she spoke of Katie. There appeared to be an abiding earnestness about her.

Fat Sal, as he came to be known in the press corps, always wore a hapless, harmless look. He was a sloppy oddball with a bulging belly and a neck the size of a bulldog's, yet he seemed benign from afar. Even with sex abuse charges leveled against him and a court date pending, no one could be certain the allegations weren't fabricated as part of the well-documented custody feud. He seemed sincere when he greeted me, and I gave him the benefit of a doubt.

Marilyn, a woman with a gigantic girth and equally oversized bosoms was, to me, the most sympathetic of the lot. She was apparently the only one among them who dragged herself out of bed each day and worked for a paycheck. While she answered none of the critical questions about Katie's obvious neglect, little of it seemed to be directly her fault. She was thrust into a role and onto a stage for which she was thoroughly unprepared—and was blowing her performance badly.

They were all, it appeared to me, brutally unlucky people, not to be condemned, but to be pitied and given a platform, if they so desired, to be heard.

It's not easy to size up people you barely know beyond a sound bite, and that was not my job. My job was to report, and on the afternoon of January 13, seventeen days after Katie vanished, I got to report on something rare: astoundingly good news.

"Get to Saxon Avenue!" the message read on my beeper shortly after midday. The assignment desk was abuzz with speculation that something big was about to break at John Esposito's house. A break in the case could mean that something or somebody was found. I had no idea if it were Katie or her corpse. Adrenaline doesn't discriminate, and mine was pumping wildly.

The scene in front of the house was chaotic. Live trucks were already on the block with their masts up, reporters were staked out and neighbors were anxiously gathered in the street—but there was nothing to report. Word circulated quickly; *Newsday* had been tipped off that something was up. Curiously though, there was no police presence at the house, not even the usual detectives who trailed John every day. It was the absence of action that was so strange and dreadfully nerve-wracking.

John's lawyers had leaked a tip to *Newsday*: Esposito had summoned his family, including his twin brother Ronnie, sister-in-law Joyce, and Joan (his brother Pat's widow). He asked them all to meet at Siben & Siben first thing that morning. He had an ominous message.

"There is something I have to tell you," John stated.

"What is it, John?" a tanned and rested Sidney Siben asked, just back from a ten day vacation in Florida.

"I know where Katie is."

"What? Is she alive?" his lawyer demanded.

"Yes."

WHAT IF?

THE TELEVISION TOLD ME it was about one in the afternoon and I heard Big John coming down the hole. The grinding at the screws in the doorway was my warning to chain myself back up fast. I actually fell asleep for a few minutes, and the groan of the ratchet roused me. But this was strange; Big John never came down this early in the day. Normally, he would come down early evening, coinciding with the evening news, to feed me and touch me. It was a steady diet of junk food and soda. Almost always there were After Eight Mints. Today, I cringe at the thought. Those thin dark chocolate wafers were all I consumed for days on end. If John prepared something for me, like a hamburger, a bologna sandwich, or macaroni and cheese, I let it rot. I couldn't be sure he hadn't poisoned the food. I inspected everything. Prepackaged food like pudding and candy—lots of candy—was the only way I could be sure it was safe.

For days, Big John had been saying cryptic things that made me wonder if he was going to kill himself, kill me, or kill both of us. Was today the day? My strategy of trying to wear him down to get him to release me was beginning to sound like a broken record he was tuning out.

"Let me go, just let me go, and I'll run far away from your house. I promise that I'll never tell anyone that you had me here. I'll say I didn't know who kidnapped me!"

It was almost as if Big John was listening to a different soundtrack. He wasn't responding to anything I said. He seemed to be thinking hard. He'd rub his head in troubled thought.

"Where am I going to go to school?"

"I'll teach you what you need to know."

"Where will I work?"

"When you are ready to work, they would have stopped looking for you, so you can go to work anywhere you want, but I'll have enough money that you won't have to work. You'll stay at home as a mom."

"So how will I have kids?"

"You'll have kids with me."

WHAT IF?

"I don't want to have kids with you!"

He seemed hurt by that comment, and I had to think fast, so I assured Big John that I loved him and that I would have had kids with him, but by the time I was ready to have children, he would just be too old. Big John seemed a little less insulted with that reasoning.

I had to be exceptionally careful. My life was literally in Big John's hands. If he killed himself, no one would ever find me. He spoke often about taking his own life and this terrified me. But he would try to assure me that when he did, he would leave instructions on how to find me, pinned to his clothes. This didn't make me feel better. I knew that if he took his life, he was also taking mine. How could the instructions possibly be good enough? How long would it take for someone to find me? And how would they ever find me down here?

I had grown up on horror movies. Little John always had on *Nightmare on Elm Street* or one of the *Halloween* movies. I knew what death looked like. I knew if I couldn't outsmart Big John, get under his skin, manipulate him into releasing me, I would be dead.

I needed to dream up just the right thing to say to Big John so that he wouldn't kill himself.

The ratchet stopped and Big John stepped down into the box. It was definitely peculiar that he was coming down on this day so early. Then I heard him speak, and my heart raced in fear. Big John was not alone; I could hear other voices. There was a man with him. All that was going through my head was that Big John brought his friends over to have a good time with me, too. I couldn't bear it.

I knew he didn't have adult friends. What adult would want to hang around with him? If they were men with him, they would have to be the type of men who would want to harm a little girl. I shook.

The door to the coffin-box flew open and Big John reached his arm in and unlocked the chain around my neck. Right behind him, in the dark, I could make out the forms of two other men. They were wearing suits. I felt sick, afraid. Please, not again.

"Katie," one of the men said. He knew my name. "It's safe for you to come out."

I didn't believe it for a minute. Not at all. Maybe Big John was testing me, having his friends play a trick on me to see how I would react to being free? If I didn't respond correctly, would I get into trouble when the trick was over? Big John was always playing the "what if" game: What if people stopped looking for me—would we be able to live normal lives together? What if police thought that I was dead? What if we moved away from New York?

Maybe this was another one of his games: "What if Katie thought she was free?" I couldn't take any chances by responding the wrong way. I was also playing a "what if" game in my head: What if I was given my freedom, but it was all a cruel joke? What if Big John took away my freedom as quickly as he had dangled it in front of me?

So I stayed put, frozen. But the men asked me to come down. "We are police," one said, in calm, soothing voice. "Are you okay?"

What? Did I hear him right? I still didn't know if I should believe him.

I slowly climbed out as I was told to do and stood in the bigger box while Big John showed the men around. Conversation with me was minimal. I just stood there, my mind racing.

One of the men then told me to gather my stuff and head upstairs. I did what he said as quickly as I could, still doubting, but realizing, as I was crawling on my belly somewhere between my last foot leaving the dungeon and my head emerging from the closet floor, that at last, I was getting out of the sealed prison that had held me.

I was the first of the four of us through the tunnel and up the ladder. When I got to the top, a uniformed cop pulled me out. I never thought I would see light again. I never thought I would see the outside again. Yet here I was, in Big John's dimly lit office, and what little light there was in that room from drawn blinds was a welcome burn to my slowly adjusting eyes.

Uniformed men led me to the living room, where Big John was now sitting, looking pale and sad. There I sat while questions were shot at me from two sides of the room. It's the first time I can remember ever seeing another adult in his house. The living room wasn't typical for a grownup. There were two couches, a table or two, and the metal spiral staircase that went upstairs to the game room.

There was no television in the living room. The only television in the whole house was upstairs in his bedroom, and the only place to sit and watch television in his bedroom was on his unmade bed. How is it possible no one thought it odd for a man in his mid-forties to have children over to his house so often and the only television was in his bedroom?

But then, no adults were ever there to notice or care. We were children left alone with a man-child. He must have smelled the scent of a lone, unattended child, the way animals sniff out their prey.

The questioners called themselves police officers, but I wouldn't believe anything that they would say until I was out of Big John's house and his presence. I was sitting on the little brown plaid couch with a "police officer" sitting next to me. Big John was on the big couch with a "police officer" sitting next to him. I couldn't pay attention to what was being asked. I was anxious, petrified that I would end up back in the dungeon after the questioning was over.

I answered the men's questions but didn't let them know that I was terrified of Big John and what I still thought could be a new round of a stomach-turning game.

Looking back, I cannot believe they kept me in the same room as my kidnapper for that long. But I *can* believe what has since been relayed to me—that, when it was time to go, I hugged Big John and told him I loved him. I have no memory of that, and it's something I wish I hadn't said to my captor. It wouldn't surprise me, though. The hole was still open, the concrete slab still dangling from a hook above the cutout in the floor only a few feet from where we sat. I wasn't yet free.

The police officers walked me outside to a car that was waiting in the driveway. "Climb in, get ready," one of them said, with a hint of excitement.

The police car slowly pulled out in reverse, through the double stockade gate that leads to Saxon Avenue. I left Big John's house behind me, not looking back. Was I free?

Beyond the gate, there was a sea of photographers now running on either side of the car, taking pictures. I had never seen anything like this before. The photographers weren't even looking into the lenses. They were just snapping the pictures high above their heads. Men with big video cameras on their shoulders ran alongside the car as we drove off. A cop in the car told me to smile and wave. I leaned my head on the back seat window and finally, wearily, closed my eyes.

The cold numbness I had felt for weeks began to lift. I didn't, or rather, I *couldn't* believe that this day had come. I was free! Finally, I could breathe!

I left that prison on Saxon Avenue with my life. But I took with me a fear of some things that will forever elicit sheer terror in me: baby monitors; the song, *I Will Always Love You,* by Whitney Houston. It had just come out and was played over and over on MTV and VH1 a hundred times a day. It made me cry each time, as I would picture Marilyn, my brother, and grandmother, believing I would never see them again; After Eight Mints; and *Edward Scissorhands.* The television version of the movie was a fixture on cable TV. Edward, like me, was trapped. The surreal story offered me hope. He escaped his captivity; I could possibly survive mine.

I had five hundred dollars with me, the bribe money Big John gave me daily, in twenty dollar bills. I had stuffed them under the pillow and clenched them in my hands as we drove away that afternoon. The police officer in the back seat with me asked me if the money was real. I didn't know. He looked at it and told me that he had to confiscate it because it was evidence. I got it back years later. It was in a crime scene evidence bag and the bills had turned blue. But it was still legal tender. I removed the bills from the bag and went shopping—for myself.

Detective Lieutenant Dominick Varrone behind the wheel driving me to freedom. (Courtesy Newsday)

My first night of freedom, January 13, 1993. It's a day I celebrate each year like a birthday. The start of my new life.

Newsday *Cover, January 14, 1993 (Courtesy:* Newsday*)*

CLOSED EYES

FOUR VIDEO CAMERAS AND two stills were trained on the small vertical window of the cell block door in Central Islip's arraignment court. John Esposito emerged, wearing a tan "pleather" jacket, purple shirt, and jeans, looking more florist than felon. He glanced at the packed gallery and then turned toward the bench, hands cuffed behind his back. He wore a defeated scowl.

"People vs. John Esposito, kidnapping in second degree," a voice bellowed.

Attorneys put their names on the record and the assistant DA was asked, "Do the people wish to be heard on the question of bail?"

"Yes, Your Honor, I do," said steely-haired and distinguished looking William Ferris. "The defendant is charged with Kidnapping Second Degree. It's a very serious charge, a violent felony. If the defendant is convicted on this, he faces twenty-five years. There has been much media attention in this case and the people are going forward vigorously with the prosecution. We are going to ask the court to hold the defendant without bail in this matter. I want the court to know the case is very strong. I want to commend the counsel in this case because what we have here is the defendant abducted and restrained this young girl from December 28 until yesterday. She was found in a subterranean vault, if you will, underneath this house."

The arraignment, as were most court proceedings in New York State at that time, was open to news cameras. Six videographers in the corner of the courtroom pressed their eyes against lenses and zoomed in tight on John's perspiring face.

"I'd like the court to know there was a search warrant executed a few days ago in this house and notwithstanding the best efforts of police, they were unable to uncover what was underneath this house. And we have information from the young girl that she tried to make noise in that chamber but she was unsuccessful because it was soundproofed. She apparently saw on video what was going on with police officers searching upstairs, but was unable to be heard. This defendant knew what he was doing. He even went to the press publicly saying he wished to find Katie. We have a person who knew full well what he was about. I am going to ask, therefore, that he be held without any bail whatsoever. The case is going forward to a grand jury, as soon as possible."

Andrew Siben addressed Judge Patrick Barton next, making a unique case for bail. "Your Honor, the defendant, John Esposito is forty-three years of age. He is a lifelong resident of Bay Shore, owner of a home in Bay Shore; he is a general contractor in Suffolk County. His only prior criminal history is an incident that occurred fifteen years ago. I can honestly say that Mr. Esposito was instrumental in the recovery of Katie Beers. Katie Beers may not be alive if Mr. Esposito did not cooperate. Mr. Esposito has shown a sense of responsibility and compassion by not fleeing when he had the opportunity to do so. He is not a threat to anyone in the community. Your Honor, it's my understanding that the purpose of bail is to assure the court that the defendant will return to court. By Mr. Esposito's own actions, Your Honor, he knows he will face serious charges and is prepared to let justice take its course."

John stood shoulder to shoulder with Siben, eyes clenched shut, biting his bottom lip.

Siben continued, "In view of his sense of responsibility, compassion and his cooperation of coming forward to help law enforcement to solve this perplexing and baffling mystery, I would respectfully ask the court to set reasonable bail. I repeat, Your Honor, without the help of Mr. Esposito, this mystery may never have been solved."

Without Mr. Esposito, this mystery would never have been created. Reporters visibly winced as they hurriedly scribbled notes.

The Sibens seemed genuinely floored by John's announcement the day before that Katie was alive and hidden somewhere in his house. The bomb was dropped by John in person. He had arrived first thing in the morning with his sister-in-law, anxiously requesting to see Sidney Siben at once. No one could believe what John was saying. Police had been all over his house. Where could Katie possibly be? In a secret room, John admitted, something like a bomb shelter. "She's behind the wall—I've had her there the whole time." [12]

Andrew Siben drove to Hauppauge and met face to face with District

Attorney James Catterson to deliver the jaw-dropping news: John Esposito had confessed that Katie was alive.

Siben and fellow attorney, Ira Kash, planned to also negotiate John's surrender and bail. Catterson, a no-nonsense, seasoned prosecutor who knew the little girl's life could well hinge on the outcome of this negotiation, was as patient as he had ever been. During the high-stakes conversation, he was told only that Katie was alive, but apparently not where she could be found.

The hours that passed while closed-door discussions were underway and Katie remained entombed would later become the subject of later public speculation and criticism. The Sibens would later say they concerned for the child's safety; if police responded too hastily, Katie could be killed in a botched rescue attempt.

John had mentioned a two hundred pound concrete slab that only he could safely open. They also knew that the matter of client-attorney privilege was at stake. They could be disbarred if they went to police or prosecutors without John's waiver. Sidney Siben, who stayed back in his office with the now potentially suicidal Esposito, got him to sign a release.

In the interim, one of the attorneys tipped off *Newsday* that Katie was alive and hidden somewhere in Esposito's house. That's how the press corps beat cops to the house. Katie was alive, and police were informed by a *Newsday* reporter. And it was a *Newsday* manager who phoned Catterson mid-negotiation, providing him with information that the two defense attorneys who sat in front of him did not—Katie was located right under their noses.

Catterson was later livid over the leak. "I'm here negotiating with his lawyers. What is Siben doing? This is like ducking out of the talks at Panmunjom and going to the press."[13] Catterson was a Korean War veteran and the reference to armistice talks was lost on younger reporters, but not the eighty-one-year-old Siben. The thickly-spectacled law firm elder made no apologies about his tactics and his insatiable appetite for publicity. He later crowed, "I wanted to have [Esposito] surrender the little girl to a *Newsday* reporter."[14]

Sidney and Andrew Siben went along with police in a small pack that followed John into his office closet as he silently unscrewed bolts, opened hatches, and cranked up a piece of the concrete foundation. In utter silence, they listened with incredulity as John pressed a button on an intercom speaker and announced, "Katie, I'm coming down."

As Katie emerged from the tomb, "… I heard a young child's voice and I knew she was fine," Andrew later said. "I told her, 'Katie, everything's fine. Everybody loves you and you're now going to be safe.'"[15]

Katie, he said, propped herself up and greeted him with a smile. "I feel good!" she said, waving to neighbors and reporters who had lined up outside. Then, she got into the back seat of an unmarked grey police sedan. Behind the wheel, breathing a colossal sigh of relief, was the chief of the Kidnap Task Force, Detective Lieutenant Dominick Varrone.

Later, Sidney Siben made Katie's time in captivity sound more like a play date than a kidnapping. "A little bruise on her knee. She was happy. Very excited. We called. We didn't hear an answer. Then she said, 'I'm here, I'm happy.'"

What was her reaction when she saw Esposito?

"She was very happy when she saw John. She likes him.[16] He's been very good to her. Her home conditions were such that she had more happiness and comfort with John Esposito."[17]

Detective Lieutenant Dominick Varrone headed the kidnap task force.
You can see pictures of Katie, Sal, and Big John on the boards behind him.
(Suffolk County Crime Lab)

Detective Lieutenant Varrone saw it a very different way. At a news conference inside an auditorium in the Medical Examiner's office adjacent to the Fourth Precinct where the Kidnap Task Force was headquartered, he told an enormous collection of cameras and reporters, "There is no way that you could describe this little girl's ordeal as anything other than barbaric. I believe she survived because of toughness, and a desire to live coming out of her own experiences growing up. I don't think his intentions were very good…we are very fortunate she is alive."

The scene outside the precinct in Hauppauge was as big a news stakeout as it gets. Cameramen toting bulky Betacams on that raw, rainy night didn't dare put them down for fear Katie would walk out any moment and they would miss the coveted shot.

Linda arrived in a wheelchair with an entourage of extended family, *Beauty and the Beast* balloons and candy for Katie.

And Marilyn, who needed to hitch a ride to the precinct from a detective, arrived poised for a reunion with Katie. It never came.

After hours of waiting in her wheelchair outside the detectives' squad room, Linda could be heard both inside and outside the building hollering, "I want to see my daughter! This is a rotten thing for you to do to me!" Cops closed the door to the room in her face.[18]

Katie emerged finally, a diminutive figure in a two-toned blue oversized slicker, clutching an open bag of potato chips. Police sneaked her out of a back door. Neither Marilyn nor Linda ever got a glimpse of her, but the media had all exits covered. This was not a shot to be missed.

She seemed to sport a smile as flashes erupted and camera shutters furiously clicked. County attorneys were already drafting court documents for Marilyn to sign, seeking temporary custody of Katie, intent that neither woman would ever lay claim to Katie again.

The next morning, John stood still with closed eyes, as his attorney asked the judge for special accommodations.

"Your Honor, I would ask that the defendant be placed in protective custody and segregated from the other prisoners, due to the notoriety this case has received. I'd also respectfully ask the court that Mr. Esposito receive medical attention due to the stress that he has undergone. I would also add, Your Honor, that Mr. Esposito has family here today—they are concerned about his well-being—and very much support him. I ask the court to again consider setting some kind of reasonable bail."

Ferris then interjected with what nearly everyone at the arraignment had to be thinking. "Your Honor, there is no *mystery*. Katie Beers was secreted in his house the entire time when the realization occurred to this defendant, we have a strong case and he stands to face substantial state time."

Judge Barton ordered Esposito to be held on half a million dollars bail. No one posted the money, so he remained behind bars at the Suffolk County Jail in Riverhead. He was placed on a suicide watch, his jailhouse cot lined only with tissue paper. In protective custody, as requested, he was shielded from a different form of justice—inmates have their own due process for child molesters.

Outside arraignment court, a crush of reporters, cameras, microphones, and tape recorders pressed into Andrew Siben.

What did you mean by that? Wasn't it your client that put Katie in danger in the first place?

"I have no comment on that; I would simply say that without Mr. Esposito's cooperation, this child may not have been found."

Why isn't he being charged with Kidnapping First Degree? Why is it Kidnapping Two? Was there some kind of deal worked out?

Kidnapping in the first degree carries a maximum life sentence. Kidnapping Two is eight to twenty-five years. The distinction is that Kidnapping One involves some kind of sexual abuse or torture. Esposito denied to his attorneys that he had ever touched Katie.

"I think it's significant that police and the DA's office only felt it warranted a charge of kidnapping in the second degree. I think that is significant."

Was any kind of arrangement worked out with the District Attorney's office?

"I will not comment on any conversations I had about this case. This case or any case."

How much time was it in between when you learned that Katie was alive and when she was freed?

Siben half smiled. He had to have seen that one was coming. "I can only say that yesterday I received a phone call from a client. And he informed me that he had information on the whereabouts of Katie Beers. I felt it was incumbent upon me to notify the District Attorney's office to see to it that the child was safe and sound. And I do feel that we helped save a human life. The end result is that Katie is alive and well."

Katie was indeed alive. But she would soon tell the Suffolk County Grand Jury that she was a far cry from well.

An eleven-count indictment was unsealed a few days later, and John was summoned back to court, this time wearing a sports jacket and the beginnings of a graying, untrimmed beard. As is standard on suicide watch, there would be no neck ties or razors. This time, Sidney Siben stood beside him and the District Attorney himself, James Catterson, sat at the prosecution table. William Ferris announced that the grand jury had upgraded the charges to first degree kidnapping and six counts of sexual abuse. Now, the stakes were higher—Esposito could spend the rest of his life in prison.

John Esposito, arrested on kidnapping charges.(Courtesy: Keith Lane)

"This case has resulted in the search for a child in perhaps one of the most intensive investigations in the history of Suffolk County. This case has attracted worldwide attention. This is a very, very strong case. For the severity of these charges—not one, but three Class A felonies—we are asking this court to hold the defendant without any bail."

From behind thick, black, square-framed glasses, Sidney Siben spoke

John Esposito at kidnapping arraignment in Central Islip, New York. (AP Wide World Photos/Alex Brandon)

passionately. In his gruff, street-smart manner that seemed to conjure a Brooklyn stickball pep talk, he made all the usual appeals for some kind of bail: John was a longtime resident of Bay Shore, never in trouble but for that one arrest fifteen years ago, but added that he needed reasonable bail so "we get him out to get him some help."

The judge technically granted Siben's request, but set bail outside of John's financial reach: One point one million dollars. One hundred thousand for each criminal count: sex abuse, kidnapping, endangering the welfare of a child, and making false sworn statements.

After the arraignment proceedings concluded, Catterson held his own court. Before an audience of reporters and cameramen, he thanked police for what he called the most expensive and most extensive investigation in Suffolk County history. Then he made what was arguably the most persuasive appeal in his storied legal career—an appeal to the media to back off.

He said he'd had the remarkable opportunity to meet Katie a few days earlier, and some of her first words to him were, "You know my name is really Katherine."

"Let me tell you a few things," Catterson continued, in a manner more fatherly than prosecutorial. "I found her to be a remarkably with-it child, an upbeat kid, but she is a little girl. She is wise, unfortunately, beyond her ten years; she is wise, but resilient, she is quick; she has a sly sense of humor…. She is in good health; I'm advised… she eats everything in sight. She sucks up love like a sponge and you can't blame her for that. In fact, she is starting to use a computer and she even told someone she may even be thinking of writing her memoirs. She had her first day of school yesterday and, you know, Katie is entitled to be a little girl; in fact, she brought a friend home with her to play. And today is another story….She is well aware of what's going on. She talks about the TV stations …and she really doesn't want to talk to the press. She wants to go to school with other kids. In fact, one of the first questions she asked the officers is, 'Will I get to go to a nice school again?'

"What does this child need? She needs to go to school regularly with children her own age. She needs a childhood. And she needs a child's routine. She needs to be silly and be playful and to be hugged and…not to be bothered. And she has to develop the ability once again to trust people, to experience childhood—a childhood that is enjoyed by most children in Suffolk County, but was denied to Katie.

"But as we speak, word has leaked out that Katie is in school, and people of your profession are out at the school trying to catch that picture, perhaps that little interview, perhaps tomorrow's story. And it really brings us down to the fundamental obligation—the media and the public's right to know, versus a little girl's right to be a child."

At the time, five or six news vans were staking out an elementary school in Springs, Long Island, after an East End radio station broadcast that it was Katie's new temporary school. By day's end, one television network and a major wire service had taken the wraps off the name and location of the school, and live trucks were circling. The tiny hamlet in the township of East Hampton now had one inhabitant who could trump the inauguration of Bill Clinton in the tabloid headlines!

"I'm going to ask the public, on behalf of the county of Suffolk, to ask the media or *tell* the media, we'd like to know she is safe, but we don't have to know what she had for breakfast."

Catterson had notes, but barely looked down. It was clear the words came from the heart and not from a rehearsed speech. "We'd like to know that she's eating well and with a family that loves her, but we don't have to know what her grades were in school. I'm going to ask you all to back off.

Give her a chance. You know, that's not asking too much. To you, she's just another story, but to Katie, it's the only opportunity she has to live a life she's only dreamed about.

"I hope that the editors that you talk to, that they have children. I have a ten-year-old granddaughter, and when I compare the two, I wonder where we are going in our society. I have a picture in my mind's eye of a little girl trying to grow up in a world where most grownups are just bad children. She was hurt by those she put trust in.

"We, as a society, must protect this child or our professed love for our own children is just a fraud, and our so-called compassion for each other is just a mockery.

"...I'm going to, on behalf of the people of Suffolk County, *demand* responsibility from your profession in letting this child alone. Let her get on the bus without a camera in her face, and let her get off the bus without a microphone in her face.

"And tell the people who tell you you've got to get the story, for God's sakes, have compassion on a little one, for after all, what are we here for?

"The County of Suffolk and the County Executive are going to ask each and every one of you to join in a conspiracy with us and the police, a conspiracy to protect Katie in the days and months ahead. And shame on those who exploit her for a cheap story. They are not any better than the person who locked her in that box.

"I'm going to leave you with a little show-and- tell, and they tell me not to do it, but I think a picture is worth a thousand words."

Bill Ferris, who stood on one side of the podium, handed Catterson a white poster board with small capital black letters. GIVE KATIE A CHANCE!

"But wait a second." Catterson ripped off a piece of paper where the name "Katie" was printed. "It says give Katherine a chance." He paused a beat and added, as if slamming a gavel on a judicial bench. "That's all I have to say."

It was a compelling argument, albeit a touchy one. Journalists don't like to be told how to behave, especially not by elected officials, but not one of us at that presser questioned his message. It sank in deeply as the news conference rolled without pause onto other topics: questions about Katie's state of mind, a possible plea deal, and John's motives.

After Katie was freed: District Attorney James Catterson, right, Assistant District Attorney William Ferris, center. Detective Lieutenant Dominck Varrone, left. They asked the media to "back off." (AP Wide World Photos)

Suddenly, our unanswered questions seemed strangely unimportant. Our curiosity would have to yield to something bigger; we were to stand back and let a child be offered love, the essential ingredient missing from her troubled life. There was not a single challenge to the notion that Katie deserved, and in fact needed, anonymity.

"We have five hundred active child sexual abuse cases right now in this county," Catterson left us with. "Perhaps this will make us all think about that."

The next day, Mike McAlary, then a columnist with the *New York Post*, gave Catterson's plea an extraordinary endorsement.

"Let us revisit the child ten years from now or perhaps even rediscover her as a college-bound treasure," McAlary wrote. "Everybody knows a truth when they hear it. I am betting that in the dither of the moment, that no one in this business was thinking about Katie Beers when they were snapping off pictures of her yesterday. That doesn't make them bad people—only jaded. You want to make life easier for Katie Beers? Shut the camera off, dummy."[19]

The very newspaper that had reportedly been hounding the *East Hampton Star* for the name and address of Katie's temporary foster family was now appealing for a collective backing off. And as radio stations and newspapers bickered publicly on the editorial pages about which ones had behaved badly, the frenzy to find Katie began to die down.

"Just as suddenly as it began, the media crush ended," declared the editorial board of the *East Hampton Star*. It dubbed the DA's message essential to Katie's recovery. "The wire service reporters and the rest folded their notebooks and departed. There were no more camera trucks roving aimlessly around the byways of Springs. This is as it should be."[20]

In fact, in the years to come, some reporters who were dispatched way east to Katie's foster home, at the direction of unrelenting news managers, admitted in confidence that when they got there, they never even knocked on the door.

Curiosity about John Esposito and the depth of his depravity was, however, considered quite fair game, and the scene on Saxon Avenue drew mobs of onlookers. It also brought out Clint Van Zandt, a special agent with the FBI's Behavioral Sciences Unit from Quantico, Virginia. The FBI had been consulted on the making of the movie *The Silence of the Lambs*.

"It's much more sophisticated," Van Zandt said, standing outside the crime scene tape. "In the movie, you've got this hole dug in the ground, and you've got Buffalo Bill keeping somebody in the hole. This is a much higher level of sophistication, so far as being able to conceal it. It was like a prison from medieval times. I've never seen anything in all my years as elaborate as this. This thing was like out of a horror movie."

How could cops have missed it?

"If someone told you that room was there, I'd put money on the line that you'd have to tear that house apart to find it."

The next day, Suffolk Police brass gathered to hold another news conference—this time with props: diagrams and a big screen, stage left. Lieutenant Varrone seemed drained as he fielded most of the questions. Esposito, he said, indicated the chamber where Katie was held was built a year and a half earlier, with Katie in mind. It begged a question.

Do you think it was used before?

"We suspect and are concerned it was used before. We may have to take the house apart piece by piece. You can imagine, if he went to this extent to create what he did, we don't know what other surprises we may find. The FBI behavioral experts were amazed. I hope we don't find anything more, but at this point it is just conjecture. Your guess is as good as mine. We don't have any direct evidence at this moment to support what I think we are all thinking."

Reporters had been told by the Sibens that Katie was relatively content in captivity, an upgrade from her sorry pre-kidnapping state. Varrone promptly put the kibosh on that spin. "In time, I think you will all know what occurred down there, but it's my belief that, at times, the girl was absolutely horrified."

What precipitated the abduction? Was it planned?

"I think this goes back to what the behavioral analysts were saying, and I'm not going to speculate on his motives, his fantasies and why this room was built, but we know that Katie was thrust in this room when there was some noncompliance. I think you are all aware of the sequence of events prior to when she was put in this room. She went to Toys 'R' Us. A video was purchased which he believed was a ruse to get her into his home. There were physical advances. I'm not going to describe them or go into them, but Katie seems to be a tenacious, feisty individual who screamed and hollered and resisted and the result being, by Katie's account, being thrust into this room."

Then, someone asked the uneasy question that had to be posed.

How it is possible that you searched that house and didn't know Katie was right under your feet?

"A suspect in the case is guaranteed certain freedoms." The answer was long and may have come from a place of deep second-guessing. But he shrugged it off and responded confidently. "We were in that house, initially, the day after her disappearance to search it. That house that Katie was in, the garage, whatever you want to call it, is actually where he lived. We were in there initially and he insisted that any police officers that stay behind go to the front house. His attorneys were adamant. We had no choice but to comply, so we were located in the front house. Right from the get-go, Mr. Esposito was obviously our prime suspect. He was the last one seen with her.

"We saw a video of her in the 7-Eleven shortly before he went to his house and she left behind her pocket book. So we knew that she had been in his room. But what we didn't know—if she ever made it to Spaceplex. That was the subject of debate, and most seasoned investigators and FBI behavioral analysts who we had group phone calls on motives and psychological theories—right from the get-go—felt that a girl from a rough upbringing who had her own change in her pocketbook would not leave that room without her pocketbook. So we all agreed on that, so we were all suspect about what Mr. Esposito had told us."

Long answers are not the norm at news conferences. Varrone had a purpose. He was taking heat in the papers about the fact that Katie was within a house the cops had been all over in top-to-bottom searches. He seemed to be fighting his own demons about the little girl who now told them she cried for help at the top of her lungs, and none of his men heard. The house, he said, "would have to have been demolished to have found her."

"We kept surveillance of him as best we could. We had detectives deployed on various sides of the block in case he decided to go through the woods. Whenever he went to go anywhere, we followed him, and I hope and I think that contributed to his decision not to harm her. I don't think Mr. Esposito anticipated the response of either the police or the media of him reporting a little girl missing. So I think that contributed. I can only speculate what his plans were—but I can tell you after viewing the room, I don't think his intentions were very good.

"We didn't believe any of the family members—any of the cast of characters. We were very tough on them. As quickly as we could, we did polygraphs on them, and we were slowly but surely eliminating all the good guys, and up to the few days prior to us finding Katie, the pressure increased on his immediate family. I think that entered into his final determination to do what he did. I feel strongly that if Mr. Esposito had not come forth, I do not think we ever would have found Katie."

Dogs, he said, would now be carefully exploring the house and yard looking for bodies.

"We believe he acted alone. It is a slow process, but obviously the lab will evaluate stains, if anyone else was ever down there. It was foul-smelling. I don't like to sensationalize, but it was barbaric. There were things in that room below the house which, I think you'll agree, were unbelievable and deplorable."

Cops propped a diagram up on an easel to the left of the podium. It showed the passageway from John's office to his underground human vault. A seven-foot-drop was connected to a five-foot horizontal tunnel, two feet high by twenty-one inches wide. It led to a box within a box. The outer box was six feet wide by six feet high and seven feet long.

Detective Captain Bill Kiley pointed to a smaller box where Katie was held most of the time. It was just two feet wide by three feet high, and seven feet long.

A grainy seventeen minute video tape appeared on the giant projection screen as Lieutenant Varrone narrated from the podium. All of us reporters were salivating to see this. The dungeon had been described as everything from a basement anteroom to a hellhole. As soon as the tape rolled, it was clear that this was no guest room.

It was a point-of-view perspective. The camera rolled as cops went through the steps that Esposito had divulged, slowly removing the red J&R Home Improvements caps from the sides of the office stereo cabinet, exposing cup hooks beneath, then slowly unscrewing the hooks, revealing long recessed lag bolts. A shelf slid out and allowed access to more lag bolts. There were four of them, and each one had to be unscrewed in order

A cross-section of the tunnel Big John built leading to the bunker. It was 2' wide by 21" high and 5' long. (Suffolk County Crime Lab)

to slide the cabinet out of the wall.

"FBI experts say they've seen a lot of these hidden rooms, but they have never seen one constructed as meticulously in such an elaborate manner."

There was dead silence in the auditorium as the video played. Casters were propped under the front of the cabinet to allow it to be slid out. The cabinet was pulled out, revealing nothing in the closet but tan carpeting. Neatly done.

"I think we would have difficulty finding this, even if he directed us to it. I think you would agree, I don't think many movie directors could conceive of an idea like this.

"Now, if you were inquisitive and you rolled back the carpet, you would find padding and the tack board around it, absolutely nothing that would make anyone in the least bit suspicious of anything underneath.

The plywood prison was 6' wide by 6' high and 7' long. Big John poured a slab of concrete and built a carport over it. Police dug it up after Katie was found. (Suffolk County Crime Lab)

Now if you pull up the padding, it reveals duct tape, which is indicative of holding the padding in pace, but you also see a piece of Velcro, which suggests something that doesn't belong. So he has a piece of Velcro on the linoleum floor and a piece on the back of the cabinet so he can lift the floor, and the linoleum would be out of the way to expose what follows."

What followed was beyond belief. The unseen detective in the video lifted the linoleum cutout in the floor and Velcroed it to the back of the cabinet, uncovering a cement square cut out of the foundation, two feet by two feet, with an eyebolt in the center. It took steel cables and barbell discs to pull up the two-hundred-pound, six-inch-thick slab and stabilize it.

"I think you'll agree it's just absolutely amazing, the amount of thought that went into this and the kind of mind it may reflect."

Below the concrete slab was a plywood cover. With that removed, you could see straight down a deep plywood shaft. The shaft was lined with two-by-four rungs placed at intervals like a ladder through a series of trap doors. Each door had to be unbolted to open.

"He had a battery-operated wrench. No adult, certainly no child, could get through this."

The final door revealed the plywood prison. The room dropped down thirty inches from the tunnel and was covered with cork squares. It was a mess of candy wrappers, empty soda cans, wires, and human excrement.

"She was able to keep the TV on all the time," said Varrone. "That was her contact with the outside world and that will contribute to her recovery, *if* she is able to psychologically recover from this."

At the Udall Road strip mall, some merchants jubilantly tore down missing child posters. Others marked the posters with "FOUND" in black letters. Scores of offers for adoption poured in from families across the country. And at Spaceplex in Nesconset, owner Gary Tuzzalo, now feeling vindicated, said he wanted to "throw Katie the birthday party she never had and invite all of Long Island."[21]

A crime scene command post bus became a fixture in front of John's house and police roped it off with yellow crime scene tape. Neighbors permitted us to enter their back yards, for a fee, to get a view of the converted garage being ripped apart. Crime lab experts hauled off carpet, padding, plywood, and the concrete hatch with the eyebolt. People, snapping photos like tourists, flocked from the city and beyond to try to make sense of the bizarre.

"He was just an average, simple, normal guy. He was just a nice guy," said a young man in a hooded sweatshirt.

One woman with hot pink lips and a perm brought her pre-teen son as a life lesson. "Just showin' him the house—pointin' out the fact there are people around like this. They look normal. They are among us, and they are victimizing children. It's scary."

A grown mother and her elderly mom came, too. "I can't tell you what I felt when I saw her rescued," the younger woman said, pressing her hand to her heart.

"We also feel this little girl should never be returned to that family," added the older woman.

Another one brought a whole vanload of kids. "We want them to know it's not only strangers they have to be afraid of. Even friends!"

The box was hauled away as well. It was pulled out of the ground by a backhoe and dangled on a giant hook, like a Playmobile toy. We stood watch over that, too. Neighbors gawked from behind the crime scene tape as it was covered in a blue tarp, gingerly lowered onto a flatbed truck, driven out of Bay Shore, and into criminal history. It collected dust in the Suffolk Police evidence hanger in Yaphank for years. No jury would ever see it.

Back in Mastic Beach, at Marilyn's house, Little John put on a tough guy face, but couldn't hide the hurt. "I just want her home," he told a semi-circle of reporters huddled around him in the bitter cold.

They're not letting Katie home because they say Marilyn neglected her, John. How do you feel about that?

"It's Sal. He's a lying, two-faced, fat slob. It's not true. She should be returned. She is a good mother."

Did you get to see Katie at all?

"Didn't get to see her at all. All's I heard is she's fine and she looks fine from the papers."

The red and yellow KISS emblem on his black baseball cap hung over his impossibly blue eyes. Little John was growing media savvy.

"I'll talk at the press conference," he said, leaving frustrated reporters behind as he walked toward a waiting limousine. Talk show hosts were clamoring to cash in on the national obsession and mocking the Beers and Inghilleris became afternoon television sport.

Montel Williams' producer offered Marilyn legal funding to get Katie back. Geraldo was pitching Linda. Sal appeared on *Inside Edition* and The Maury Povich show erupted into an audience assault on Marilyn's character. Sally Jesse Rafael, *Prime Time* and the morning talk shows were circling.

Meanwhile, John Beers escorted his grandmother, Helen, into a waiting stretch limo that seemed ludicrously out of place on Mill Drive in Mastic Beach. They were whisked to a chopper and delivered to the set of the *Phil Donahue Show* in Manhattan. As the limousine pulled away, it passed a home on the block where a white sheet hung crookedly from tacks pushed into the vinyl shingles. "Welcome Home Katie" was handwritten in multicolored bubble letters.

For Katie, this would never be home again.

My story on the evening news that night went like this:

With one bizarre mystery solved, police are now digging through John Esposito's home to see what other surprises they may unearth here. So far they say they have found photographs and video tapes of children, but won't comment on their nature.

Police dogs, meanwhile, are sniffing for bodies because police say they believe the underground vault where Katie Beers was kept was not built for her alone. The lead detective in the case suggests Esposito had a method to his madness.

"He works slowly, he gains their confidence, and he showers them with gifts to include their families," Detective Lieutenant Dominick Varrone said.

But while law enforcement paints a picture of a monster, Esposito's attorney says Katie Beers owes him her life.

"Without the cooperation of Mr. Esposito, this child possibly never would've been found," Andrew Siben, John Esposito's attorney said.

Prosecutors dismissed the notion that Esposito did anyone a favor. "Mr. Esposito is being charged with taking her and abducting her against her will. For whatever reasons and I can't go into them now, he held her for over two weeks. At this particular time, I think that really speaks for itself," William Ferris, the Prosecutor, said.

The man who held Katie Beers for sixteen days is now himself being held on half a million dollars bail. According to police, he had built an elaborate prison for his captive. Ten-year-old Katie was at times bound to a wall by a chain around her neck, handcuffed and able to see police searching for her through closed-circuit TV. Soundproof walls kept police from hearing her. The room lay beneath a bookcase. Police had to unbolt the bookcase, roll up the carpet and lift a two hundred pound slab of concrete to uncover the crawl space that led to the tiny cell where Katie was kept.

This man, the head of Suffolk's Big Brother Organization, rejected Esposito as a member and warned Katie's mother years ago that he fit the profile of a child molester.

"I happened to have had a little more knowledge about his background and I didn't think that this was a random incident. I knew that somebody had to be involved that knew her. Most children are abducted by people they know," Paul Freedman, Suffolk Big Brothers, said.

Esposito's neighbors say he was a mystery to them before the arrest and even more so now. "Just to see him coming home and late at night having that across the street, it's just weird."

Make you frightened?

"Yeah, it does. Exactly."

Meanwhile, a criminal behavior expert with the FBI is now studying Esposito's secret cell, and he says it's reminiscent of the movie, The Silence of the Lambs, only in some ways worse.

"This is a much higher level of sophistication as far as being able to conceal it and I tell you what, if somebody told you that room was in there and you went in to look for it, I'd put money on the line that none of you or I would be able to find that unless you almost tore that house apart. It is concealed so well," Clint Van Zandt, FBI, said.

What's next for Katie? She's survived, but can she ever recover? In Bay Shore, Carolyn Gusoff reporting.

HOME

THE DRIVE TO THE police precinct seemed to take forever. When we pulled in, it was night, and the flash of cameras hurt my eyes, which hadn't yet adjusted to life. I was so embarrassed. I hadn't showered in over sixteen days, and I was wearing a soiled nightgown and swimming in a man's extra-large jacket.

The cops brought me down to the police station's basement, where I talked endlessly to a uniformed woman named Debbie. First, I needed fresh clothes. She handed me a neatly folded pile: yellow sweatpants and a T-shirt. They draped my frame but I was relieved to finally be out of the urine-stained Dalmatian nightgown I had worn for over two weeks.

Then police prodded me for details—lots of them. I don't remember how long we talked or much at all about what was said, but the questions kept coming at me and so did the snack food. I was starved, and the fluorescent lights burned my now-aching eyes.

After Debbie and her barrage of questions, I was brought to what I now know to be Schneider Children's Hospital in next door Nassau County, for what I was told would be an evaluation. I remember everything was hurried—a blur of hospital staff rushed me into an exam room right away. They had cops standing outside the door at all times. I asked a nurse if I could bathe, and she told me that as soon as I was done being examined, I could shower.

They took some vaginal swabs and took blood from a big needle stuck into the crook of my little arm. I now know they even took a pregnancy test. The nurse brought me some orange juice in a paper cup, and it was the best-tasting liquid I have ever had. Even so, I was skeptical, being poked, my legs opened, my insides checked. I didn't exactly know if I was in safe hands.

It was around midnight when I was brought to a private hospital room and uniformed cops were posted inside and outside the door. The curtains were drawn and I was told not to open them, not even in the morning. Someone asked me if I was hungry and what I wanted, saying that they would open the hospital cafeteria for me to get something to eat—but I only wanted Chinese food. Pork fried rice and wanton soup.

It was the first real food I had eaten in seventeen days. It appeared and I devoured it.

Sleep came fast and hard. I woke after a deep, long rest, and someone broke the news to me. At first, I thought I didn't hear it quite right.

"What did you just say?" I asked.

"You're going to a foster home for the time being, Katie. That means you won't be going home…yet," one of the social workers said.

Not going home to Marilyn and Little John? I would not be seeing Grandma Helen either? I didn't understand. What had I done wrong?

Now the guilt resurfaced. I had done something wrong and was being punished. It was my fault I was kidnapped and Big John wanted me. I was dirty. My stomach churned and my breathing quickened. I was very upset because Marilyn's home was the safest place I thought I could be. The tears came next. I wanted to go home, even though I wasn't sure which place *was* home.

Home was an ever-changing concept for me. The Inghilleris, who had said they were boarding with us temporarily, were in Grandma Helen's house at 12 Higbie Drive to stay. And there, Aunt Linda's wrath would surface regularly. When one of her Blue Pomeranians, LuLu or Tiki, got out of the house, Aunt Linda would scream her head off chasing the dogs and trying to catch them. That was when she still had both her legs. I would stand frozen, inside the house, scared to say a word as she fumed. She looked back at me once and yelled, "You little bitch, come help me catch Lulu."

I remember hurrying outside the house and trying to catch Lulu, but the dog darted into Udall Road, a busy county road one block away from our side street. Aunt Linda ordered me into the street. Lulu was in the middle of the road, with cars flying past her on both sides. Aunt Linda gestured to the road and ordered me to go fetch. I tried to explain that I was not allowed to cross the street without someone holding my hand.

"Get the fuck in the road and get the dog," she barked. So I braced myself for a mad dash, ran out into Udall Road between the rush of cars, grabbed Lulu, and then raced back to the sidewalk, where Aunt Linda was simmering as she watched me. As I handed her Lulu, she pulled my hair and told me that if I ever disobeyed her, she would beat the crap out of me again.

After she lost her leg to diabetes several years later, I became her little errand girl. Beginning at four years old, I would do all of the cleaning. I had to dust and clean the floors on my hands and knees, bathe the dogs, and clean the bathrooms with a nauseating batch of bleach and ammonia that I was ordered to mix myself. From her upstairs room, Aunt Linda would summon me with her errand demands and I would dutifully comply. If I wasn't in the house when she needed me for a chore, she would scream out the window for me.

Sal and Linda always found a reason to yell at me. Sal would yell for not being his servant in a timely manner or for not being "available" when he wanted me to touch him. And Linda usually yelled because she was too lazy to do anything for herself, if I didn't bring her the right snack, or if I didn't fold the laundry properly.

The pizza place was a frequent detail. It was across the street and down one block in a small strip mall on Udall Road. Her standard request was Sicilian slices with pepperoni. But one day, without warning, her standing order changed. She wanted plain pizza this time—cheese only. After I paid for the pizza and left, I realized my terrible mistake. I had accidentally ordered the slices with pepperoni out of habit. I started to cry while I was walking home, knowing I'd be in big trouble. So I stopped at Harry's, the strip mall deli. The girl at the counter asked me why I was sobbing, so I told her that I messed up Aunt Linda's pizza. Together we picked off all of the pepperoni as she assured me it would be just fine.

It wasn't fine, not at all. Aunt Linda immediately noticed the cheese was missing in some places and beat me. She commanded me to come over to her, yanked me by the hair, and hit me with solid punches to the back.

I spent so much time at the stores at the strip mall that everyone knew me. I was good friends with Harry at the deli. When a gun shop opened, I soon became friends with the people who worked there too.

Harry's was a frequent stop, and one time Aunt Linda wanted a dessert cake from his deli. Her request was a pack of Yodels, but when I got there, they were out of Yodels. I picked her up a pack of Ding Dongs because they were basically the same thing, just a different shape. I brought them home and explained to Aunt Linda that they were out of Yodels.

She was not happy about that. She grabbed me by my ponytail and beat me with both sides of a paddle hair brush—the wood side first, then the bristle side. She beat me for over five minutes because they didn't have the right snack cake. I was crying and between breathless sobs, explaining there was nothing that I could do because they simply didn't have what she wanted. She screamed back at me that she didn't give a shit; I should have gone somewhere else to get her what she wanted.

"The closest store is across the highway!" Even I knew I was too small to cross Udall by myself. She then threw the Ding Dongs back at me and ordered me to get her what she wanted. When I got to the bottom of the staircase, Little John was there. He had heard the screaming and offered to walk with me across the street to get Aunt Linda the right snack cakes. I had welts all over my arms, legs, and back because of the beating. My brother hoisted me up on his shoulders and held onto my legs tightly as we crossed Udall together, without saying a word.

Marilyn needed to work two jobs to pay for everything in the house, since Aunt Linda and Sal lived there for free. In between her day job, driving the taxi, and the night job, watching the old lady, she was dead asleep in the room she had grown up in upstairs. She would always leave John and me an allowance every week, usually five dollars, for whatever we wanted. I would usually use my allowance to buy Aunt Linda a pack of Virginia Slims.

Yes, the stationery store around the corner would sell cigarettes to a five-year-old because Aunt Linda had written me a note once saying that the cigarettes were for her, and not me. The cigarettes were usually around three dollars, so I had about two dollars left over. Most of the time, with whatever was left from my allowance, I would buy M&Ms for my grandmother. Every day, Grandma Helen would sit in front of the TV, from the morning test pattern to *The Tonight Show*, downing beer and frozen M&Ms.

Sometimes I'd buy a magazine for Little John or a trinket for Marilyn— something that said "Mom" on it. I don't call her "Mom" now. I know it's a title she doesn't deserve.

Aunt Linda and Sal bled every penny out of that house in West Islip and eventually my grandmother had to walk away from it with next to nothing. Marilyn had allowed them to come live with us because they said they would help out with the bills and help watch John and me—but neither Marilyn nor my grandmother ever saw a nickel from them.

Aunt Linda rarely went downstairs. If she needed something from downstairs, she would either scream for me, or use a broom to beat on the floor to get my attention and summon me for a chore. She would walk from "her" bedroom to the upstairs bathroom naked, her fat and breasts hanging loosely. She'd walk to the bathroom to get into the shower to "cool off," and she would do that several times a day. When she was done using the shower, she would walk back to the bedroom without drying herself off, dripping water everywhere. Eventually, the bathroom floor rotted from the ever-present puddles and literally fell into our living room below.

No one had enough money to pay for the repairs, so Sal took out a loan, with my grandmother co-signing, using our house as collateral. But the loan was larger than Sal needed to make the repairs on the living room ceiling and bathroom floor. We got the upstairs bathroom repaired, but there was a lot of money left over, enough to make the minimum payments for a few years.

Instead of using the money to pay off the loan, though, Sal bought a new tow-truck and lots of porn. My grandmother and Sal got into constant fights because she wanted Sal to pay back the loan, always arguing that Aunt Linda was the one who "broke" the house. But Sal never gave in and instead used the money for himself. A few months later, unable to make the payments, Grandma Helen had no choice but to put the house on the market. We stayed as long as we could, even after the new owners took title. Eventually, we were evicted from the house that my grandfather built.

There was no *home* after that.

So when the social worker at the hospital told me I wouldn't be going *home*, I had to think for a moment. *Where is home, anyway?*

From my hospital window, I sneaked a peek out of a small opening in the drawn curtains. I could see an encampment outside, around the semicircular drive that formed the entrance to the children's hospital.

HOME

There were big news vans and at least a dozen antennae sticking high up in the air, almost as high as my window. Cameramen toted gear on their shoulders and reporters stood in front of tripods gesturing and speaking words I could not hear but knew were about me.

A woman who told me she was my "case worker" wanted to get me out of the hospital without being noticed, so she told me to lay on a gurney—and be very still. Orderlies pulled a sheet over my head and the gurney was pushed into the elevator. Something went wrong and they wheeled me over to the wrong car. When we finally got into the correct car, somehow unnoticed by the throng of media, I climbed into the backseat, and off we went.

We drove for hours. I remember wondering where the heck they were taking me. No one told me where we were going. It was Sunrise Highway and the road went on forever and ever. Straight ahead for miles on end, past strip malls and gas stations, and then farm land and barns. Finally a sign read "Southampton" and the road kept going…and going.

There were so many trees everywhere! It was getting dark; dinner time. We pulled up to a house. It was a huge house with a two-car garage, cedar shingles, and it looked like a storybook farm house. Only this was real, as was my exhaustion. I rang the doorbell, hiding behind the caseworker's leg, and a smiling couple invited us all inside.

I didn't grow up in a house where there was a Mom and Dad, so the first few minutes felt to me like something out of a television show. The only family I ever knew was from *Growing Pains*. I sat down at a fully set kitchen table surrounded by three kids, a mom, a dad, and a pizza. The pizza was warm and so were the welcoming faces.

But I had an anxious feeling in my gut. I felt like I couldn't breathe—as if a rope was tied around my lungs and heart. I couldn't inhale. The rope was tight and painful. I've had many anxiety attacks in my life since then, but that was the first one.

That night, at dinner with the foster family, I didn't talk much. I tried to breathe slowly and calm down. I was skeptical of the adults at the table, Barbara and Tedd. They tried to be very, very nice, even buying a belated birthday cake for me—a Carvel ice cream cake. And there were presents.

But I was very rude. I was presented with a *New Kids on the Block* Donny Wahlberg doll, but took one look at it and announced that I didn't like *New Kids on the Block* anymore.

"Kid stuff," I snapped.

The next day, the father, Tedd, came back to the house with a Steve Urkell doll for me. Urkell was the star of the then-hit television show, *Family Matters.* I politely thanked him, but still wondered when I would be going home to my real family.

MAKEOVER

T HE PRESS WAS NOT kind to Marilyn. A *Post* headline was especially pitiless: "Disgusting Marilyn Beers" a big woman with bad teeth.[22] Mike McAlary, the acerbic Pulitzer Prize winning columnist, had a New York way of seeing it and saying it straight:

She is a sad figure, really. But then you remember that this woman gave up her child to a house run by an admitted pedophile, Sal Inghilleri. She lost two children to the deranged lust of John Esposito. On occasion, Beers sent her own kid out into the cold with bare feet....No one can save Katie Beers from her first ten years. But we should be damned as a society if Katie Beers is returned to this loutish lot.

So when Marilyn initially signed over temporary custody of Katie to Suffolk County, then changed her mind the next day, there was no one, at first, volunteering to walk her through the minefield that was Suffolk Family Court. No one but John Jiras. Tall, white-haired and sixty-something, Jiras began his career as a TV and film makeup artist but decided, ten years into his chosen vocation, to attend law school. After earning a name in Hamptons' homicide cases, he was referred to Marilyn by her psychic, John Monti. He took the case with gusto.

"All future questions about Katie should go through my office," he instructed reporters on the first day Marilyn appeared in Family Court to attempt to win back custody of her daughter.

The jockeying for Katie's custody had actually begun in earnest days earlier, on the talk show circuit. Linda had no legal standing in the tug of war, so instead, she made her case via satellite on *The Montel Williams Show*.

"To me, there is no difference between John Esposito and Marilyn Beers," she said, as the audience raucously stood and cheered. "They both have claimed to love [Katie] but in a sick way. John had her living *under* a garage and Marilyn had her living *in* a garage. But Katie and I have shared a *real* love, a *real* home, and *real* tears to be together forever."

Marilyn, who appeared live in the studio, admitted on national television that she didn't know the identity of Katie's father. "So crucify me." The jeering crowd nearly did just that.

Linda's argument may have gone over with daytime talk show addicts, but in court, it was only Katie's biological mother who could stake a claim to custody. And the stake was planted, albeit tenuously, in Suffolk Family Court on January 21, 1993.

Ms. Beers, are you willing to let Katie stay in foster care?
Are you satisfied with the arrangements?
How often will you get to see your daughter?
Ms. Beers?

I stuck a mini recorder under Marilyn's chin as she walked into court, with Little John's father, Teddy Rodriguez, at her side, lips clenched. Not even a hello.

Reporters were allowed into the proceedings, but had to leave video cameras outside, so when the brief session ended, we catapulted out of our seats, beat the lawyers outside by hustling down stairwells, and waited in a pack in the only part of Family Court's exterior that is not an arctic wind tunnel—just steps from the revolving front doors.

"You got it all inside. What else do you need?" Anthony DiSanti, a young county attorney assigned as Katie's law guardian, asked. "The case was put off until February 11th and there is an agreement between all parties."

What's the agreement?

"Can't tell you. That's part of the agreement. I can't tell you any more."

What are the allegations against Marilyn Beers? On what grounds can the County take Katie away?

"Can't tell ya."

A passing attorney muttered something about there being a letter "N" on the docket number, indicating an allegation of neglect or abuse.

But Katie stays in foster care?

"Yes, the child is in foster care."

And Marilyn can come back at any time and request custody?

"Yes, she can request that."

It was actually quite a bit of usable sound-on-tape for a "no comment." Marilyn came out next.

C'mon guys, down in front, make room for Marilyn.

MAKEOVER

Marilyn, are you giving up custody of Katie?

Jiras, who stood beside her, cut in. "We are not here to make a statement. I'm here and the Suffolk County attorney is here," he said, gesturing to Jeffrey Adolf, who made the common mistake in the legal community of exiting the courthouse in the bitter cold sans winter coat, and going slowly numb as reporters' questions dragged on.

Adolf added, "The law prevents us from discussing the contents of any information contained in court documents…"

But what about the allegations of neglect against Marilyn….?

"Can I please finish? A child protective petition," he explained, "alleges neglect, abuse, or both. Can't tell you which of those, but it's one of them."

What the lawyers did reveal was that the county and Marilyn had agreed to the following: supervised visitation with Katie three times per week, with the matter being revisited by the court in three weeks. Additionally, both Marilyn and Katie, now referred to in court as Katherine, would undergo psychological evaluation.

Jiras didn't even try to hide his motivation. Rumors were swirling about big-money movie deals with the networks. The county had floated the idea of assigning a legal property guardian to manage the piles of money that were sure to come Katie's way.

Marilyn agreed to a county money manager for Katie, saying she wasn't interested in the inevitable riches; she only wanted her daughter back. But Jiras, by all accounts, was pushing Marilyn to sign over the rights to her story to movie producers. He reportedly turned down a three hundred and fifty thousand dollar offer for the rights to Marilyn's side of the story, insisting on a million dollar movie deal.[23]

No one believed Marilyn could make a dime off her perspective, except perhaps Jiras.

Do you expect to sell Katie's story for big money?

"Is the Pope Catholic?" he quipped.

If it was supposed to get a laugh, no one in the tight circle of journalists huddled around him cracked a smile. McAlary wrote in his *Post* column the next day, "after that remark, I promised Jiras, 'You, sir, are a dead man.'"[24]

It was the last time Jiras would represent Marilyn in court. Even she could recognize a public relations disaster. "I'd rather be poor and have my daughter."[25]

Eight years later, Jiras was crossing Main Street in East Hampton on his way to meet a friend for dinner at Sam's, the "Cheers" of the East End. It was dark out and he may not have seen the Nissan heading south. The driver told police she just couldn't stop in time. Jiras didn't make it, and neither did his anticipated riches for Marilyn or Katie.

Meanwhile, any mystery about exactly what kind of home Katie was living in was solved by the Suffolk County Sheriff. He volunteered to reporters that Katie's foster father was a longtime sheriff's deputy and decorated Vietnam veteran, and her foster mother was a homemaker with four other children, who was herself adopted as a child.[26] And the principal of Katie's new school gave interviews out on the front lawn. Peter Lisi said Katie was doing very well.

"If folks would just leave her alone, she would be on the road to recovery."

The three weeks passed and we were all back at Family Court outside, staking out arrivals. This one, though, was not anticipated. Wheeling up the walkway of the sprawling modern courthouse was Linda, being pushed by her mother, Ann Butler. Linda was uncharacteristically cold to reporters, to whom she had poured out her heart in the previous month. She stared ahead, as if camera crews tracking her ride were invisible. Instead, a tall, blond man toting a legal briefcase answered for her, but continued to walk with purpose.

"We are just here," George Harkin said, "as interested observers."

This time, Judge James F.X. Doyle granted the media's application to videotape the proceedings. It was rare for Family Court to be open to the public, much less news cameras, but the judge's ruling mentioned something about the fact that everyone already knew the parties involved. Katie's identity was no secret, so any privacy issue was moot—and the public could use a lesson in the workings of Family Court.

A heavy-set, neatly dressed woman entered Judge Doyle's courtroom and sat down at the defense table. She had a shoulder-length perm with bangs reaching to the top of her aviator glasses, and wore a neat black blazer. Marilyn Beers had undergone a complete beauty makeover!

She had done more than lop off a foot of hair. She had cleaned up her Mastic Beach garage apartment, too. The day before, she invited news crews in to show off her squeaky clean digs. The dirty dishes were gone; the floors were mopped and cleared of the piles of magazines, beer cases, and trash.

But the upgrade in appearance did little to change the custody arrangement. More visitation was requested, but denied. Disanti, who represented Katie, told the judge he would side with the request for more visitation, but the judge was not moved.

Linda positioned herself on a bench in the back of the courtroom. Harkin had filed a motion for custody, but the judge would not allow it to be heard in court.

Outside, Disanti again was the first to emerge.

How is Katherine feeling?

"She's in good spirits; she is in a very good foster home. But she loves her mother very much."

Does she have a preference?

Where does Katherine want to live?

"She has indicated to me her desire; that is all I'm going to say."

Linda came out with a scowl and no comment. Ann, who held a cigarette between her teeth, opened the front passenger seat for Linda, bumped into a cameraman and barked, "Hey, want me to get you for damages to my car?"

Linda was caught in the camera frame of a dozen news crews and couldn't escape as Ann hurried to remove the wheelchair legs.

Were you here to make your own custody petition? Did you get to do that?

Nothing.

Linda, if Katherine is watching this, is there anything that you'd like to say to her?

With that, Ann slung a purple windbreaker over the passenger side window, blocking the cameras' view as Linda propped herself into the car looking more dejected than usual. After the car sped off, Harkin stuck around.

"She is seeking custody of Katherine. The Court would not hear her application at this time. Certainly she is disappointed."

Marilyn's new attorney, a short blonde with a perky bob, was more upbeat and optimistic. "She wants custody of her child and she is willing to do whatever it takes to create the least pain for this child that has already had enough pain," Andrea Lannak said.

"We are working toward gaining their reuniting. It's our understanding that Katie wants to be with the mother."

Is Marilyn happy with the visitation?

"Marilyn Beers will not be happy until she is with her daughter."

Are you concerned with Linda Inghilleri's claim for custody?

"No, not at all. I don't know why you all keep giving Mrs. Inghilleri so much notice. She is in no position to be applying for custody of this child. Nor is she capable. I don't even think it needs to be addressed."

She claims she raised her.

"People claim all kinds of things."

Adolf, refusing to offer specifics, managed to give just enough to confirm that the case against Marilyn wasn't going away.

Will the county pursue its neglect case against Marilyn?

"The case is continued till March 1. It's continuing. It never stopped."

March 1st came with new charges that Marilyn was an unfit mother. The assistant county attorney revealed in court that Suffolk was now not only seeking to take Katie away from Marilyn, but also had a neglect petition against her for failing to send John Beers to school.

And Katie, Judge Doyle said, would be taken away permanently if the county could prove she would be in imminent danger to her life or health if she were to stay with Marilyn. The motion for permanent removal would be argued in a full-blown trial in eight days. With tears in her eyes, Marilyn bit her lip and walked out of the courtroom, navigating her way through adjacent District Court, ducking out on the waiting cameras outside.

Lenny Kostas, a stringer photographer, was helping Marilyn out with her image and stood before the microphones fielding a barrage of questions. Marilyn, he told the gathered press, was seeing a therapist to turn her life around. She was stunned, he said, that she was being accused of failing both of her children.

Eight days later, Marilyn's prospects were even worse. Suffolk was now formally accusing Marilyn of allowing Katie to be abused by both John Esposito and Sal Inghilleri. Kostas, again speaking on Marilyn's behalf, held several pages of handwritten notes. He read, often interrupted, what he said was a statement from Marilyn. But he prefaced it with some words of his own.

"Every time she says something, it is misconstrued or twisted, and it causes the public to form a false judgment about her. This is a very high-profile case, and every time a rumor or hearsay is reported, it's almost construed as fact by the general public and, even though it's proven false down the road, they remember that rumor or allegation. They believe what they read in the papers. When you are reporting, remember that a ten-year-old child is watching everything that's going on. And that's her mom you are talking about. She loves her mom. She wants to be home with her mom right now. She doesn't want to see her mom on television being crucified. ..."

The gathering of reporters bristled at the suggestion.

What have we reported that's not true?

Didn't she allow her daughter to go to Linda's with Sal in the house?

Didn't Linda's husband sexually abuse Katie?

She knew Esposito was molesting her son?

"We are not going to try the case out here. We understand the media and the public has the right to know, but we have to be very careful..."

We deal in truth and people do trust us, and we try our best to be accurate, and we take that responsibility seriously. What is it that she thinks we have been inaccurate about?

"There was an article that called Marilyn a whale, worst mother of the year."

That was a column. What have we reported that is incorrect?

"But it appeared in the paper and people read that."

But it was an opinion piece.

Teddy Rodriguez took a turn. He had been accompanying Marilyn at every court date, and now stood outside next to Kostas. His big blue eyes, identical to his son, John's, searched in vain, trying to offer examples of what he felt had been misreported. Finally, a somewhat defeated looking Kostas retreated to the pages in his hands and read Marilyn's rambling statement, condensing as he hopscotched in and out of questions and answers.

"I'm tired of the media twisting and misconstruing my words to suit their purpose. I would like to straighten out a few things for you, your readers and your viewers. The first thing is that I never gave Katie, my daughter, to Linda Inghilleri's care when Katie was two months old. I love my daughter very much. I would give my life for my children. The second thing is that my life was threatened if I did anything to take my daughter away from Linda. I tried to do the best for my family. The third thing ...."

Who threatened Marilyn's life?

"Sal Inghilleri did."

When?

"The third thing," Kostas continued. "Sometimes I get so frustrated, I feel like a victim of the system. They are using me as an example, for what reason, I don't know why. I believe all this negative publicity is really hurting Katie deeply. I used to work long hours to support my family. I always tried to do the best for them. There is one paper, I believe, that said if I were a professional person, I would be considered ambitious, but as a working single mother I am considered neglectful.

"People think of me as a cold and uncaring person because I don't show my emotions. I guess I am afraid to show my feelings to the outside world but that doesn't mean I don't feel anger, pain, love or happiness. I'm a person with very deep feelings. It's hard for me to show them to people I don't know. I am a loving and caring person. I have always tried to be there to help my friends, if they ever needed me.

"I let Linda and Sal stay in my mother's home when they needed a place to stay. They were not giving us anything. My only mistake was the judgment of choosing the wrong people to care for my children, Katie and her brother John.

"I know the system believes it is doing what's best for Katie, but I believe what's best for her now is to be home with her family, which is where she wants to be. We all love her and we miss her very much."

Kostas was a passionate advocate for Marilyn and continued his damage control even after some of the reporters and cameras had pulled away the mics and rushed off to edit their stories for the next newscast.

"She's making a lot of positive changes in her life. She moved into a three bedroom apartment, and ..." he said to the remaining reporters.

Are these changes for show for the custody hearing?

"Most people who have missing children don't ever see them again. And if they do find them, they are not alive! She has an opportunity to do things over, and do them right! Marilyn Beers seems to be a real good person. She doesn't project well in the media. Marilyn has a second chance here. And she is going for it. She will not give up."

Marilyn Beers and Teddy Rodriguez, Little John's father on the right, outside a Family Court hearing in Central Islip, New York on January 21, 1993. (AP Wide World Photo/Mike Alexander)

The court, meanwhile, had other concerns. It was sidetracked on an issue quite separate from the custody of Katie Beers. The media was petitioning to keep cameras in the courtroom, but virtually all the other parties wanted the proceedings closed. The judge got to hear from an adamant Katie herself on the matter, in a handwritten letter.

> I Dont Want People to Know What HAPPENED to ME, because its None of THERE BISINES. A MEAN Little Boy Was Saying Things About ME Last Week And It Made ME Sad. If Everyone Saw MY life on TV it will Upset ME AALLOOTT. Please Dont Put MY CASE On TV, Its BBAADD Enough That Its In The Papers.

Judge Doyle's decision allowed reporters and cameras to stay in the courtroom for the custody trial, but with limitations. Media would be excluded from the courtroom during Katie's testimony and anything else he ruled "sensitive." The county, unsatisfied, appealed the decision to the New York State Supreme Court Appellate Division in Brooklyn. Until the case was assigned a date on the busy appeals calendar, the custody trial was on hold.

While the cameras in the courtroom debate took center stage, things were not going well for Linda. First, a judge ruled she could not visit Katie. Next, her custody petition was thrown out altogether. The court dismissed her motion, ruling she had no standing in the case and was a "legal stranger" to the girl.

Katie's wishes, at least concerning cameras in the courtroom, were heard loud and clear by the five Appellate Court justices in Brooklyn. Katie didn't appear in court personally, but attorneys for her, her mother and the county argued that cameras in the court, as allowed by New York State statute, could cause great harm to Katie. Assistant Suffolk County Attorney Robert Cabble argued, "Katherine...does not deserve to have her life brought out as an abject lesson in the workings of Family Court."

The attorney pleaded with the justices. Katie, he said, had already been hurt by public knowledge of her case.[27]

The decision of the panel was unanimous. The Katie Beers custody hearings would be closed.

Thus, when all parties agreed to a settlement on June 12, 1993, reporters had to learn the specifics via sources and what little Marilyn would acknowledge. She was required to admit that she had been a neglectful mother, that her "lax" supervision had created conditions that made the kidnapping possible. The county, in return, would drop the abuse allegations against her. Marilyn was giving up custody, but just for a year, and was not giving up hope.

The arrangement was supposed to be periodically reviewed. But Marilyn's makeover was short-lived. She was evicted from her new three-bedroom house for alleged failure to pay rent. Later, she faced misdemeanor charges for allegedly hiding work income to collect unemployment benefits. None of this helped her custody claim.

Eventually, lawyers closed the book on the Katie custody case. A small blurb on the one-year anniversary of the kidnapping appeared in *Newsday*'s "Letters to the Editor" section. It was entitled, "Thinking of Katie."

MAKEOVER

...After being an integral part of Katie's life since she was an infant, I am now considered by the courts to be a complete stranger to her. Katie was not the neglected waif the media portrayed her to be; she was and always will be deeply loved by myself and my family—her family. Katie always had lots of clothing and toys, material possessions were as abundant as our love for her. Katie was always kept clean and well taken care of when she was with us.

Katie is still being held prisoner after more than a year. First by John Esposito; now, held prisoner by the county. She's not allowed to make phone calls or write letters to anyone who shared in her first ten years of life. A year has come and gone since we celebrated Katie's 10th birthday—a family celebration with all the trimmings, then an outing to the movies to see Aladdin. *Two days later, tragedy struck. Katie disappeared. As the nation tensely awaited news of Katie, my family's and my torment increased hourly.*

Katie's cries are not being answered now any more than when she was in that horrid dungeon. I will continue to petition the court for at least visitation of Katie. I will push to let Katie know we are still here, still loving her, and still waiting for her to be released from her captors.

Ann Butler
West Islip

The matter of Katie's custody never made news again.

A WHOLE NEW WORLD

LIKE A SCENE FROM *Oliver*, I suddenly entered a picture perfect new life. I didn't want that; I wanted to be back with Marilyn. I was scared to death, having problems breathing. But Uncle Tedd and Aunt Barbara, as they asked me to call them, immediately enrolled me in fourth grade at Springs Elementary School and treated me as if I were the newest member of the family—the youngest of their five children. They wasted no time. Monday was Martin Luther King Jr. Day, so the next day, a Tuesday, an unmarked police car waited for me in their driveway.

Detective Brown drove me up to the Springs School and drove around to the back, taking me inside through the exit. He told me he would wait for me, and that until further notice, I was to enter the school through the back exit. There were camera crews in the front.

I hadn't been to school in a very long time and it smelled good. I didn't know it then, but the children were briefed on me. They had an assembly prior to my arrival and a letter went home with parents. They were not to ask me any questions about my kidnapping, but that didn't stop them.

"I heard you were held between the walls of a crazy man's house," one girl teased me.

"No—that's not true," I snapped back. I didn't bother with an explanation. No one could possibly understand.

Mrs. McGintee showed me a seat in the front of the classroom. Jason, one of my foster "brothers," was in my class, and everyone else seemed to know I was coming.

She showed me my cubby and where I could put my coat. The day moved quickly through music, art, gym and everywhere I went, I was warned never to walk through the front hall of the school. I would have to walk around the long way. There were large picture windows in the front and photographers, in the frigid cold, were camped outside what amounted to a giant fishbowl.

I was very far behind in school, especially in math, but Mrs. McGintee didn't pressure me. She had her daughter, who was in seventh grade, come in during lunch and after school to help catch me up.

Upstairs at the foster home, I shared a room with Cassandra, an eighth grader and the younger of the two daughters. Cassandra was very tall and pretty with blonde hair, blue eyes, a muscular athletic build, and ever-present pony tail that swung as she knocked the heck out of a volleyball.

Rebecca, the oldest of the four children, was away at college. Jason, my age, was adopted into the family from foster care, and Jesse, sixteen, shared a bedroom with Jason down the hall. It was the first time in a very long time I had my own bed, and at first I was afraid to sleep. I wasn't sure these people had good intentions, nor did I understand why I wasn't with Marilyn.

Years later, I would learn that I wasn't the only sleepless person in the house. Barbara, having been warned I might run away, spent the better part of a year struggling to stay awake at night to make sure I didn't disappear again.

It was easier for me to talk to Aunt Barbara than it was to connect with the others in the house. I didn't talk to the siblings very much at first; I'd always connected better with adults anyway. They were doing their best to assimilate me into my new life. Tthey took me shoe shopping and clothes shopping—all new experiences.

I had never had anybody caring just for me. These people were concerned about my hair and my clothes and my comfort—did that fit right, was I hungry, what did I like to eat, and was I tired? No one had ever before asked me anything about my comfort.

Despite their efforts, I felt very uneasy alone with Tedd at first, especially during any trip in the car with him. I remember he drove me to the dentist's office, a forty-five minute trip, and I could hear my heart thumping as I edged as far away as I could from the driver's seat. *Just get this over with*, I thought. *Please don't touch me.*

This didn't last very long. He treated Aunt Barbara with the utmost respect. I soon learned he was a gentle and caring man; the first one I ever knew.

As the newest member of the family, I had to learn basic hygiene. I had never been taught to brush my teeth, and my mouth was a disaster. My teeth were yellow and rotting.

Years earlier, Linda and Sal had taken me to an emergency room in the middle of the night because of an excruciating toothache. It turned out a gaping cavity needed to be filled. The long Novocain needle terrified me and I would not sit still, fighting the dentist and the nurse, my arms and legs flailing.

Someone went to tell Linda in the waiting room that I was resisting the needle, and she instructed them to give it to me any way necessary. I had three people holding me down and the ER dentist stabbing at my gum with what felt like an ice pick. It was the last time I complained of a toothache.

Now, living under Uncle Tedd and Aunt Barbara's roof, I was introduced to a new ritual: brushing teeth before bed, every night and every morning. I was given a toothbrush and told what it was and what I was supposed to do with it. Visits to the dentist came often. My fear of needles was respected. I would get all the work done with sweet gas. Needles were banished from my new life. My feelings mattered. And a steady diet of school was introduced.

School had previously been optional. The only grade that I remember attending on a day to day basis was kindergarten. Once Linda and Sal moved in with us, I stopped going to school with any regularity. Most mornings, I would eagerly get ready for school. The bus would come, but Linda would bang on the floor with her broom and summon me upstairs to buy her a pack of cigarettes. Then she'd call school, tell them I was sick and send me to the stationery store to do her errands.

Truancy called the house once in a while questioning where I was, so Sal would drive me, stopping at a desolate parking lot to pleasure him before dropping me off.

I always loved school. When I did go, I could be a kid. No wondering if Aunt Linda was going to need me, or if I would get in trouble because I didn't hear her calling me to do a chore or run an errand. I could pretend for a small amount of time that I was child with no responsibilities. I wouldn't have to worry about doing the laundry, cleaning the toilets, making the meals, or servicing Sal.

When I did attend, I never had the right clothes and Marilyn and my grandmother were constantly being called in to discuss my attire. I would wear summer clothes in the frigid Long Island winters, outgrown pants and skimpy shirts that were bought from the dollar store or Cheap Johns. Once a year, Marilyn would buy me a new top at Caldor for class picture day. I would wear it over and over again, and I could hear the kids at school call me behind my back "Dirty Katie" and "Cockroach Kid."

That's me in the middle with my new shirt. (Suffolk County Crime Lab)

I did have this one friend growing up: Roseanne. She lived around the corner from me in West Islip. We would ride bikes, play dolls, and swim in her plastic above-ground pool. I had such fun with Roseanne, until Sal ruined it. Sal knew that I was friends with Roseanne, and also knew that he had control over me. He instructed me to bring Roseanne by his bedroom window; he wanted to show her something.

I put it off as long as I could, that is, until Sal threatened to beat me and my grandmother. He picked a morning for the task. My instructions were to bring Roseanne by his window, and he didn't care how I did it; he just wanted it done. I told Roseanne that we were going to play "McDonald's drive through" on our bikes and that Sal would be at the window to pretend to be the McDonald's employee giving us our food. When we got to the window, Sal was there wearing a robe. I "ordered" my food and then it was Roseanne's turn to order.

Roseanne went up to the window, and before she could "order" her food, Sal's robe was on the floor and he was standing there naked, asking her if she wanted to play with him. Roseanne sped away from the window screaming and crying. Sal ordered me inside. He was furious Roseanne did not play with him, so instead, Sal raped me.

I tried to go to Roseanne's house a few days later to play with her, but her mother came to the door and informed me that I was no longer allowed in because of the "event that occurred the other day."

Child Protective Services was at our house a few days later asking me questions. I was so scared of Sal that I lied about what had happened. I told CPS that Roseanne was the one who was lying and that something probably happened at her own home. I did not see Roseanne after that and things for me only got worse.

There were also allegations of Sal abusing two girls for whom Aunt Linda babysat. For some reason, Sal would come along on the job, and so would I. The girls and I were playing "house" with their older brother. I was playing the role of the mother, the girls were the daughters, and the brother was the father. While we were playing, the brother and I were pretending to sleep.

Sal summoned the girls to come out of the room. They went with Sal and came back a few minutes later, crying hysterically. I could surmise what had happened, but asked anyway. They said that Sal touched them, and made them touch him. They also said that this wasn't the first time it had happened.

Then, they reluctantly revealed Sal's threat. If they told anyone about the "game they played," he would hurt their parents. He didn't have to elaborate. They knew he meant what he said. Their brother also admitted to me that he had been physically abused by Sal and that he got the same lecture about not ever saying a word about it, or else "someone would get very badly hurt."

I'm not aware of any charges ever brought against Sal for molesting these little girls. His threats apparently succeeded.

When we lost the West Islip house, Linda and Sal moved to their house in Bay Shore, and Marilyn to the Mastic Beach two-car converted garage. Sal and Linda took me with them because Marilyn was still working two jobs and figured she couldn't care for me. They took in my grandmother Helen, too, because they needed my grandfather's social security checks.

One day, while Linda was napping and Sal was out of the house, Marilyn came and took me away.

"Katie, you're coming with me," she said. "Get your stuff."

It was right after Marilyn filed charges against Sal. She said little. I had no toys, just some clothes. I let Marilyn and her boyfriend, Teddy, in through a back basement door where my grandmother was staying. They stuffed all my things into black plastic garbage bags and threw in what little Helen had, too. Then they took me and Grandma away. I was kicking and screaming.

Since Linda abused me, I thought: *She is going to blame this on me. She is going to beat me the next time I see her.* That is why I was panicking. Sitting in the back seat of Teddy's car, I stared out the window, going all the way down Sunrise Highway, crying. *I'm going to get beat real bad.*

Marilyn enrolled me in fourth grade in Mastic at the Tangier Smith Elementary School. I don't remember any of my teachers, from any grade. I never asked anyone for help. I didn't know I should have or could have. No one, in those days, discussed these things.

When I did go to school, I got a wicked case of head lice. It was so embarrassing because everyone already thought I was a dirty child—then I got lice to prove it. I was sent home for treatment—stayed home for a few days—then returned to school, only to be examined by the nurse, who found my head still full of nits. After a few more days, I snuck back to school and the nurse sent me home again. That's when my long, beautiful hair was chopped off. Marilyn took me to get it done.

"If you want to go to school, Katie, you have to get rid of that mop," she said.

The salon was in a strip mall in Shirley, near the house in Mastic Beach. They had to use special sanitized scissors as they cut as close to my scalp as possible. I had always had long pretty hair. Now I looked in the mirror through glassy eyes and saw my nearly shaved head. My hair had been the one thing that was ever really tended to, with braids or ponytails and barrettes. All that was gone in a pile swept into a plastic dustpan.

BURIED MEMORIES

The haircut and the repeated doses of RID didn't even work. I still had lice. Marilyn seemed to do everything she could to kill them. She gave herself, Little John, and Grandma Helen the treatment. She treated the house, the sheets and my one stuffed animal, but I still had lice.

The nurse would call the house next door, and the neighbor would come deliver the news. Grandma Helen would then walk the one mile to school, collect me in the nurse's office and we would leave together, returning on foot to the garage apartment the four of us shared.

As she held my hand, she would say, "Katie, I know you want to be in school, but we gotta have this lice taken care of."

Helen was soft-spoken and gentle, the most special person in my life. She was the only person who ever hugged me or physically expressed love, because Marilyn just wasn't around.

Grandma Helen and I used to walk to the grocery store, and it wasn't close to our house. She tried to pay one time, but the store clerk wouldn't let her use a check because the one before had bounced. When we returned home empty handed, Sal was so angry, he not only beat me, he also hit my grandmother.

She was a petite woman. There wasn't much to her. She would shake her head and say that if Grandpa Stewart were alive, things would be different. Then Sal would chime in saying it was a good thing Stewart wasn't still living, because he would hit him, too. Sal was such an angry man.

Grandma was a wonderful soul, but she was too weak to save me. Uncle Bob later told me the home he and Marilyn grew up in, Helen and Stewart's home, was a "madhouse." Having come from one, I can only imagine.

Helen died when I was thirteen years old. I was at summer camp in my new life. My foster parents didn't want to call me and break the news over the phone, so they waited to have the services and funeral for when I got home. I hadn't seen her much after the kidnapping. Marilyn, when I did see her, never wanted to go the hospital to visit her mother. When we did go, Grandma would hang out the hospital window smoking cigarettes, and Marilyn would sneak smokes downstairs. Helen Beers died of lung cancer.

To Grandma's wake, we had a police escort with silent lights as if we were something special. At the viewing, the laid-out body looked nothing like my grandmother. In life, she was thin and frail—there was nothing to her. When you pass, you retain water. She looked bloated and made up. She had never worn make up. As I looked at her in that box, I thought, *I never really knew this woman.* I certainly never understood how a grown woman could be so helpless.

I don't think about her much anymore. I have no desire to see or speak to any of them. I don't want to hurt Marilyn, so I try, once in a while, to keep in touch.

EVERYBODY'S CHILD

WITH READING GLASSES PROPPED on the end of his nose, Judge Joel Lefkowitz read a note aloud.

"We, the jury, have reached a verdict," he said, and then shot a glance at the bailiff.

"Okay, bring them in."

As the jury filed in, Sal, seated at the defense table, took a deep breath and leaned back in his chair. The camera in the corner of the courtroom picked up the sweaty sheen on his multi-folded forehead above shaded aviator glasses. He wore a wide paisley tie and his shirt collar was unbuttoned at the top to accommodate his extra chins.

Sal, now forty-one years old, was facing two counts of sexual abuse in the first degree and two counts of endangering the welfare of a child. They were enough to put Sal away for at least a dozen years.

Prosecutors offered him a generous plea deal of only two-and-a-third to seven years in prison if he admitted to the top count. The deal was intended to spare Katie the trauma of having to take the witness stand and relive the years of abuse. It was to be a package deal: Esposito and Inghilleri. If they both agreed to plead guilty, Katie would never have to testify.

But Sal insisted on his day in court. Against the advice of counsel, he demanded a trial. He stuck to his story: he was innocent of molesting Katie and she was a liar.

Sal got his trial, and along with it, a slew of new allegations: He had assaulted Katie's grandmother and brother, he had defrauded Helen Beers, he sexually abused three other children, he cheated on his taxes, he bashed Katie's cat's head against a wall and made her watch.

"I did not kill no cat," he said, sauntering past reporters in the hallway of Criminal Court in Riverhead.

Katie would have something to say about that. On June 28, 1994, Katie Beers, ushered into court through a back entrance and stairways, propped herself upon a pillow on the witness stand of Judge Lefkowitz's courtroom. Three telephone books supported her feet. She wore a lace-collared pink dress and her hair was now shoulder length and wavy. She held tightly the hand of Mary Bromley, her therapist.

"I was scared of Sal…because he was always beating up on people and animals."[28]

For four hours Katie calmly answered questions. She described how Sal made her "touch him on his private. He put his hand over mine. He moved my hand up and down." In court, Sal quickly moved his hands away from his chin and clasped them in his lap beneath the defense table.

"I don't remember dates," she confidently told the prosecutor, "but I remember it was often on a Sunday."

Now eleven years old, Katie was unshaken but for a small grievance she expressed to the judge during a break. "Can you make him stop looking at me that way?"

Sal was always sitting back in his chair, glaring. When her testimony was over, Katie bounced out of the witness stand and waved goodbye to the judge and jury. The court officers shuttled her to the back of the courtroom, the route usually reserved for legal staff, and out the courthouse back door.

Members of the news media never got the picture of Katie for which they had been staked out. For most of us, her brief courtroom appearance was the first and last time we would ever lay eyes on the girl in the headlines.

The *New York Post* cover the next day shouted in all caps: "COURAGE OF KATIE."

Outside the courtroom, Sal crowed, "Everything she said in there is all fabricated. Believe me—I'm not going to lose no sleep over this."

His attorney, Thomas Klei, later implored the jury to be "brave" and not judge Sal by his unlikable looks. Sal, he told reporters, was originally tricked into signing a confession by police, whom he claimed withheld his nitroglycerin pills. Then, the defense floated, Sal became the victim of an unyielding press, thrown into the spotlight only because Katie had been kidnapped.

Go, go, go!

Reporters spilled out of the courtroom, raced down the hallway to alert their cameramen court was in recess. I flipped on the microphone and my mini-cassette player.

"The jury has to see that my client is human. That he is not the monster he's been made out to be in the papers," Klei said as he and Sal walked the long corridor toward the elevators. It was a daily dance. Sal would pace as quickly as his two hundred and seventy pound frame would allow, muttering, "No comment." A horde of cameras and reporters like me, in nineties shoulder-padded blazers and too-big button earrings, would scamper in high heels alongside him, arms outstretched with microphones and recorders.

I was now working as the Long Island reporter for WNBC in New York City. The promotion gave me a certain sense of ownership over the beat. Whatever happened on Long Island was on my watch, and in July of 1994, the Katie Beers case was squarely back on the front pages.

Sal would say nothing until he could go no farther, boxed in by the closed elevator doors and the sea of cameras. As he would stand there, waiting for the interminably slow courthouse elevators, a torrent of questions would wash over him, like the tide rolls over a beached whale.

You think you've been vilified, unfairly painted?

Sal, how you holding up?

Sal, do you think the jury believed you?

Sal, you got anything to say?

"Can't read their minds, just hope it's a good outcome."

You think you can convince the jurors that you never had Katie touch you?

The elevator came and we followed him in.

Sal patted his breast pocket. "Got my cigarettes. I'm gonna need 'em."

Sal had made the risky move of taking the stand in his own defense. DA Catterson was prosecuting the case himself, and let Sal wriggle on the stand through question after question designed to expose him as slime. Catterson emerged from the courtroom with a grin.

You got pretty emotional in there!

"Don't we all get emotional about little ones? What is a little girl supposed to do? She was betrayed. We have an obligation as a society to protect kids; we have an obligation to kids to protect them."

Catterson didn't need prodding. One question wound him up.

"Maybe the tough life she had helped her get through this. She's doing as well as can be expected. She's gonna have a lot of problems. The grandmother couldn't help her, her mother wouldn't help her, and Linda didn't help her. She had no one to protect her. She was nobody's child, but she is really everybody's child, and we have an obligation to protect her."

Sal was in way over his head. He would arrive each day at court trying to look the part of an upstanding citizen: a suit and too-short tie, an unbuttoned dress shirt, the aviator glasses. He carried an attaché case and tugged on a cigarette as he lugged his heavy frame past cameras and reporters outside Suffolk Criminal Court.

What do you have to do today?

"I'm gonna go on the stand."

Are you nervous?

"Not at all."

He paused for another cigarette, heaving as he leaned on a garbage pail, nervously chewing gum.

I walked up to him, camera rolling.

Just want to know how you feel, Sal, going into this. You sure about taking the stand?

He paused, blew out some smoke and said, "No comment."

Really? I'm surprised. You're usually so talkative.

"When it's all over, I'd be happy to talk to yous. Up until that point, no comment."

When it *was* all over, Sal was, in fact, in handcuffs, two pairs needed to make it all the way behind his hulking back.

Sal wasn't the only accused molester in that courthouse that summer. John Esposito, simultaneously, decided to go a shorter route and take the plea deal.

"For what purpose was this room constructed?" Catterson grilled John in court, to elicit the allocution required for a guilty plea.

"It was constructed to hold Katie," he answered sheepishly.

"It was constructed to hold Katie?"

"Yeah."

"When would you say construction was completed, sir?"

"Actually, it wasn't really completed."

"When did construction begin?"

"It was approximately a year before."

"Was it your intention a year before to place Katie in that room?"

"Yes."

"Now, prior to December nineteen twenty-eight, to your knowledge did any other person or persons besides Katie and yourself enter or visit those premises? Just yes or no. I'm not going to ask you any names."

"You said nineteen twenty-eight."

"Nineteen ninety-two. Excuse me."

"What was the question again, sir?" It was a peculiarly polite exchange.

"All right. Before Katie went in the room on December twenty-eighth, nineteen ninety-two…"

"Yeah?"

"Other than yourself, had anyone else visited that room?"

"No."

"After arriving at your residence, did there come a time when you decided to restrain Katie, intend to prevent her freedom, her movement? If you could answer the question. Did you make up your mind…?"

"Yes."

"At some particular time that you were going to hold her?"

"Yes."

"And that in holding her you understood that would limit her freedom, her movement?"

"Yes."

"And at that time, did you formally intend to put her in this room?"

"Yes."

"And you knew at that time that this was a place where, but for you, she was not likely to be found by anybody else because nobody knew about it and you knew that at that time?"

"Yes."

If found guilty of first degree kidnapping, John could have been put away for twenty-five years to life. The plea deal would make him parole eligible after only fifteen years. Katie would have a say each and every time he was up for review, but the plea would give him a shot at one day dying in freedom.

"And how long was Katie kept in that room?"

"Approximately sixteen days."

"Sixteen days. During that time, did you know that from time to time she was crying?"

"When I was there, she wasn't crying. I didn't know that she was crying when I wasn't there."

"Did she ever ask you or tell you that she wanted to get out of this place?"

"After a period of time, yes."

"Did she ever beg you to let her go?"

"After a period of time, yes, after four or five days."

"And you knew, did you not, that she was in terror, afraid of being in the dark?"

" I…It wasn't really dark. But she was afraid, yes."

"You knew you were keeping her against her will, did you not?"

"Yes."

"And in keeping her against her will, you did intend, did you not, John, to prevent her liberation by keeping her in a place where she was not likely to be found; isn't that correct?"

"That's correct."

"And you knew that you were interfering with her liberty?"

"Yes."

"At any time when she was in that room, did you place a chain around her neck?"

"No."

"You never did?"

"No."

Catterson wasn't stopped by apparent inconsistencies between Katie's account and John's. He was ticking off required elements of Kidnapping One and was satisfied the threshold was being met.

"When Katie Beers was in the room, could her voice or shouts or cries for help be heard by anyone?"

"No."

"Did you insulate the room to make it soundproof?"

"Yes."

The judge cut in, satisfied. "Continuing under oath, John Esposito, as to count three of the indictment charging that you, on or about December twenty-eighth, nineteen ninety-two, in Suffolk County, abducted and restrained Katherine Beers for a period of more than twelve hours, with the intent to terrorize her, kidnapping in the first degree, an A felony, how do you wish to plead?"

"Guilty."

The coy child-like carpenter hung his head in shame.

On sentencing day, Tuesday, July 26, 1994, John would receive "a sentence that could never atone to Katie Beers for the crime that was committed," Catterson spoke for posterity.

"It's an artificial sentence at best," he said reflectively, "but the balance of two interests. This defendant does present a patchwork personality. He is seemingly inoffensive, harmless, perhaps even inadequate. But in my estimation, he has committed one of the greatest crimes of all time…to terrorize a child and betray a trust, this is unforgivable.

"To use other human beings, not as if they were human beings— an unfeeling utilization of another human as if they were an object— is absolutely one of the most heinous sins, let alone crimes, I could contemplate. He had no concern for the far-reaching effects on this child, what nightmares and terrors she will suffer in the future because of his actions….I will agree to spare this child another spectacle—another ordeal. It is amazing that one child should suffer so much betrayal in such a short life."

The District Attorney was speaking as much for the members of the media, squeezed tightly into benches in the courtroom, as he was for the record that would accompany John to Sing Sing Prison. Future parole boards would review Catterson's words for the duration of John's incarceration.

"Her trust has been severely damaged, we know that. She feels she hasn't been protected, she feels violated. She cannot judge the trustworthiness of others."

Katie, he said, had recoiled recently when he leaned over to simply offer her a grandfatherly goodbye kiss.

"She put up her hand to me. She doesn't trust men!" the skilled prosecutor suddenly boomed. "It's going to be a long time before that child can recover the trust of mankind."

Katie then had her say: a few handwritten words on a folded piece of paper, read into the record by Assistant DA Eileen Powers.

He made me feel dirty. I didnt know what he was going to do to me. Even though now Im safe, I still worry all the time. I worry about being taken away; I worry that someone might hurt me. John Esposito should go to jail for as long as he can. If another little girl were kidnapped or sexually abused, I would advise them to talk to an adult or go to the police. They should talk about everything with their therapist if they have one and they should try to be brave. I learned to be brave for being on my own. Now I feel safe with my foster family. Other people who made me feel safe were the district attorneys office, Mr. Catterson, Mary Bromley, the police, my friends and my family.
—Katherine Katie Marie Beers

It was all Katie would say publicly about John Esposito—for two decades.

Catterson then took the unusual step of commending defense counsel for their handling of the case, saying they *were* instrumental in convincing Esposito to, in the end, do the right thing. Andrew Siben offered a deferential head nod and spoke on behalf of his visibly crushed client.

"I have spent many, many hours with John Esposito since the charges have been brought, and I am struck by his profound regret. In fact, before John took a plea, he repeatedly told me he didn't want to cause Katie any more pain or suffering. John is a strange and perhaps perplexing individual, a sad individual, perhaps, some would say, a lost soul. There was no physical harm brought to Katie," he maintained. John Esposito was not a terrible monster, but a person "who conceived of an idea which he believed was helping Katie Beers' future."

The floor was then handed to John, who spoke in a soft murmur, in a sing-song voice.

"This is the first opportunity I have had to talk to you or anyone else who is interested in this case, including, and most of all, Katie Beers. I know you know from reading my probation report a lot about my life and a lot about my personality, the things that have caused me to be the person that I am. I also want you to know that I am not the monster that people think I am. When I was in jail, I got to review articles that were written about me and I am not at all angry at them about the things that were said about me. If I was in their position, I probably would have thought the same things that were written about me.

"Your Honor, believe it or not," he fought back tears, "Katie Beers is a very special person to me. In my own strange way…two years ago, I believed in my mind that I was in some way going to help Katie Beers for the future. I knew full well, and I admitted in court, that what I did frightened Katie Beers a great deal. I knew that for sixteen days she was living in terrible fear and dread, and it was very, very hard for Katie to believe that she was going to be released to the world again.

"I think Katie knows I'm sorry. She didn't deserve this. I hope she comes through this okay. And I am happy she is with a family who truly cares about her. After being in jail for more than a year and a half, I have thought about Katie many, many times and what I did to her. I realize how terribly wrong I was.

"Not only did I really hurt Katie very much," now he was sobbing, "I hurt my family, Katie's family, I caused the police many, many problems. The one thing that keeps me going is my intent to make it up to everyone when I get out. When my mother was alive and Katie was over my house, Katie would make things for her and talk to her. Katie always made my mother feel good. Later on, my mother would tell me, 'Son, you should do something to help Katie.'

"So not only did I let down Katie, I let down my mother." His voice was now cracking. "People think I'm not sorry for what I did. I'm very, very sorry. They're wrong! It hurts me deeply knowing what I've done. People who know me know I have always cared about children. My only hope is one day Katie will find it in her heart to forgive me and let the real John Esposito, the one that really loved and truly cared about you…. I pray God blesses you and makes you grow, and Katie, I'm very sorry," he sobbed. "Thank you."

Judge Lefkowitz would have the last word, calling John Esposito "a classic case of arrested development."

He had read the probation report, which chronicled his over-protected life. It traced Esposito's decline from coddled child to broken man.

John was a child who had been a complete surprise to his parents, Rose and Ralph Esposito. Rose delivered a full term baby on May 14,

1949, but her labor mysteriously continued. She had no idea she was carrying fraternal twins. Baby Ronald was strong and healthy, but John was a sickly three pounds and was not expected to live. His first days were touch and go, but John survived and Rose doted on him as he grew, always shy and skinny.

Her coddling seemed warranted. She had lost her first son, Ralph, in a sudden and dreadful manner. The child ran out to catch the ice cream truck and was hit by a car on Saxon Avenue. He was just five years old. Little Ralphie died in the street on Rose's birthday.[29]

John never moved from that house on Saxon Avenue. He converted the garage into an apartment while another brother, Patrick, and wife Joan lived in the front house with an increasingly ailing and overweight Rose.

In 1990, Patrick died without warning. The Medical Examiner ruled it a cocaine overdose. Just a few months later, Rose also stopped breathing. John tried to resuscitate her but to no avail. He fainted in the hospital when doctors broke the news that his mother wouldn't make it, and sobbed uncontrollably at her funeral.

He spoke about suicide and hating God. The loss of a mother and brother in less than a year left him shattered. That's when he began constructing the underground bunker.

Pale, his head down, John scampered through the courtroom door without looking back.

"Case on trial, the people versus Salvatore Inghilleri. All parties are present. Ladies and gentlemen of the jury have you reached a verdict?"

"Yes, we have."

Two weeks after John's sentencing, it was now Sal's turn to learn his fate.

"The defendant will please rise and face the jury."

"Count one, sexual abuse in the first degree?"

"Guilty."

"Count two, sexual abuse in the first degree?"

"Guilty." The guilties continued until Sal sank back into his seat, wearing a vacant look. He was sweating profusely. It again took two pairs of handcuffs, linked together, to lock his hands around his back.

On sentencing day, Sal shuffled into that courtroom wearing drab prison green and staring up at the ceiling. The aviator shades were gone. One look at her son dressed as an inmate and Sal's mother, suffering heart palpitations, fell out of the courtroom doors and into the hallway. An ambulance rushed her to the hospital.

DA Catterson was merciless. "I have searched long and hard to find some counterbalancing compassion or socially acceptable traits that would merit Your Honor's mercy," he said before sentence was pronounced. "I found none. I find a man who has blamed everyone he has encountered but himself. He has blamed his wife. He has blamed society. He's blamed his health, the publicity. He has blamed his own appearance and the child's mother, but not once, just possibly, did he say he might be a little bit at fault.

"He has blamed an eleven-year-old child for concocting lies against him. How low can one person sink? He has robbed her of her childhood. He systematically looted her grandmother of her meager pittance of a social security—forcing her to take a mortgage he knew she couldn't pay off …a man who has flouted the laws of this state. He wasn't paying taxes for eight years, either, a total disregard for the laws of society.

"I ask Your Honor to send a message to the community that each and every one of us, no matter what our personal failing may be…we cannot victimize children and the elderly. I ask you now to consider sending a message to the Salvatore Inghilleris of this world that a civilized society will not tolerate his conduct, his abuse of children and the elderly, and the flouting of the laws of this nation and community.

"This man has no socially redeeming character or talents. He deserves whatever the law can impose upon him…. I wish that I had the courage to ask that child to go back in and seek a superseding indictment that would have told the *whole* story. It was bad enough she had to testify, and for that act alone he should receive the maximum penalty.

"Oh, before I finish, under the law, the victim is allowed to make a statement—her feelings about this defendant."

Eileen Powers again stood and read Katie's handwritten words aloud.

The truth is he was a big fat liar. He should go to jail for as long as he can. I know he is guilty of a lot more things. I was afraid of him all my life and everybody in my house was afraid of him. He was a fighting man, always fighting with someone about something. Some nights I could barely get to sleep because of his fighting with Linda. One time he asked me to lie to the police because he and my brother were fighting. I always knew when it was going to happen. I could just feel it. I just wanted to get it over with. He should have gone to jail a long time ago. If some other girl or boy were living in that situation, I would advise them to talk to an adult or go to the police.

—Katherine Katie Marie Beers

Sal surprised everyone when asked by the Judge if he had anything to say prior to sentencing. He looked squarely into the camera lens pointed his way, shrugged his shoulders and opened his mouth.

"First I'd like to say I'm sorry to everyone for putting yous all through this situation. I feel sorry that little Katherine Beers had to take the stand and testify. But I guess it was my only alternative to try to clear my name." He shrugged again. "I ..I don't know the right words to say this, but uh, I accept whatever verdict or sentence I get. I'm sorry this situation had to take place. I'd like to say to my family in the courtroom, I'd like to thank them for standing by me and hopefully I can get my life back together after my time is served."

The probation report was brutal. Judge Lefkowitz read parts into the record:

There is little of a positive nature to be said about this defendant who reportedly has a history of preying on weak and vulnerable individuals. Inghilleri…is a manipulative and amoral individual who has little insight into his behavior or the consequences of his actions on others.

Sal's smug gamble had failed miserably. He was sent upstate for four to twelve years instead of the two-and-a-third he had been offered if he had spared Katie a trial.

Outside court, a woman wept. I asked her to comment. "It's not enough," she told me. She had a stake in the case. Her own three children said they were also abused by Sal when she hired Linda as a baby sitter.

"He got one year for Katie and one year for each of my three. It wasn't enough!" said Linda Butler, her name a strange coincidence.

How would you describe Sal Inghilleri?

"As an animal."

What would have been an adequate punishment for him?

"Twelve years is not enough. When he gets out, he'll just do the same thing to another child."

Together we did the addition. Sal would be forty-nine when he would be eligible for parole and Katie would be in college, if she were able to overcome the damage and lead a normal life. Linda Butler hung on the word "if."

The first four years passed without a mention of Sal Inghilleri in the headlines. Not even his contentious appearance before the parole board at the Collins Correctional Facility in 1998 made news.[30] He told the Commissioners he had sexually abused Katie only once.

"Why did you commit this crime, sir?"

"It just happened."

"Don't give us that. We don't want to hear that. Things of this nature don't just happen."

"I was standing in the bathroom," Sal said, as he spoke before the panel, "the little girl came in, I was standing there and I had just come out of the shower. I was standing there nude, and she looked at me and— she just looked at me and I said to her, what are you looking at, and she says I'm looking at you. I said you act like you want to touch it. And she continued to look at me and then…"

"She what?"

"She continued to look at me, and I says, please leave, and she didn't leave right away. I says, well, since you're not leaving, why don't you touch it, and she did, and I allowed it to happen."

"Do you believe your story that you're telling us today?"

"Yes."

"You really do? That is a pathetically woeful story."

"Well that's…"

"It needs a lot of work."

"That's what happened."

The Commissioners were not buying it, and Sal was too slow to get it.

"You didn't call this child into your bedroom when you were lying in your bed naked?"

"She was never in my bedroom. That child was never in my bedroom."

"She was ten at the time?"

"Yes, I believe she was ten years old, she had just turned ten."

"Okay, you never asked this child to put cream on your penis and rub it?"

"No, I had—let me explain something. I had—when I came out of the shower, I still do this to this date; I put baby oil on it, cream on it, cream moisturizer. I had the cream on already when she came in. The house that we lived in had no door locks. They…they just used to come in and out."

"And this child was so infatuated with your body that she wanted to touch your penis?"

"No."

"Is that your story to us?"

"All I'm saying is that she was looking at me and I asked her, what are you looking at, and she didn't answer me and she didn't leave right away. I…I says, well, since you're—you know, you're staring at me, I just asked her, said she looked like she wanted to touch it. So I said it twice and…"

"Why would you say that to a ten-year-old girl? Why would you even say that, you look like you want to touch it?"

"Sir, I don't know what possessed me to say that."

"All right."

"And all I know is it ruined my life and it ruined the little girl's life."

"Did you get any sexual gratification from this?"

"No, sir, absolutely not."

The story spiraled further down a ludicrous path.

"…When I realized what was happening, I pushed her hand away and she—you know, she went, because I started yelling for my wife. My wife lived upstairs."

"This was a naughty little girl who saw a grown man come out of the bathroom in the nude…"

"I was…"

"Let me finish. This was a naughty little girl who saw a grown man come out of the shower in the nude and she decided to come over and manipulate your penis, is that your story to us?"

"No, my story is that I was coming out of the shower and she came into the bathroom, probably not realizing I was in there, and she caught me in the nude drying off and…"

"And when she caught you in the nude, she was so interested in your body that she decided to manipulate your penis, is that your story?"

"I don't think she was interested. I think she was just more scared than anything else and she didn't move and I…"

"So in fear, she decided to manipulate your penis?"

"I don't think there was any fear there, but I did entice her to do that. I did entice her."

"You did or did not entice her?"

"I asked her."

"Okay, you asked her. Now, back to my basic question. Why would you want this child to do that, for what purpose?"

"I have no idea, sir, why I did that."

"How come you have no idea? You are the best person to ask that question. Isn't that true?"

"Yes, it is."

"Then how come you have no idea why you did that?"

"I don't know, because I never did this type of thing before."

"Have you been involved in sex offender counseling?"

With that, Sal admitted that he had failed to attend mandatory sex abuser counseling in prison, because the counselor didn't believe his story, either. Despite promises to try to make himself a better person upon release, parole was denied.

The ruling was succinct:

> *It was apparent that you have not yet come to terms with your criminal conduct, which you severely minimize. You displayed an abject lack of insight into your criminal behavior and have failed to fully participate in recommended therapy. Until you fully address the psychosexual dynamics of your criminal behavior, you will continue to represent a massive risk to public safety.*

Sal must have taken note of that last line and returned for parole review in 2002 with a completely different story. This time, he admitted to sexually abusing Katie twice.[31]

"I never mentioned, you know, to the commissioners in my previous appearance, but when I took the counseling, the sex offender program, she was very good at getting things out of you, and I myself was abused as a young child and maybe I just started to do to another child, I don't know. Family members, a grandfather, uncle, you know, there was—they used to tie me to the benches out in front of the house. They, you know, like they used to buy other things for other children and that just progressed and progressed and as time went on, as I grew older and older, I believe until the age of twelve or thirteen, I had two of my aunt's brothers, they used to try to take me down in my uncle's basement and they used to—wanted me to do things.

"They used to touch me, and the family that I came from, the children were supposed to be seen not heard, and every time I tried to talk to, you know, my mother about these things we were always just, you know, pushed to the side. So I guess in my mind, you know, I—over the years—I suppressed these feelings and maybe it just came to a head one day and I, you know, I did what I did."

"Obviously, the things that occurred to you as a young boy, I would certainly assume you derived no pleasure from those things occurring to you?"

"No, I didn't."

"All right. Then why in God's name would you ever want to do this to another person after you have been demeaned and injured in that fashion? I mean, this is an unspeakable, horrendous thing that you did."

"Well, like I explained to you, I think, you know, it just came to a point that maybe I wanted to do it to another child but that's, like I said, not the right way and I can't take back what I did. All I could do is, you know, improve my lifestyle and try, you know, if and when I do go home, just try to be a productive citizen of society and of course, you know, I know I have to, you know, seek counseling."

The Parole Board commended Sal for taking a big step with his admissions, then asked him if he ever had child pornography to which he answered, "I don't even look at porno books."

Parole was denied yet again. Sal skipped the hearings altogether in 2004 and 2006,[32] where parole was again denied.

After serving the maximum of twelve years, New York State Department of Correctional Services had no choice but to return him to society. Sal moved back to Bay Shore and settled in a room at 501 East Main Street, better known as The Econo Lodge. He never registered, as required, as a high-risk sex offender and warrants went out for his arrest.

In October of 2007, Sal was picked up in North Carolina and brought back to Suffolk County to stand trial for the parole violation. Police said he had been living there with a girlfriend and her very young children.

FORCED MEMORY

I WAS TOLD I had to remember details. Dates were absolutely necessary, too. Investigators with the DA's office took me to the Riverhead Library to browse through old newspaper archives on microfiche. Sal used to get the newspaper every day, so if I could simply recognize a headline or a comic strip, they could have the needed date and I could be assured Sal would never hurt me or anyone else again.

But neither the headlines nor the comics could jog my memory. All I knew is that Sal had been violating me for as long as I could remember.

Three days a week after school, I would go to Mary Bromley's office to regain the memories. I never minded going to Mary's office—she treated me more like a teenager or an adult than a previous therapist had. The first therapist, who I saw briefly, was geared more toward kids. I *was* a kid, but I didn't have kid problems. So my foster parents quickly changed gears and brought me to Mary.

Mary's office was big, with a lot of windows and wraparound book shelves. There were two couches, a big comfy chair, which Mary usually occupied, a coffee table, her desk, and a little table that was kid-sized. The kid-sized table was where I would do arts and crafts, color pictures, and play games. I usually sat on the couch with a pillow planted in my lap.

There, I could talk about anything and everything without a care. As I got older, my foster mom would come to some sessions, as would Marilyn. Not that Marilyn and I ever resolved much. She was the child and I was the grown-up. I was the one always making excuses for *her*.

As I grew and made friends and the court cases ended, I went to Mary's office twice a week until it dwindled down to once a week; eventually, I would go once every other week. I liked talking to Mary; she was a safe person to confide in, and for the first time in my life, I didn't have to worry about protecting anyone but me.

Mary always reminded me of how strong a person I already was. Everyone from the DA's office, too, would tell me how strong I was to pull through. Most kids who went through what I had gone through, they assured me, would have never been able to withstand a trial. No matter how much preparation they received, they wouldn't be able to have done that. They told me I was special.

I tried to regain the memories as requested, but it was hard to do after blocking them out for so long. Blocking thoughts was my only way of controlling Sal's behavior, and later, Big John's. If I didn't think about the dirty things they were doing to me, they wouldn't happen as often. And even if they did, it was as if it wasn't happening to *me*.

And so, I willed the memories to disappear. Of those that lingered, almost every memory that I have of my childhood is of the abuse I endured. Very few memories make me smile. Most make me cry.

Unfortunately for me at the time in therapy, memories were summoned to reappear. Even worse, in court, I had to talk about the abuse publicly. It was the hardest thing I ever had to do.

I was ushered into a big room with a lot of chairs. The grand jury room was empty except for me, Mary, Mr. Catterson, and a few other people I didn't know. Mr. Catterson asked me questions about what Sal had done to me. This was something we practiced a lot to make sure that I was comfortable answering Mr. Catterson's questions.

At this point, I was as comfortable as I was going to be. It wasn't easy to tell people—strangers—that Sal made me "move my hand up and down on his penis after he made me put lotion on it." Hell, I was only ten and eleven years old; I wasn't comfortable even saying the word "penis"!

But I moved along with my testimony, answering the questions that were asked. I was asked if I remembered the dates that the abuse occurred—I didn't. I was then asked to recall a few specific incidences that didn't occur at my house in West Islip. Instead, I told them about the time when Sal was supposed to be taking me to school—he pulled off into a nursery off of Udall Road. I guess that was specific enough for members of the grand jury.

I was then asked about the nights that I slept on the couch because Linda wouldn't let me come up to the bedroom, having missed the cut-off time. I answered flatly, on those nights that I awoke face-down to Sal on top of me, I pretended to be asleep because I wanted it to be over quickly. Sal would take off my underwear and hump me, rubbing himself between my butt cheeks. After he had ejaculated, he would wake me up, and tell me to go clean myself off.

I told the grand jury one time after this happened, I threw up. Usually, Sal would come with me to the bathroom and clean himself up, too. I was disgusted with what had just happened, and now I had to witness him cleaning himself. It was too much to keep down.

I'm now grateful that no one woke up in the middle of the night to witness the abuse, because Sal probably would have killed them. I told the grand jury how, when I didn't make it upstairs in time, I would sneak into my grandmother's room and sleep in bed with her, but Sal would still find me and march me to his room. There was no escape.

I traveled a lot to Riverhead during preparations for Sal's trial—a few times a week. As I sat in Mr. Catterson's office, with him and Assistant District Attorney Bill Ferris asking me questions, Mary was always by my side, usually holding my hand to make me feel at ease. Even now, when I am in an uncomfortable situation, I need something in my lap, either a pillow or my coat, a stuffed animal—something—a little piece of Mary always with me.

The dress I would wear to court was the most beautiful thing I had ever put on—rose colored, with a white lace collar. And the buttons: pearl all the way down the front. But as strong as prosecutors assured me I was, nothing could prepare me for Sal's burning glare. He was staring me down, leaning toward his attorney to get a better look at me.

I tried not to pay too much attention, but it was hard because he was in my line of sight as I answered Mr. Catterson's questions. His eyes were like knives aimed at me. If those eyes could talk, they were saying to me alone, "If I don't go to jail, you're finished."

The searing stares unnerved me. As many times as I was promised Sal would go to jail, I wondered if somehow he would find a way to avoid it and come find me at my foster parents' home in East Hampton. Suffolk prosecutors, in my many visits to their offices, served me bowls of mint chocolate chip ice cream, and assurances that Sal would never do this to anybody else.

I would walk from office to office in the DA's Riverhead headquarters, greeting everyone. Bill Ferris became my friend for life. He still calls me every year on my birthday. But I'm also often visited by Sal's burning glares. They come back to me in my nightmares. Even when I knew that he was going to go to prison, I feared he would get out one day and make me pay for speaking the truth.

Somehow, in all the questioning, in all the courtrooms, in all the conference rooms, and on all the prosecutors' couches, it never came up that I was raped.

Maybe all the grownups were afraid to ask me straight out. Maybe they didn't want to traumatize me any more than I had been. Perhaps they *did* ask me and I just don't remember. Although I'm pretty sure no one ever asked me if either John or Sal had penetrated me.

And therefore, I didn't tell. I wanted to forget that the rapes ever happened and I thought that if I didn't talk about being raped, it didn't happen. I felt dirty enough already with just being touched and forced to touch them. I didn't want to feel dirtier by admitting to being raped. I was too young to understand that Sal and John both would have both faced far more serious criminal charges if I had mentioned the rapes.

Instead, the rapes faded away, like the scars on my arm. No one knew that I had been raped and there was a good chunk of time when even I didn't have an understanding or a word for what had been done to me.

There were a lot of suppressed memories that came to light after starting to spend time with Mary. Little things would jog a memory. Most of my early childhood memories were suppressed. I blocked out whole years and fragmented images: my silent, helpless whimpers as Sal beat my brother; the deep searing pain of a lit cigarette touched to my skin, and the angry rants from Linda when I cried; the invasion of my most private parts that began when I was two years old.

It seems unreal to me now that as such a young child, I was hurt by so many different people and I didn't have a mental breakdown or turn into a heartless monster. Erasing the memories was only one coping mechanism. I also developed the ability to cry away the pain.

As a little girl, I would often cry my eyes out. I still do. Sometimes I find myself having a "good cry" and don't exactly know why. Afterwards, I am drained but recharged.

Sal's conviction was on the cover of a New York City newspaper when I was in fifth grade. My gym teacher showed me the paper. I felt instantly weak and sick and rushed to the school nurse. I needed to go home right away.

Rebecca was home from college and dropped everything to get to the school and bring me home. I went right upstairs, closed the blinds and made the bedroom as dark as possible. When Aunt Barbara got home from work, she came to check on me—and immediately knew that something was very wrong by the appearance of my bedroom, dark like a cave. I didn't want to talk about why I was upset, but finally I could speak.

Seeing that headline and Sal's picture, I told her, put me back in a place I wanted desperately to leave behind. School was supposed to be a safe place for me, and the teachers were supposed to know how to keep me safe. I don't know what was going through my gym teacher's head when she showed me the article. Maybe she wanted me to know that Sal was going to jail. But it was Sal's glare all over again, just as I was trying to forget about all of them and start to live my life—a life that I had never been able to enjoy until now. I wanted to forget about their existence and the pain that they caused me. I wanted a childhood.

News of Sal's conviction and John's plea never came up again in my presence. My foster parents never let me see a newspaper or watch television coverage of the cases. They wanted me to get on with living a normal childhood, and not think about anything from my past. The memories were finally allowed to retreat and I was allowed to reinvent myself.

It is because of them, I am certain, that I am the woman that I am today. Had they not become my parents, I would have been bounced around from foster home to foster home. At the time of my abduction, Barbara and Tedd were actually getting ready to take a foster infant into their home. They called Child Protective Services and put in a revised request: When Katie Beers is found, and if she is going to enter the system, could she be placed in their home?

A few days later, I was rescued and assigned to their Springs home, where there was one other adopted foster child, Jason. They had chosen me!

I wasn't the easiest foster child for them. I lied a lot from Day One. I lied about the smallest things—for no reason. I don't know why I lied; perhaps it was a coping mechanism. I had learned well to lie to Linda about a lot of things to keep her from beating me. Barbara and Tedd never once gave me a reason to lie to them. I did it because it was a hard habit to break.

I remember one time, I ate toast as a snack, and Aunt Barbara asked me if I had eaten all of it. I confidently told her that I had. She asked me again, this time with a hint of disbelief, if I had eaten all of it, and once again I assured her that I had. But she was an experienced mother and was wise to me. The leftover crust was sitting on the top of the garbage. Why I lied about this petty offense, I don't know—the only thing that I can come up with is that Linda would always yell at me for throwing away food.

Instead, under the foster family's roof, I was punished not for the failure to finish my food, but for the failure to tell the truth. One week of grounding from friends' visits and phone use for smaller infractions. One month grounding for lying about where I was.

The message in the home was clear. For the first time in my life, there were principles and values.

At first, the consequences of breaking their moral code had little effect on me. I would withhold the truth without thinking. To me, not telling the whole story was not a lie. My friends and I would go to the movies on weekends. Aunt Barbara would ask me who I was going to be with, so I would list a few friends, omitting the fact that boys were in the group, promising to call home when the movie was over.

But instead of calling right away, I would wait a little while so that I could hang out in town. I didn't realize that Aunt Barbara could call the theatre and find out what time the movie was over. The lies flowed freely. It was the only thing Linda had taught me to do well.

I was thrown into a house that had many rules. I didn't really know what rules were. If Linda hadn't liked something that I had done, she would simply beat me, sometimes with a smack in the face with her hand, other times with the paddle part of a brush, or she would have me bend over her knee so she could spank me. I would literally have to brace myself on her lap for her to hit me because part of one leg was amputated. And the beatings were based on rules even she couldn't explain.

Marilyn didn't subject me and John to any rules. Only Sal made rules, and everyone else lived in fear of how he would apply them.

In my new home, there was barely a voice raised in anger. There was a rotating schedule, and I was expected to chip in with small chores. One child had to take the laundry hamper downstairs when it got full, and another child had to clean the bathroom once a week. We also had to set the table every night for dinner. Uncle Tedd gave us each an allowance—three dollars per week if we did all of our chores. As I got older, I also had to clean my bedroom and help with vacuuming and dusting.

I enjoyed cleaning my room. With Rebecca in college and returning home only during school breaks and the summer, for the first time in my life, I had a room I could call my own. Uncle Tedd and Aunt Barbara bought me a new bunk bed, new soft sheets, and a new cozy blanket. These were precious to me for one reason: they were bought with me alone in mind. They were mine.

It was indeed "a whole new world." I was reminded of the Disney movie theme song. After I began my new life, everyone told me that they were under the impression, based on news reports, that the lyrics to the song, *A Whole New Word*, had deep meaning to me.

Truth be told, I had no attachment to that song at all. It was another one of Linda's self-serving fabrications.

F amily came first in my new home, and Uncle Tedd and Aunt Barbara always put the needs of their children ahead of their own. They taught me what it was like to be in a functional family. An involved dad, a mom who was there to put us on the bus every morning, brothers and sisters who would play with us and help us with our homework, and of course, what perfect family doesn't have a dog or two?

They reconditioned my thinking and taught me that you have to work hard for the things that you want. In junior high, I so badly wanted to fit in with the popular kids, I tried out for the volleyball team. But with my spindly legs and lack of training, I couldn't make the cut. So instead, for three years straight, I took the decidedly unglamorous job of equipment manager.

Finally, in tenth grade, determination paid off. I not only made the squad, I was named team captain. It gave me confidence to try other sports. I played tennis for several years, and I was a cheerleader. Uncle Tedd and Aunt Barbara taught me that hard work, dedication and practice had satisfying payoffs.

Growing up, my coping skills revolved around having to lie, while enduring grave injustices. My new family gave me loving support and the confidence to achieve what I wanted through dedication and hard work, concepts that had been completely foreign to me.

Most of all, they were there for me. For a game, a play, a teacher's conference, they were always there. Uncle Tedd, newly retired, made Jason and me a hot breakfast every morning. There would always be French toast or eggs, a neatly packed lunch, and his company at the breakfast table. There wasn't much said. There didn't have to be many words. The message was evident. They gave of their time freely and were involved in my everyday life. This was the greatest gift.

But as my new family steered me down a new path, seeing Marilyn and Grandma Helen was a constant return to the dead-end childhood I had escaped. I visited with Marilyn for many years. I liked going on visits at first. Like the therapy sessions, it was three times a week, then two, then just once a week.

There were certain things that Marilyn and I were not allowed to talk about during our visits. My foster family was one of those off-limits topics, other than general information. What happened to me during the kidnapping was also off-limits.

At first, I would tell anyone that would listen to me that I wanted to live with Marilyn again. The response was always that the court was going to do what was "best for me."

The visits with Marilyn, though, continued to take me back to a place I was beginning to see more objectively. Now that I was enrolled in school and attending every day, I wondered why I hadn't attended before that. I used to beg Linda to let me go to school, but she needed help at the house. I didn't go to school a good part of my third grade year because we had moved to Bay Shore, and Linda couldn't legally enroll me in school; Marilyn had to.

But Marilyn never enrolled me either because she wanted me to come live with her in Mastic Beach. She thought that by not enrolling me in school, the authorities would get involved and take me away from Linda. They never did. Now, attending school regularly for the first time, I realized that school was not optional. I was beginning to see that Marilyn's solution was short-sighted and kept me in harm's way.

FORCED MEMORY

Perhaps there was a turning point, when my memories began to be paired with more mature understanding. I slowly began to see Marilyn in a different light.

Not surprisingly, while Marilyn was busy going to court trying to keep custody of me, she missed a lot of our scheduled visits. She would only make it to about one out of five visits. I was seeing her less and less, and it was sad for me because I looked forward to seeing her and my grandma, Helen.

My caseworker, Ginny, was creative. When Marilyn would miss a visit, Ginny and I would do something special—it was usually playing a game of "let's get lost" which consisted of us driving around aimlessly with me telling Ginny where to turn.

Missed visits took a real emotional toll on me. When Marilyn would miss a visit, my heart would sink and I would sadly say to myself, "Not again."

There were also nightmares, stomach aches, heart palpitations, and anxiety. I would get this feeling in my chest like someone was tying a rope around my heart, and every time I inhaled, the rope would tighten and I couldn't take a deep breath—the pain was excruciating. I often yelled in my sleep, furiously. I still have dreams about being abducted or being sexually violated.

To this day, every now and again, I will have a dream that either I am in the bunker or being held against my will. The dreams are vivid—I am ten years old, in the little coffin-box where Big John held me, chained by my neck—but in my dreams, I am not smart enough to find the key to the padlock, so I am chained twenty-three hours out of the day, lying in my own filth, not able to move.

Another dream that I have is that while I was kidnapped, something happens to Big John—either he is arrested, because I was presumed dead and he was the only suspect, he dies, or moves, and the dungeon becomes my grave.

I sometimes dream of the abuse that I endured by Sal—but this time I am an adult, and he is still violating me because I don't have the mental capacity to get away. The dreams don't scare me anymore. They are not real. They are my memories struggling to emerge.

Very gradually, visits with Marilyn lost their appeal. Playroom visits at the Social Services Office in Riverhead or Ronkonkoma became supervised outings to the mall, the outlets, or out to dinner. When Marilyn, Grandma Helen, and John moved to a new house in Patchogue, I was able to have home visits there. We would do homework, bake, make dinner, and watch a movie, for three hours twice a week.

But as I got older, the visits were even further reduced to once every other week and were usually on Saturdays in East Hampton, because I just didn't have time to carve out of my high school schedule. My new reality was being involved in school sports teams and being on the stage crew, and I had neither the time nor the desire to visit with Marilyn anymore.

By the time I was thirteen years old, I understood that I would never go back to living with Marilyn. It was a sad realization, not because I wasn't happy in my foster home, but because my entire life I only wanted to live with Marilyn. It was a deep longing for anyone to love me. And now, even if Marilyn had the means to "take me away," she no longer had the legal ability.

I also came to understand why Marilyn did not rescue me from Sal and Linda when I was younger. You didn't mess with Sal because he would follow through with his threats—and Marilyn knew this. I think that if Marilyn had been aware of the physical, emotional, mental or sexual abuse, she would have gotten me out of the situation quickly, but she was blind to it. I didn't tell her because I was ashamed of it all and I didn't want to worry her. Again, I was the adult.

I was getting ready for high school graduation when Aunt Barbara mentioned that she felt that it was important for her to finally meet Marilyn. She didn't want it to be awkward at the actual ceremony if that was to be the first time that they actually met.

Mary arranged for them to be introduced at her office. It was a civil, but surreal meeting. Marilyn thanked Barbara for taking such good care of me. Tedd didn't meet Marilyn until just before graduation. He wasn't as sold on the idea of "one big happy family." It was awkward for everyone, but it was something that Mary agreed should happen. For me, it was a freeing moment. The hand-off was complete. I was liberated from my sad past and a longing for something that would never be.

FORCED MEMORY

From that day forward, "Uncle Tedd and Aunt Barbara" would be my "Mom and Dad."

Whether revelations about Marilyn's failures as a mother came out of my years of therapy or from finally living in a functional, happy family, I do not know. What I do know is that I would never be able to leave my child with a virtual stranger, like Marilyn did to me.

When I turned eighteen, I got to choose when and if to see Marilyn. I now had a steady boyfriend, my own car, and was getting ready for college. Since then, I have seen Marilyn, at most, once a year.

I never saw Linda again. At one point, when I was thirteen years old, someone from the Social Services office phoned and told me Ann Butler requested a visit with me. Did I want to see Linda and/or Ann? I told them that I had no desire to see either of them. Linda didn't protect me from Sal—in fact, she defended Sal, saying he would never abuse a child. She stood by her husband and denied being told about the abuse before Sal was arrested.

And Ann, she was just the gateway to Linda. I was old enough to know that Linda needed to stay out of my life.

On high school graduation day, an elderly woman showed up with a younger woman and a small child. She followed me inside. I was pretty sure I had never seen this woman before in my life. I actually thought that it was a news reporter, so I turned around to get a better look.

"Do you recognize me?" the old woman asked. "It's me, Mom."

I looked at her long and hard and thought, "Who the heck is this woman?" And then suddenly, a light bulb went off. It was Ann Butler.

"Get the fuck away from me. I never want to see you again," I snapped. I walked away but she followed me. So I got into my best friend Caitlin's car and had her just drive me around for a good long time until I was certain she would be gone. I had no desire to see her and she knew it.

Ann had always treated me well; I liked going to her house because she was like a grandmother to me, always spoiling me. I would go to bingo with Ann, or to the flea market—she treated me like I was her granddaughter. I had no ill feelings toward Ann, but did not, on my graduation day, want a trip down an agonizing Memory Lane. And I didn't want Ann to know what type of car I drove, or worse, to get my license plate number. I also didn't want her to know where I lived.

Later, during the graduation party at my house, I had to tell my parents that I had seen Ann. I was so ashamed when I told my Mom what I had said. I thought she would be furious and disappointed that I had been so disrespectful, and cursed at this elderly woman. I shudder to think that at any point in my life I may have disappointed the woman who means the world to me. I was almost in tears when I confessed to her exactly what I said.

There was no anger. Instead, my mother extended her arms and offered me a loving hug. "Good for you, Katie," she softly spoke, "for standing up for yourself."

I was free of the people who had hurt me, and free of the memories that could have defined me.

I was a clean slate and I wanted it that way. The only thing I kept from my early childhood was my name: Katie. Once I said I wanted to be called Katherine. It was a threshold thing, moving from single to double digits. I said it once, and Linda put it on my birthday cake. Linda thought she could say and do whatever she wanted.

I'm Katie Beers—and always was.

I was regaining the lost memories, safely and slowly, with Mary's help. She said it was important for me to remember. They came back at unexpected moments, like when I met Harvey Weinstein.

The first time I met Harvey, I was awed by how tall he was. Mary invited him to our sessions several times. Harvey had the most captivating voice; it was so deep, but soothing at the same time. I was so happy that Mary brought us together. Harvey was such a special person.

Harvey went through something strangely similar to me just a few months after I was freed. A man in his late sixties, Harvey was the owner of a tuxedo manufacturing business. He was known as "The Tuxedo King." He told me every day he would have breakfast at the Mark Twain Diner in Jackson Heights. One day, while he was walking to his car in the diner's parking lot, he was approached by a long time worker, a man who sewed tuxedo pants at his factory and had always been a loyal employee.

But on this day, the worker had in mind a plan to make millions. He and his brother, armed with knives, forced Harvey into a waiting car, blindfolded him and drove him to Upper Manhattan where, on a small island between the Hudson River and the Henry Hudson Parkway, they threw him into a fourteen foot deep, five foot wide dirt pit and covered it with a steel door weighted by cement blocks. They shoveled dirt on top of it and left Harvey for thirteen days with nothing except water and a couple of pieces of fruit.

The kidnappers demanded ransom and Harvey's family got together three million dollars in one hundred and fifty dollar bills. When the kidnappers picked up the ransom, police arrested one of them, who must have given up the location where Harvey was hidden.

Police were standing just over the ditch when they called Harvey's name and he weakly answered, "I'm here. I'm here." Dirty and disheveled, Harvey was pulled out of the hole by two cops. After thirteen days of captivity, Harvey's first words were, "Thank God you're here—and I'd like to have a cigarette."

Harvey told me he wasn't worried about his body surviving. He was a trained Marine. He knew he could get by long enough on the little bit of water and fruit. He was most worried about his mind. And he would speak aloud each day, remembering his life story, chapter by chapter.

It helped me to learn that I wasn't the only one who had gone through an ordeal like that. When I think of him, I am inspired to help other people, like he helped me.

Harvey died in 2007, but I can still hear his deep voice. In fact, it was Harvey's voice that unearthed a lost memory.

Behind John's house, there was a hole in the ground. Little John and my cousin Jason were jumping in and climbing out of it. Big John said it was going to be an "underground bunker." I was too small to join the guys, so I was just standing on the edge of the deep hole, laughing. I was six, maybe seven years old. We were all playing in it, this big open pit in the ground, partially covered with a blue tarp, jumping in and out and laughing.

Later, John poured a slab of concrete and built a carport over it. I never thought of that hole in the ground again until Harvey Weinstein mentioned the hole where he was buried alive. I was sixteen years old and I suddenly realized that I watched the construction of the bunker that would later be my prison. In fact, Big John's neighbors and family may have watched as well, and no one thought a thing about it.

Later, when I was kidnapped, no one put two and two together. It was a long-term plan to steal a childhood, hatched in plain view.

FEMALE ANDERSON

THE PHONE RANG AND was picked up quickly—after just one ring. It surprised me that Marilyn Beers would have a cell phone, a luxury for someone I guessed would be flat broke by now, almost twenty years after Katie's kidnapping. The voice was instantly familiar.

"Hello," she answered brusquely.

"Marilyn?" I asked.

"Who wants to know?" Predictable, I thought, even after all these years.

"It's Carolyn—Carolyn Gusoff—the reporter—I'm working with Katie—she said it would be okay to give you a call."

"Oh, yeah," she said, her voice just as gravelly as it was in 1993, her vocal chords charred by lifelong chain smoking.

"How've you been, Marilyn?" I asked with genuine interest.

"Alive."

I chuckled courteously. "Well—that's better than some others." It was no joke. Many of the people at the center of the kidnapping case had since died.

We made a date to meet the following Wednesday—her day off. She quickly put the kibosh on my request to meet at her house. We agreed it would be somewhere neutral.

"I'll treat you," she offered, "to coffee."

Her yellow cab, emblazoned with the words "Sunset Taxi" on the doors, was parked in front of the MVP diner on Montauk Highway in West Babylon, a beacon indicating I was in the right place. Marilyn, seated in a booth, looked much the same as the last time I saw her, nearly two decades earlier, pacing the halls of Family Court trying to retain custody of Katie after the kidnapping. Her long, stringy, dirty-blond hair was now streaked with gray. While her face had not changed, there were two startling differences.

She appeared to have lost most of her enormous weight, and the skin on her arms hung loosely like sleeves where rolls of fat used to reside.

Even more astonishingly, she was not smoking. The woman who two decades earlier had a cigarette permanently affixed to her lips had given it up cold turkey, she announced, on January 29, 2003, at ten to midnight. Took the last drag of USA Gold Light 100s with a half carton left in the house, she told me.

That didn't stop her from hacking over her meatloaf and mashed potatoes lunch. Often. The damage of past sins wouldn't easily let go.

"Are you sick?" I asked.

"No," she answered. "I don't know what that is."

Then she volunteered, "Katie is the kind of person that will tell you what she thinks you want to hear. I used to tell her, 'Tell me the truth; if it hurts me, it hurts me, but I won't care.' And she would tell me what she thought she wanted me to hear—not the truth. She would tell Linda one thing and when I asked her she would tell me something totally different. She didn't want to hurt my feelings."

Marilyn said she had no idea anything was "going on with Sal or Linda. No matter what I asked her. I used to get annoyed at that. If it hurts, it hurts. I wanted the truth."

I was amazed, all these years later, that Marilyn may have quit smoking, but seemed to have acquired little insight into the barrage of abuse her daughter was enduring under her nose. But I had come to hear her out.

The one-sided conversation continued.

"Linda acted as if she was Katie's mother. I missed a lot. I have a lot of regrets," Marilyn lamented. "If I had to do it over again, I would never have become friends with them. They were bad people who found one another. They deserved each other."

"Why would they pick on a child?" Marilyn suddenly asked, and then answered her own question. "Because a child cannot fight back."

Especially, I thought, one whose mother hen had left the nest unattended.

I was glad to get out of the diner. Marilyn took the lead in her taxi, as I followed. We were going to visit some places from the past. She led the way to the house on Higbie Drive, where she grew up and "raised" Katie. She drove with purpose, zigzagging in and out of side streets to avoid Sunrise Highway, the vast six-lane route that starts in New York City and traverses the underbelly of Long Island's south shore.

Her cab, number one hundred thirty, had "Airport Service" stenciled on the back windshield, and I couldn't help but wonder how many folks around here could shell out one hundred bucks for a taxi ride all the way to the city airports. We passed cookie-cutter strip malls, naked maple trees and streets without sidewalks frosted with a hint of snow, black with slushy winter soot, melting into the sewer grates.

We finally pulled up to a small, white cape perched on a corner. It was topped with a brick chimney, and statues of Mary and Jesus were nestled into the front shrubs. I remembered this place.

"This is it," she said and proceeded to point out which was her room and which ones housed Sal and Linda when they were all packed into the little house like sardines. She turned and gestured to the corner strip mall, visible a block away from the front yard, where Katie was frequently sent to do errands and the family laundry.

"That," she emphasized, "was for Linda. I never sent Katie to do laundry—not at five years old. John, yes, when he was about thirteen, I may have asked him to go to the local laundromat. I was very naive," she added. "I never believe anything anybody tells me anymore."

What about the physical and sexual abuse? Did she know what was going on under this asphalt gray shingled roof?

"I never knew about it. Katie never told me nothing." But then she added, "She could have always gone into my room. Hindsight," added Marilyn "is a terrible thing."

Marilyn walked me around the tiny patch of property, and then walked me through a long lead up to the loss of her daughter, Katie, literally starting at the beginning with herself.

The name card above the bassinet in the newborn nursery at Fordham Hospital in the Bronx read simply "Female Anderson." The baby girl was premature—only five pounds—born on September 2, 1949, to an unwed mother from the Midwest who, with the help of a young man from California, created a child no one had planned. He wanted nothing to do with his mistake, and the young mother fled to New York, where her sister lived, to deliver the baby—then instantly turned the newborn over for adoption.

For three months, Female Anderson lingered at the Spence Chapin Foundling Home, unwanted.

At the same time, a young couple in Bayside, Queens, Helen and Stewart Beers, was trying to conceive a child of their own. Stewart, a thirty-six-year-old claims adjuster for Liberty Mutual Insurance Company and a WWII veteran, was told by doctors that he was the problem, with a low sperm count. Helen, who had been Stewart's secretary, was thirty years old and refused to give up on her plan to have a baby. They visited the Foundling Home in the Bronx and were asked if they wouldn't mind a little strawberry blonde baby. Female Anderson became theirs. They named her Marilyn.

Two years later, on August 10, 1951, Helen and Stewart returned to the Foundling Home and this time chose a baby boy. Two-month-old Alfred Distefano was christened Robert Beers. Marilyn now had a baby brother and the Beers family was complete.

Helen had no intention of telling her children of their beginnings, but Marilyn altered the plan when, at age five, she dreamed she was adopted and confronted her parents with the question. A stunned Helen, never one to show much emotion, reluctantly admitted to Marilyn that she was neither brought by the stork nor came from Beers stock. She was, in fact, adopted, and Marilyn was forever convinced that her vivid and frequent dreams provided her with special psychic insight.

Growing up, Marilyn was shy and introverted. Her low weight at birth was short-lived, and soon Marilyn was a stout child with low self-esteem and no motivation to please anyone, least of all her teachers. Five days before her eleventh birthday on August 28, 1960, the Beers family moved out of the only home Helen had ever known and into the less crowded suburbs.

The Suffolk County neighborhood of West Islip was indistinguishable from so many others that had popped up in the fifties and sixties. Tracks of Cape Cod homes were constructed hastily on slabs to accommodate young families with enough money to finance a small mortgage and leave the New York City boroughs. Nassau County, adjacent to Queens and less than a one hour railroad ride into Manhattan, was the prime choice for white-collar garment center workers, businessmen and returned war veterans who flooded the new western Long Island communities.

But for those without the financial means and those whose livelihoods were not dependent upon proximity to Manhattan, the prudent choice was the more remote Suffolk County.

Twelve Higbie Drive in West Islip was a small cape with four tiny bedrooms and two bathrooms on a coveted corner lot. By city standards, it had a big backyard. Its aluminum siding made it look well cared for, and its flat shingled roof blended in with the winter sky. It had a small hedge that gave the Beers family privacy, and for only fourteen thousand, five hundred dollars, they felt as if they had landed a piece of the American dream. Marilyn liked it there so much, she became a permanent fixture, firmly rooted.

Marilyn's teenaged rebellion began in her preteen years. She started smoking at age eleven and by twelve was consuming a pack of cigarettes a day in the woods behind the Udall Road Middle School. She dropped out of high school, and when Helen and Stewart offered to pay for community college or trade school, Marilyn refused their offer, claiming she had no aspirations.

While Helen worked in a school cafeteria, Marilyn took odd jobs as a filing clerk at a local insurance company, driving a school bus and filling in as home health aide. As her size grew, so did her smoking habit, some days blazing through five packs of Marlboro 100s. She made no attempt to curtail her drinking, either. Vodka and tonic with a twist of lime.

Marilyn would get so drunk at local watering holes, she got pregnant twice accidentally and couldn't be sure who fathered her second child, but she was happy to share the good news with Helen and Stewart that they would be grandparents.

In fact, she was living in her parents' home on Higbie Drive when she gave birth to John Carl at age twenty-seven. Marilyn delivered John much like she did everything else in her life: alone. She said her mother was too busy taking care of her ailing father to accompany her to the hospital, and so she cabbed it to the delivery room.

Soon after, Stewart's lungs gave out to decades of tugging on Old Golds and Silver Thins. Grand Pop Beers died of asthma and emphysema on a Saturday, a month before Marilyn drank her way into the conception of a second child.

BURIED MEMORIES

Even before she was born, Katie demanded attention. Twice she was nearly lost when Marilyn, at age thirty-three, was diagnosed with borderline toxemia. She became a frequent visitor at the Bay Shore Health Center for a "cattle call," as she considered it, to have her blood checked for poisoning from the pregnancy. And her enormous pre-pregnancy size didn't help matters. Her hands, ankles, back, and knees ached from arthritis as she lingered long past her due date. Marilyn's legs swelled up like sausages, from her toes to her panty line, eliminating any hint of ankles and making for an oppressive month of extra gestation.

Finally, on December 30, 1982, three and a half weeks after her due date, Katherine Marie Beers entered the world. The little girl was named for her maternal great-grandmothers. Marilyn was awake and alone in the delivery room, but for the staff and doctors at Southside Hospital in Bay Shore. She had been alone for the labor, alone for the birth, and she and Katie went home from the hospital alone, in a cab.

She had no layette or the usual abundance of baby supplies that accompany most suburban births. Instead, she was given a hand-me-down bassinet and some used onesies from a concerned neighbor. Taking virtually no time off, Marilyn continued to work double shifts driving for Sunset Taxi in Babylon. She said she had no choice. She had two children and a widowed mother to support and was too proud for a public handout.

Although she failed to save a single photo of either of her children, Marilyn recalled that Katie was beautiful. She had vivid recollections of Katie's jet black hair that hung an astounding two inches in straight locks framing her equally black eyes. She and her older brother, John, were christened together at United Westminster Presbyterian Church. Their single mother was not fond of services but was a staunch believer in God. Thereafter, she named her best friend, Linda Butler, godmother.

Katie was a happy baby and as she grew, her personality evolved into the utter opposite of that of her insecure mother. She would learn to be unafraid of strangers, as Marilyn would take her along on taxi runs. Marilyn was working twelve-hour shifts, six in the morning to six in the evening, and her new baby didn't slow her down. She worked for a fifty-fifty split commission and paid for gas. On some nights, she added in a shift as a home health aide.

The long hours didn't leave much time to tend to John and Katie and so Helen, her mother, now well into her seventies, tried to fill in. But it was Linda who really took over.

Linda Butler, a frequent cab fare, had quickly became a close friend. She was five years younger than Marilyn, and at age twenty-eight, lived in a single room on Deer Park Avenue in Babylon—near the Long Island Rail Road station and worked occasionally as a school bus matron. The two had much in common and always seemed to have plenty to talk about as Marilyn drove Linda to her mother's house in West Babylon and back to her apartment.

Linda didn't have a driver's license. She was, Marilyn now concluded, "plain lazy and a con-artist. Conned everyone she knew out of everything."

At the time, Linda offered to watch Katie when Marilyn was exhausted from working double shifts. Linda would offer and Marilyn would gladly accept. The first visit turned into an overnight and soon Katie was spending days, sometimes weeks, with Linda, and was referring to both women as "Mother."

It was Linda who introduced Marilyn to her friend, Sal Inghilleri, a car mechanic with a pot belly and a chain-smoking habit to rival Marilyn's. Linda suggested she could fix Marilyn up with Sal, but Marilyn had no interest. Even she had standards and knew there was something about Sal she didn't like. So Linda and Sal became an item instead and eventually married.

Linda Butler became Linda Inghilleri, and the portly couple moved into a rented house on Myrtle Avenue in West Islip—not far from the Beers' house on Higbie Drive.

Katie could be found at either home with no apparent schedule or rationale. Sometimes she would be a ward of Helen Beers while Marilyn worked double shifts. Her grandmother meant well but didn't have the strength for a toddler and gave Katie little attention or notice.

When Marilyn or Helen needed a break, which occurred often, there was always Linda—ever eager to take Katie for a night, or several days—however long, no one cared.

Katie would split her time between the Higbie Drive house and wherever Linda and Sal were living, often missing school in the transition. The changeover wasn't always friendly. Several times Marilyn would show up to reclaim her daughter and Linda would refuse. Police were called on a few occasions.

Marilyn recalled one Thanksgiving when she appeared at Linda's home to retrieve Katie for a holiday dinner only to find the apartment dark—no one home.

What about the way Katie was dressed, no coat in the winter?

"That never happened on my watch. I always made sure she had a coat and shoes."

Marilyn continued to allow the visits with Linda because Katie, she thought, seemed to be happy with Linda. And it enabled Marilyn to pay the bills because no one else in the family was working.

In 1987, Sal let the insurance on his car lapse. "He was always good for that," Marilyn sniffed.

As a result, he lost his driver's license. In the summer of 1988, his income evaporated, too. He could never seem to hold onto a job. Once in a while, Sal would repair a car in the driveway, but the work was sporadic and incoming money a rarity. Sal's pudgy five-foot-six frame packed on more than two hundred seventy pounds, and in his mid-thirties, he collapsed one day. His heart stopped working and even though he survived the heart attack, he stopped working altogether.

Linda also gave up on work. Diabetes set in and she stopped getting out of bed much at all.

Linda and Sal always seemed to have trouble paying their rent and would often ask Marilyn if they could stay at her place on Higbie Drive. A couple of weeks would turn in to a couple of months and eventually the Inghilleris would move on, only to get evicted from another apartment and return to live with Marilyn. It was a cycle that repeated often.

Helen was miserable with the Inghilleris as non-paying boarders. The house was too small for six people, three of them over-sized, and everyone lived in terror of Sal's temper. In Marilyn's opinion, they were abusive and nasty, and nothing bothered her more than the fact they paid nothing toward the upkeep of the house.

Not that much upkeep was ever done. The house was falling apart. Sal would often erupt into temper tantrums, yelling, cursing, "beating the crap out of Linda," and just as often, Linda would need a lift to the hospital to be treated for raw bruises. Sal would swing a baseball bat with such force he left holes in the walls, "ticked off over any little thing imaginable." Not even Helen's black eye would end the Inghilleri's free ride.

Marilyn asked her mother how it happened, and a humiliated Helen muttered that she had fallen. Marilyn, of course, didn't buy it, and eventually Helen had to admit that Sal slugged her during yet another quarrel over money.

The house was overrun with dogs and cats, as many as twenty-two living inside and in the yard. Marilyn now insisted that most of them were outdoor cats, but conceded there was more than the average share of four-legged creatures. She also confirmed the odd sleeping arrangements.

Upstairs, Marilyn occupied her childhood bedroom and Linda took over what had been her brother, Robert's, room. Sal slept downstairs in a bedroom with John. Helen had her own cramped bedroom, also on the main floor. Little Katie had no formal room assignment. She was left to find a place to sleep at night. The child had no room and no bed to call her own.

Marilyn said she often called the cops to have the Inghilleris thrown out, but because the house was not in her name, she was powerless. And her mother, Helen, who legally owned the house, was paralyzed with fear of Sal, too afraid to ever press charges. So the abusive occupation continued.

Sal often badgered Helen to sign the home over to him. He insisted she take out a fifty thousand dollar home equity loan and lend half of the money to him. Under extraordinary duress, a petrified Helen took out the loan and handed over half to Sal. While she was afraid to refuse his demands, she would not agree to sign over the house. Instead, she simply stopped making the payments.

The house on Higbie Drive was now unaffordable because of the increased mortgage. If Helen had made the higher payments, she would have had nothing left to live on. She had no choice but to sell the house for a below-market eighty-one thousand dollars.

Marilyn packed up, leaving behind all family photos in the process, and moved into a garage apartment in Mastic Beach, thirty-five miles east of West Islip. The Inghilleris rented a house on Ocean Avenue in Bay Shore and Katie and Helen were assigned to live with the Inghilleris.

The move meant yet another interruption in Katie's already intermittent education. She would be registered in the school district in which Marilyn was living, and if Marilyn were home, Katie would attend school. But when Marilyn was working, which was the case on most days and nights, Katie was home with Linda.

School, said Marilyn, only seemed to get in the way of Linda's needs. When school would call to question why Katie was not in class again, no one would bother to pick up the phone. Later, with bills unpaid, there would be no phone.

On one of those twelve-hour days driving for Sunset Taxi, Marilyn picked up a new fare, a sweet elderly woman named Rose. Marilyn and Rose got to talking and Rose said she also had a son named John—John Esposito. Her John was single and worked with a "Big Brothers" organization. She learned Marilyn's John didn't have a male influence anymore because his grandfather had passed away, so she suggested that the two meet.

"Big John," as he quickly was dubbed, came over and met Little John, who was nine years old at the time. The two hit it off.

To Marilyn, Big John appeared to be a gentleman. Every week, he and Little John would get together, play games, watch videos. Big John would lavish gifts on his new friend—a twelve hundred dollar stereo and eventually even a trip to Disney World.

Little John never provided Marilyn with any details—just that Big John "touched him." That was enough for Marilyn. She no longer let her children near Big John and reported her suspicions to the Big Brothers organization. Her antenna was up.

But not high enough.

Marilyn teared up as she spoke about the hand-off on the day before Katie disappeared.

"I had told Linda, 'Do not let Katie go with Esposito.' She was told. She insisted that Katie go. Katie didn't want to go. I said, 'Take her, but on one condition that she is not to see John Esposito' and that she be home the next day."

Katie's taped message was indisputable. "Once I heard that tape," said Marilyn, "they asked me what I thought and I said, 'It doesn't sound like Katie's playing games.'"

Days after Katie vanished, Marilyn had a psychic drive her around Suffolk County. They stopped in front of John Esposito's house and the psychic said she got a sense that "Katie is in the dark, she is underground, and she is all right."

Marilyn now wept openly over her empty plate where meatloaf and mashed potatoes had been positioned around a pool of brown gravy. "I trusted the wrong people. I never got her back. I couldn't even see her that day she was rescued. I was like garbage. Like I wanted to kill everybody just to get a hold of my daughter. Just to *see* her. It was horrible. I was called 'uncaring' because I didn't cry on demand. But then they didn't see me while I was by myself, like *THIS*."

"But yes," she added, Katie's new life was filled with much more opportunity "the way things worked out."

She looked up, regained control of her breathing, put down the fork and said firmly, "I do not regret the judge's decision. That's why I didn't fight that hard. I gave up my rights because I wanted what was best for Katie. I was not stable, and if she could be with a stable family—that was best for her at that point. She knows I never wanted to give her up. She knows I always wanted her back with me. But I believe to this day that I did do what was best for her. I thank God every day. Katie survived because of a strong will and a very good therapist who helped her through a lot.

"As for me, well, I'm a loner. Always was, always will be. You can overcome bad things. You can overcome just about anything. No matter how bad something is, just remember there is someone else who has it worse. I am not wishing it on anyone, what I went through, I wouldn't wish it on anyone. I just hate it when people come up to me and say, 'I know how you feel.'

" No, you don't. More than anything else, that bugged me the most. 'Cause even if you went through the same things that I went through, you don't know how I feel." Now Marilyn was resolute, even angry.

"Of course, I *am* proud of her," she backed off.

Marilyn left the diner as I had always known her to be. Alone. There was something frail and sympathetic about what she had exposed of her soul—housed in a distracting exterior—her arms covered with scaly red sores, her teeth crooked and yellow, skin hanging around the ghosts of lost obesity.

In her eyes though, and partially toothless smile, there was more than a flicker of human frailty. She was repentant and admitted to her failings, and wanted nothing in return. Suddenly, I had an inkling as to where Katie's resilience may have, in part, come from. For it is clear that Marilyn, like her daughter, is a survivor.

THE CHIEF

I NEVER STAKED OUT Springs Elementary School on the East End hoping for a Katie sighting. I agreed she should be allowed to grow up out of the news. Some felt differently and they had their reasons. The attorney who represented Amy Fisher, the Long Island "Lolita," tried to pitch Marilyn the notion that the story was perfect for Hollywood. Proceeds of a movie would ensure Katie's future. He would broker the deal. And books about the kidnapping were dished out like short order burgers.

But her foster parents wanted no part of it for Katie, and declined all media requests through the sheriff's department.

Even years later, after I began working at a different network and the stakes had grown even higher, I chose not to seek out Katie on birthdays and anniversary dates of the kidnapping, when the papers would revisit her case. She was a child, and technically would be for at least another eight years. Even more important, she was a victim of sex crimes and she had the right to anonymity.

It wasn't until I was covering the arrest of Sal Inghilleri in North Carolina on parole violation charges that I did the arithmetic and realized, for better or worse, that Katie had grown up.

With her decision to collaborate on a book, and with her permission, I sought out the one man I thought could fill in some of the gaps in her memory: Dominick Varrone. The Detective Lieutenant was now Chief Varrone, the man who led the kidnap team in Katie's disappearance.

I had low expectations as Varrone dug a machine out of a cardboard box he had pulled out from the bottom shelf in his cavernous office at Suffolk Police Headquarters in Yaphank. The tape recorder was vintage eighties: big, black, and covered in a visible coat of antique gray dust and home to years of mold spores.

If there were anything worth listening to on this tape recorder, I guessed the audio quality would be marginal, at best.

His office was a throwback to a different era, when space was not considered a luxury and offices spoke of rank and experience. Varrone had both. He had been on the Suffolk Police Department for thirty-eight years and was currently the Chief of Detectives on a force of more than twenty-five hundred sworn officers, one of the biggest in the country.

The paneled walls of his office were a testament to that experience with barely an inch of space between the collage of black framed photographs, plaques and awards: photographs of Varrone shaking hands with Rudy Giuliani, posing with George W. Bush, and standing with Joe Biden.

The framed newspaper headlines were a journey through Long Island criminal history. One read, "Hunt for the Killer." Varrone was the tactical patrol commander in the summer of ninety-four, when a sniper took aim at random people—shooting through the crosshairs of a high-powered rifle as one victim ate at a diner and another filled the tanks of suburban gas guzzlers at a service station. Still another woman was shot as she wiped tables at a busy Wendy's. Thousands of interviews and still more ballistics checks led to an arrest and thus another success for the up-and-coming detective.

A year later, Varrone helped orchestrate the multi-agency response to wildfires that swept through Suffolk's "Pine Barrens"—an expanse of pine scrub that burned out of control during the end of the summer of ninety-five. The Hamptons were cut off from the rest of the island for days as a line of fire burned on both sides of Sunrise Highway. A black smoke plume could be seen as far away as Manhattan. Seven thousand acres of low pines and shrubs were charred for a generation, but not a single life was lost.

The next year, Varrone was overseeing the response as the wreckage of TWA Flight 800 was pulled from the Atlantic Ocean and later being reassembled like an impossible giant jigsaw puzzle. Investigators were trying to determine why the Paris-bound jet liner, filled with two hundred and thirty souls, blew up in midair above the county's Atlantic Ocean shore on July 17, 1996. The plane was reduced to metallic confetti just twelve minutes after takeoff.

In fact, Varrone was in charge at most of these sentinel Long Island events where I, quite often, was scribbling down his words.

I had known the chief for the better part of my two decades covering Long Island for, at this point, three televisions stations. Yet, even after countless press conferences and interviews, this was my first visit to his second floor office. I knew the weight of his title, if not the path he had taken to attain it: Commanding Officer of the Second Precinct, Commanding Officer of the District Attorney's Rackets Bureau, Commanding Officer of the Hostage Negotiating Team, Assistant Chief of Patrol, and now—Chief of Detectives.

Photos of swearing-in ceremonies lined the modest book shelves, but my eyes were drawn to the bookcase to the left of his massive county-issued desk. Here were framed pictures of what had to be his family. I asked about his wife and kids.

He started haltingly, "This is my wife, and these are my kids. I recall at the time of the kidnapping my daughter was about the same age and, you know, because of the similarity, same name, Catherine..." he sighed. "My son was a little older at the time and sort of got involved in the investigation—what little I was home—because my son was very into video games, and there was a video game aspect of the case, I tapped his knowledge of some of the games. My daughter was the same age as Katie, nine going on ten. It was just a coincidence...but...."

Varrone stopped, obviously uncomfortable. "I hadn't prepared to do this."

I moved quickly back into his comfort zone and we talked about Katie and what prompted her to finally tell her story after so many years of silence and anonymity.

"You sure this will be good for her?" he asked.

For some reason, the chief always reminded me of someone familiar, although I couldn't place the face, and this was especially true at that moment. Maybe it was his eyes, with a softness that defied his authoritative position. Or maybe it was the way he answered a question, going the long way around to get to the end point. The soft spot I always had for the hard-nosed investigator was reinforced at that moment when I realized that under the blue armor was an active heart.

This, quite obviously, was a man who sincerely cared about the victims long after the newspapers had yellowed.

The largest headline on his wall hadn't lost its crispness a bit. My eyes zeroed in to the top right corner of the back wall. There, in a simple black matte frame, was a front page of *Newsday* with a full page picture of Katie.

She looked dazed, wearing the over-sized blue rain poncho as she was ushered into a waiting police squad car. The headline screamed, "ALIVE!"

Just above the "Alive" headline was one more framed photo of Katie. That was the face I knew well. It was Katie's high school graduation picture.

Chief Varrone headed the kidnap task force when it was newly formed in the wake of the 1989 abduction of a mentally disabled Suffolk County boy.[33] Thirty-nine cops were each trained to respond to different aspects of a kidnapping case, from phone tapping to interrogation. Varrone, who was a precinct commander when Katie disappeared, was suddenly thrust to the helm of an investigation that would mean life or death for a child his daughter's age.

He kept mementos of what was obviously one of the highlights of his law enforcement career. One of them was a framed clipping—this one included his own picture. The headline read, "A Comforting Face." And there was a framed photo of Katie, sitting in the back seat of a detective's car moments after being rescued, with Dominick Varrone behind the wheel, whisking her to safety.

Dominick, as he soon gave me permission to call him, apologized for not going through the cardboard box before I arrived and led me into the conference room. He plopped it down, causing a dusty cloud to rise, and began sorting through its contents. There were tan folders and aged manila envelopes, pads of white pages scribbled with notes and the vintage black tape recorder. He plugged it into the wall with a long industrial extension cord, then fiddled with the buttons for a few seconds and asked, rhetorically, if I was ready. Then he hit play.

Dominick had casually informed me earlier in the year that dramatic audio tapes existed of Katie in captivity.

"Tapes?" I was incredulous.

Why would anyone have recorded her days in captivity? I vaguely remembered a mention of tapes in a McAlary *Daily News* column after Katie's rescue, but it seemed to me anecdotal. McAlary wrote of a law enforcement friend who heard tapes of Katie "sleeping and snoring"[34] in the dungeon. They seemed insignificant.

I never saw the subject of tapes ever mentioned again in the press. If they contained a treasure trove of insight into the crime, as Dominick was now suggesting, how was it possible that they had never leaked out? I was floored but tried to mask my anticipation.

"John had a mini-cassette player on the shelf in the bunker," he told me. "Now you are the only reporter who knows that."

"And you've kept that to yourself all these years? How? Why?" I asked in complete amazement.

"To protect Katie," Dominick said, more like a father than a cop. "She should never hear them. It wouldn't be good for her at all."

Instantly he moved on to a thick pile of eight-by-ten crime scene photos—there had to be well over two hundred of them. I began to flip through. The first one showed an opened red and black *Home Alone* video game box on the floor of John's chaotically cluttered bedroom. Bureau drawers were haphazardly ajar, dirty tube socks strewn all over the tiled floor, opened Pepsi cans and snack bags on the tables, and the casters of an unmade bed were propped up on folded newspapers.

"We now know Esposito made Katie an offer. She liked to drive the car, so he made an offer to pick her up and to take her to Toys 'R' Us. He was going to let her drive. So on that morning, he comes to pick her up—he sets it up the day before—he allows her to drive, sitting on his lap. They go to Toys 'R' Us and they buy some items, which ultimately we document because we knew what some of the items are. Nobody goes to Toys 'R' Us and buys the same four or five items. So we were able to backtrack and document that they did, in fact, go to Toys 'R' Us and to confirm exactly what he said he purchased. And we now know that he took her back to his bedroom and allowed her to play *Home Alone* and then made the sexual advances on her, pushed her down on the bed. He got on top of her. He began to kiss her and she fought back and screamed. With that, he brings her around to the entrance way to the underground bunker which he had prepared, and he throws her down the hole to the bunker and then he comes down with her. And he has a small voice activated recorder. He makes a recording of her saying that she got kidnapped.

"This is the actual recording," Dominick continued, like a seasoned cop commanding a press conference, delivering information with purpose, not waiting to field questions. He remembered every minute detail of this case and wanted the record to be clear and accurate.

"Later on, he goes to Spaceplex to report her missing. We now know he goes to this Amoco gas station which is right near Spaceplex and he goes to this telephone booth and dials Linda Inghilleri's number—he might be aware of the fact that she is incapacitated in a wheelchair and she doesn't usually get to the phone—and he leaves a message—what he actually wants her to believe is that it is actually Katie calling. And everyone, including us, initially believed it. So this is the call that Linda receives on her answering machine."

He fired up the tape recorder, hitting play. There was a loud hiss of background noise, then a telephone answering machine beep followed by Katie's tiny trembling voice from the distant past.

"Aunt Linda, a man kidnapped me and he had a kniiiiiiife...ooooooohh ohhoh...Oh NO here he comes—I gotta goooooo." Her voice trailed off like the ending to a sad song.

A click is then heard on the tape followed by Linda's voice, said with urgency: "Katie???"

"Now, from an investigator's perspective," the Chief continued, "it is somewhat problematic because this actually was played for me the first morning when the kidnapping was activated. As soon as I got to the Fourth Precinct where we set up the command for the kidnap team, I listened to it just as you are listening to it now."

He played it again.

"Now all of us—and Marilyn Beers and her mother all agreed—when you hear it there is no question it sounds like a young girl in distress. Really, that is hard to feign. My first impression when she said 'a man kidnapped me'—I was disturbed by the fact that a nine-year-old would say a 'man *kidnapped me.*' I would expect her to say 'a man got me' or 'a man took me.' Somebody's got me. So 'a man *kidnapped me*'—that bothered me.

"And then," he rewound and hit play again, "Ohhh oh no—here he comes—I gotta gooooooooo." The tone in Katie's little voice is heart-breaking.

"And he *had* a knife. That's past tense. And that's something we learn in statement analysis. The tenses don't match. A little girl would not say he *had* a knife—you know? He's got a knife. A man kidnapped me! He's got a knife! For the past tense, that was problematic."

Again he punched the play button.

"You hear the sobbing? 'I gotttaaa gooooooo. Oh no, here he comes, I gotta go.' And the big problem we had with that was, how does a nine-year-old in the clutches of a kidnapper—how is she able to get to a telephone to make a call? It's just—that was extremely bothersome. However, the fact is that this was clearly a girl in distress. Obviously you are concerned for the well-being of a nine-year-old child and you knew she was in trouble. But there were some issues. Now, at the time, we didn't know that this was a recording—a playback of a recording we thought this was her live, talking into a telephone. And we didn't know until it was sent to an FBI lab that this was, in fact, a recording and that he was playing it, and then we were able to determine actually where that incoming call came from—but that was all days later.

"But the other thing that the FBI picked up on," Dominick added, "if you listen to the beginning of the recording—and we didn't pick up on it, but the FBI did—you can hear an arcade game prior to her speaking."

Again, he rewound to the beginning of the tape.

"Beep ... bom bom ... "

Again. It sounded musical, like notes in an amusement park ride.

"'Bom bom bom,' you hear that? The FBI brought that to our attention. We asked them what they thought that was and they said clearly it sounds like some kind of an arcade game, which was, well, a dilemma for us because it supported the Spaceplex theory, where you play these arcade games. As it turns out, children, when Esposito would have them over the house, would record things on this tape recorder for fun, and they would always be playing these games. And if you ever pause one of these Nintendo video games, da da ... bom bom bom ... so this was a recording over a tape that apparently had something previously on it from the kids at Esposito's house. We determined this after."

The chief then recalled the morning after Katie was first reported missing and John was being grilled.

"I'm listening to the tape, it was eight or nine o'clock in the morning, and we know that imminently we are going to get a phone call from an attorney because his family is aware we have him all night. The attorney will tell us that we are on notice to stop talking to him without counsel present and we know that's about to happen. We kinda thought John Esposito was involved. We just weren't sure how. Initially we thought that he cooperated in her abduction. We actually thought that he participated in some way, perhaps unwittingly, because we thought he may be a pedophile.

"We learned he would take boys, children, to Spaceplex. We envisioned this pedophile hugging onto boys as they played video games and we were disturbed. But we quickly learned from interviewing boys that he was very childlike himself, that he would go and play the games himself. So once we learned that, we figured that—guess what? She could have been abducted!

"In investigations, there are numerous hypotheses that you float and try to confirm. So the other theory was that people knew Esposito and knew his M.O. and the fact that he went to Spaceplex, and once he got there, she'd be off on her own and someone who knew them both could just take her. 'Come with me, Katie.' And now he's left holding the bag. So we considered that possibility.

"But I still felt he was involved, and I asked him, 'What do you think happened to Katie?' and I'll never forget it. He said, 'I think something *dirty* happened.' And I thought that was odd. Very, very odd and troubling. And it made me feel even more that she was the victim of some sexual abuse."

Something dirty. It is an odd thing to say.

"Certainly that was an inappropriate remark to make," the chief continued. "My question to him then was, 'Well, why do you think that? What do *you* think happened to her?' He wouldn't say. I played into it. 'Well—she called Linda,' I said. 'Does she have *your* telephone number?' He walked into that. He wanted to show me she trusted him—not knowing where I was going with it. 'Yes,' he said, 'Katie knows my telephone. She always calls me, and I call her.' I said, 'Well, John, do you think if she manages to get to a telephone again that she might try to call you?' And he said yes, so I had my opening.

"So, I said, 'Well, then, we have to set up on your phone. We have to set up a recorder on your phone because she may call and we will want to trace the call.' And he had no choice but to say yes. And that became very critical to the investigation because it allowed us to be able to put detectives in with him, in his home, to monitor Esposito, up close.

"They were able to get into that house and feel him out and their impression was that he was extremely nervous. He wanted them out of there. When they are in the back garage, he became very uneasy—now we know why. They are literally above where Katie is. On the ground level—they are back there. He is just beside himself. But ultimately we hear from his attorney and they say they want us out of the apartment.

"We explained what we were trying to accomplish. And they said, 'He is shy, he's nervous, he wants his privacy. By going to the front house,' his lawyers argued, 'you could monitor the phone from there.'"

Dominick continued through the thick cache of eight-by-ten images with meticulous details that were obviously etched in his memory.

It was at that moment that it occurred to me. Dominick reminds me of a younger version of my own father. It was his hazel-brown eyes. Like my father's, they showed deep compassion. He and my father shared the same even tone, which conveyed a soft-spoken wisdom. There was something familiar to me in the way he steered me though the story with clarity, unspoken moral outrage, and humanity.

While I was comforted by his familiar decency, I knew instinctively that his monologue would contain dreadful details. I couldn't have been more right.

"This is the bed where he first made his advances on Katie. And here is some more evidence of the disarray, and his storage closet is full of games that children would enjoy playing.

"This is also the truck she drove sitting on his lap."

It was an eighty-nine Nissan pickup. I remembered it well. The next photo was a close-up of the peak of the converted garage where Esposito lived.

"This is the gable. If you look real close, and we didn't find this till after Katie was found, there is a video camera lens secreted in the back of the gable vent. Without a light you would never see it—it was darkness. He actually has the video camera secreted in the attic, so that when he is down in the bunker he would be able to observe anyone approaching the house. So when Katie was first held, she was able to see the detectives the night she was reported missing. The next morning, they actually went with him to his apartment and this is the day she observed the detectives approach, and she was banging and screaming at the top of her lungs because she knew there were detectives in the house.

"The detectives never heard a thing, but interestingly enough, John Esposito relayed to us later that, when he was with the detectives, he could faintly hear her screams for help, so he was very nervous. He was talking most of the time and trying to obscure the sounds.

"After we found Katie, we went down there and put a detective—put one in the bunker—shut everything up the way Esposito did and, if you made a lot of noise, you could faintly hear the sounds."

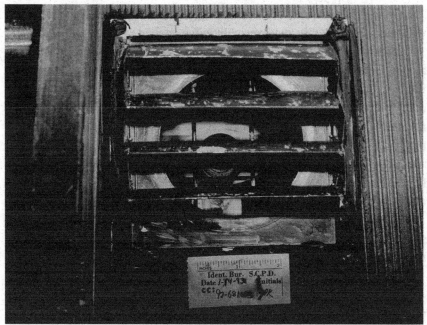

A camera hidden behind an air vent enabled Katie to see police searching for her, but they couldn't hear her screaming for help. (Suffolk County Crime Lab)

I could sense the chief had regrets.

"This is the downstairs of the garage apartment outside the office, the living room area, and it's noteworthy how much neater this is."

What do you make of that? I managed to get a question in.

"It's a cover, a setup. The bedroom has all the junk food, the Nintendo games, partially because this is how he lived but also because he continually entertained numerous boys—they played guitar, video games, ate snacks, and therefore the room is a mess. Now, what I like to tell investigators is that this is the little bar area that is obscuring the entrance to the underground bunker. Notice how neat everything is and, you know," he paused and sighed, "is that a clue that we missed?"

He answered his own question.

"Perhaps. When most of the place is a mess and you go to an area and you see order—that's a clue.

"Another clue," he moved on, "her coat. Her coat is found in his truck and we were bothered by the fact that in the winter time a little girl would leave her coat in the car. But then we come to know that Spaceplex is quite warm with all the video games, and he says she left her coat in the car because it's so hot in there. And those of us who have kids know that, and I had a daughter that age and can relate to that fact, and I had been in Spaceplex and know that it is hot in there. I could understand that. Of course, her coat, the reason her coat and her hat are in the car is because he wants to remove evidence from his apartment and make it look like Spaceplex is actually where she is missing from—so he is planting his own evidence. These were props to dupe us into believing she was with him in Spaceplex—trying to support his own story that that's where she was actually abducted from. We know he put her coat back in the car and that she never made it to Spaceplex. We didn't know it at the time. This is what he does to try to point us in the direction of Spaceplex."

He was now shuffling through the photos quickly, like a giant deck of laminated cards. Then, from out of the dusty box Dominick pulled a small, handwritten note. He blew off the film and explained that it was that note that was found in a book in Katie's room in the Inghilleri house. It was located, not by his team of detectives, he reminded me, but by a psychic that was brought into the case by Linda to get a "vibe."

"I was a little disturbed that my detectives didn't find it," he confessed softly as he read aloud words I vaguely remembered.

To Aunt Linda,

I love you. You are my favorite person in the world. But I am stuck in the middle of You and Marylin. I love you both but I love you more than Marylin. You and I have a lot of good mermies to share. But you got to understand I am only ten years old so it is very hard for me to decied who I want to live with Becaus I have lived with yo both.

Love Always, Katherine

p.s. I love you

"We now know and believe it to be authentic."

Dominick explained that the hand-scrawled note created an investigative dilemma. If it were real, it actually supported the theory that Katie may have run away. Maybe, though, people who were aware of the horrible situation in which she lived, and the fact she was like a Cinderella child to the Inghilleris and might be being abused, had staged the abduction.

"That complicated things for us as investigators," he said.

"The other thing we found disturbing were the lips and the keying in on the lips," he said as he pointed to the left side of the note, where there was an image of an oversized, crayoned red mouth.

"You know," he said gravely, "that could be indicative of a sex abuse victim because how many children—or how many pictures from a nine-year-old—would you see such large lips? Interestingly, when we went through a lot of the video tape that Esposito kept of boys and children over the years, he would zoom in on the mouths of the young boys. And knowing now what we know about him, it's obvious why. He had an oral fixation.

"There are two types of pedophiles—there is the preferential pedophile, where he or she prefers young children. They relate better to children—their goal in life is to cultivate relationships with children and that's what John Esposito was. And there are many more situational pedophiles—these are pedophiles that do not have this inherent desire to be with children, but because of a situation they are in, they take advantage of that.

"Sal Inghilleri is the perfect example of that. He is in a situation—he has a wife who had a leg amputated—was incapacitated—you can only guess as to what their sexual activity was, and Katie was at his disposal. He utilized Katie to engage in sex acts on him."

Dominick's voice cracked slightly as he said, "So how horrible is it that a nine-year-old child would have both classes of pedophiles in her life? That is very unusual—and very, very unfortunate."

My mind returned to the image of the predator smelling the scent of unprotected young prey. Then, I wondered aloud if, ironically, Katie had been helped by her numbness. Perhaps she could cope with the kidnapping and the repeated sexual abuse while in captivity because she had learned at an early age how to shut off the hurt.

As abhorrent as the sexual abuse was that she endured, in a way, maybe it equipped her for the second predator, who also had a nose for an unattended vulnerable child.

Dominick nodded, "That's exactly right. It certainly contributed to her survival and we don't think that many children could have endured sixteen, seventeen days underground with the sensory deprivation and the sexual attacks regularly. But because of her upbringing, the sexual experiences, the abuse, and street smarts and toughness, she was much more advanced than the normal nine-year-old, and we believe that contributed to her survival."

Dominick then reached into the dusty box and pulled out a sheet of paper. "This is something … "

He looked down through reading glasses.

As I said: something happened to me. I find it very hard to write everything. It started when I was between five and ten years of age. At that age I was always afraid of everything. I don't even remember Mommy or Daddy ever kissing or holding each other. I remember they were always fighting. I remember Mommy never slept with Daddy. I don't even remember them sleeping together until I was about twelve years old. Mommy always slept with me. I was very young. I think it was early in the morning I remember being touched. I think I was touched a lot while I was asleep. I know it's hard to believe, however, around five years ago I asked Mommy if anything ever happened when I was young. She looked at me and wept, but didn't say. I think she wanted to, but couldn't. She told me God is punishing me for what she did. I don't know why she picked me, instead of Ronnie—maybe because I was always afraid. She knew I wouldn't say anything. I think Daddy knew what was happening. I remember he was always mad at me. I hope you understand why I was so angry and odd. I want you to know I still loved Mommy. I think she needed someone and I was there.

Dominick dropped the letter and looked up. "It was written by John Esposito. So this is kind of an admission that he was abused. We find that that's not unusual for pedophiles. You find that most pedophiles were abused themselves."

I had suspected that John was probably abused himself, but the letter was a rare *mea culpa.* As a news reporter, I've overdosed on the lethal consequences of bad decisions, selfish acts and ruthless crimes. I conduct daily door-knocks at the homes of people who have a penchant for dishing out pain to others, who deliberately cause harm, or unwittingly hurt and then fail to own up to their mistakes.

I am invited into living rooms and bear witness to the pain of those whose lives are scarred, altered or taken for no apparent reason. Survivors, sentenced to an indeterminate term of grief, speak of their unyielding suffering; yet perpetrators, even when there is nothing left to lose, often remain stoic.

I have sat attentively at the sentencing of killers longing for a moment of elucidation that never materializes. Every so often, there are brief, faint words read from a crumpled script on jailhouse legal paper, but they are rarely words that explain *why* harm was done. These courthouse apologies are rarely proportionate to the enormity of the crime committed, and often leave victims feeling victimized yet again.

Explanations can be found only in textbooks: Psychopaths harm, the experts say, because they don't feel empathy,[35] and pedophiles abuse because they were abused.[36] But until this moment, I had never been convinced.

If Katie could apparently recover from childhood sexual abuse, why couldn't John Esposito? Two abused souls and one recovers but the other perpetuates the cycle of abuse. What is the difference?

"You don't know to what extent the letter he wrote is self-serving," Dominick, more pragmatist than psychologist, brought me back to the moment, and right back to the photos.

"This is a command post, this is the ... "

As he spoke, I was distracted, wondering when, if ever, we would get to the audio tapes of Katie in captivity. But the chief continued in a slow and deliberate pace, chronicling the story through the photographs with dogged attention to detail.

Somewhere between the command post photo and the bunker tunnel photo tour, I realized what was going on here. The particulars of the investigation and Katie's survival were catalogued like locks of baby hair in a parent's scrapbook. The chief was deeply invested in this case. Katie didn't have a father when it may have mattered most. The men early in her life violated her body and soul. But Dominick, years after the case was closed, was still Katie's protector.

I was heartened by the realization that Katie, whether she knew it or not, had a father figure.

Tedd had also embraced the role, albeit at times stoically. As Katie was becoming family, he was assigned the unenviable job of escorting both John and Sal from prison to court as part of his detail as sheriff's deputy. He later told me he endured the assignment as a professional, and never uttered a word to either one of them. Had he known the details of the abuse Katie had suffered, he may not have been able to maintain his composure.

"I viewed John Esposito as a very pathetic man who needed to be punished for his crime," he revealed to me. "I didn't feel the hatred for him, as I did for Sal Inghilleri. Sal needed to spend the rest of his life in jail. He was a monster, a bully who preyed on the weak. Not only did he spend twelve years in jail, but I am sure he did hard time. He probably spent most of his years in segregation. Jail time for child abusers is hard. You are at the bottom of the pile—the worst of the worst. There is a place for him in hell."

The year after she was kidnapped, I lost my own father. Soon after Katie was found, his brain tumor recurred. His speech vanished after experimental stereotactic radiosurgery. Doctors kept reassuring us he would speak again, but he never did.

I would recount for him the stories I was covering each day, but was never really sure he understood my words. As I sat beside a morphine pump and the hospice bed where our dining room table had been, at 7:10

in the evening of May 17, 1994, my fifty-nine-year-old father took his last breath.

Days and weeks later, the murder of Nicole Brown Simpson would lead the news. His beloved Rangers would go on to win the Stanley Cup for the first time in fifty-four years. I know he would have been captivated by the wall-to-wall coverage.

His death left me without a father, but with an abiding sense of what was expected of me. I wondered what becomes of people who do not grow up with a captain of the ship, a moral compass—people like Katie.

Dominick was pointing now at an image of John's office and the entryway to the bunker.

I asked if I could hold the photos—and I thumbed through them. I could see the carport, and Dominick explained that the bunker was located directly under the carport. Esposito, he said, poured the slab of concrete himself and put an oil tank in there. He built all of it and even put a car in the carport so that no one would imagine what lay beneath.

"This is the outer room with soundproofing covering the walls and ceiling; this is the coffin-like room where Katie was secreted most of the time. Katie," he said, "had been complaining that she was having trouble breathing, and he made a hole for her in the side of the box. And there is the makeshift toilet, with plastic in it. And this gave him the excuse that every time she came out to use the toilet, he fondled her and dried her.

"I would like to hear what she has to say now, to see how consistent it is with what she told us," he said. I wondered which version of events he would consider to be more reliable: the details she gave when she was ten years old or the ones she remembers now, as an adult looking back two decades. Would they be the same, or, I wondered, does time erase the most agonizing details?

I was hopeful the tapes would answer that question. But I was beginning to wonder if the tapes truly existed.

"This is one of the chains he used around her neck. This is the inner room, and you've seen photos of this. This is the TV, and it was always on twenty-four/seven. The TV was very important. It provided light. It provided heat. Don't forget she is down here in December and January in the cold winter months with no heater inside. It provided light, heat and what I think is the most important piece—it provided psychological support. The broadcasts that were repeated all day—she knew we were looking for her and that gave her hope. I don't know that she shared that with you."

She had shared that with me. In fact, it was the reason, I believed, that Katie entered into our partnership. She knew of me from my news reports, my presence on the small cathode-ray tube inside her coffin-box.

"When Marilyn or her brother appeared on the TV, she would hug and kiss the TV. She gave us a very poignant description of what she endured down there and how she survived. I think that TV was critical to that—she remained in contact with the outside world."

Holding up the next eight-by-ten, Dominick continued, "This, it took us a while to figure out what this was."

I could see what was coming.

"It was just lying there," he said, as he pointed to the photograph of a wooden box.

"We weren't sure what it was at first. What it is, is a head box."

It was as evil as it sounded.

"It's very well-constructed. There are air holes. This is the mechanism for a guillotine, slide it up and place the victim in, then drop this down under the chin, hitting the victim at the bottom of the neck so as to immobilize the victim from the neck up."

Dominick explained that the captor would then have access to the victim's body and have the ability to observe the victim's face, without the victim seeing him.

"I didn't know the genesis of it, but there was actually a girl out west who was abducted in Washington State and held captive for years, and a head box was built to hold her in place. We think it's meant for an adult—it's certainly big enough and heavy enough, and the FBI noted that the coffin-like box is big enough to accommodate an adult, so we don't know if his fantasy was to have ultimately taken an adult. But we know it was made for an adult."

Was it ever used?

"There is no evidence it was ever used. Katie never said it was used."

But you know he built it?

"We absolutely know he built it. And I now know that he built it based on a book. We know that John Esposito read the book because the book makes reference to the number of juveniles reported missing every year, and there are so many that eventually the police just forget about it. We think this is where it instilled the idea in his mind that he could abduct a child, and that after a while the police would stop looking."

Until this point, I was largely unaware of the twisted details of the story of Colleen Stan, a story that most criminologists consider one of the most extreme cases of sexual torture ever. I am well aware of that horror story now.

In May, 1977, Colleen, a twenty-year-old free spirit, was hitchhiking through Northern California. She accepted a ride from Cameron Hooker and his wife, Janice. They had their baby in the car. Colleen, who had passed up two other drivers, reasoned it would be a safe ride.[37]

The next seven years were filled with brainwashing and unspeakable torment. Colleen was hung by her wrists, whipped, stretched naked on a board and raped by her sick, sadistic captor. She was threatened that if she didn't submit to the torture, her tongue would be cut out. Her captor also told her that if she resisted, she would be nailed to the ceiling beams—or even worse, her family would be tortured and killed. She signed away her life in a sex slave contract, was given the slave name "K" and spent years imprisoned in a coffin-like box under the Hookers' waterbed.

Hooker's signature handiwork was a wooden box lined with egg-crate insulation. When placed over Colleen's head, it engulfed her in total darkness. Holes allowed her to breathe, but insulation rendered her mute to the outside world. Her gasps and anguished pleas could be heard only by her own ears. The box was locked over Colleen's head as the rest of her body was kept inside the coffin-like chamber, twenty-three hours a day under the bed where Cameron and Janice had sex, and where Janice gave birth to a second child.

In fact, Colleen lived in that box, her head locked inside the head contraption, for an unfathomable seven years, eventually only being let out to do domestic chores inside the home and to submit to sexual torture.

Dominick showed me the book, *The Perfect Victim,* written by the prosecutor in the Colleen Stan case.

"By the time I became aware of this, had I known, I would have searched his house for this book, gone to the library to see if it was ever signed out to him. But we are convinced he read the book. I read the book myself and came upon a quote:

"Like so many missing persons bulletins, this one elicited no response. It was filed and forgotten."

"So this is a portrayal of another criminal, but I think it is giving another predator an idea. And I'm convinced Esposito read the book. I'm convinced that's where he got the idea of the head box, and this is where he starts thinking that if he takes a child and she is reported missing, there are so many cases, it will just be filed and forgotten. And he had no idea; he was overwhelmed by the response, the kidnap team, all the media attention. No one would just let it go."

He paused. "We are quite lucky he didn't use it."

The chief changed the subject as quickly as he flipped to the next picture.

"This is the drop down into the bunker. Now in between, you crawl forward. And in that hallway, there is a trap door and a secondary barrier to prevent escape, and he wedged a board here. So even if you were able to get out of the first box, you would have that obstruction, not to mention on the top, he had a heavy six-inch thick piece of concrete. It was certain that no one could escape.

"Here," he pointed out, "are eyebolts with nuts. Every time he left, he closed it like this and all of these eyebolts had nuts on them. He had an electric wrench to remove the bolts. You'd hear them—the grinding of the bolts. You can just relate to the horror that this sexual predator was coming, and when he left, as well. And I'm not sure which was worse. Because now she is deprived of any human contact and realizes she is really locked in."

What happened to the bunker? It was my understanding it was being kept for forensic education.

"We kept it for quite some time. Eventually, we needed the space." He didn't elaborate further, but was lost in thought.

"This is the side vent here. This provided ventilation for the underground—something else we missed."

They missed the significance of the baby monitors, too. One part was positioned inside the bunker and the other, in the living room upstairs, where detectives had searched repeatedly.

"The monitor—we actually saw up there! And you recall that his sister-in-law lived in the front house. When the detectives asked him what that is, he said, 'That's connected to the front house.' That's another clue we missed."

You beat yourself up about that?

"No, it's bothersome to know she endured as many days as she did. Seventeen days underground. But we also know that had it not been for our efforts, it could have been far worse for her.

"Here are the handcuffs." He showed me a glossy of the cuffs John had installed to lock Katie to the coffin-sized box.

Then he extended to me a photo of an open grave.

"This was a low point in the investigation, when a psychic found a grave and told us it was Katie. Turns out," he paused, "it was the grave of a dog."

And the tapes?

"I'll look for them," he said. "They are buried here, somewhere."

John Esposito's living room. You can see the baby monitor on the table. He told police it was hooked up to the main house. The other end was actually inside the bunker with Katie. (Suffolk County Crime Lab)

LOST LOVE

I HAD ASKED MARILYN who my father was many times, but never got a straight answer. If not for my brother, John, I would have written off men altogether. John was my brother and father rolled into one. We were six years apart, so we battled often, mimicking the TV wrestlers we watched every weekend, pulling each other's hair, stabbing at each other's eyes, and yelling our heads off. But we were very close.

The only happy memories I have of growing up, I can count on one hand. And John is a part of all of them. He was the first person who believed me when I got the courage to speak up about the abuse by Sal. I will always love him for that, even though it backfired badly.

I tried to tell Aunt Linda when I was old enough to speak up, maybe seven or eight years old, but she yelled at me and called me a rotten liar. She said there is no way Sal would ever do that. So one day, I climbed onto the roof and refused to come down. I stayed there until Linda hollered every curse and threat at me through her opened window; I eventually climbed back into the house, and until I moved in with Marilyn in Mastic Beach, I never uttered another word to any other adult about what Sal had done to me.

No one, I was sure, would take my side, and anyway, I probably deserved it. My brother, John, didn't see it that way. John knew firsthand about Sal's ferocious temper and mean streak. So when I told him I needed to talk to him one afternoon, he brought the radio into his dinosaur-tented bed, turned up the music, and in a hushed voice, asked me what was wrong. We were still living in the West Islip House, and I was eight years old.

John could tell that I was nervous as I whispered so no one else would hear.

"Sal makes me touch him."

John asked me to elaborate, so I got up the courage to tell him that Sal makes me touch his private parts. John asked me if there was a specific time or place that Sal made me touch him, and there wasn't—it was sometimes when no one was home other than Linda because she never came downstairs or just my grandmother, but she had no purpose to go into Sal's room. It happened whenever Sal wanted, which was all the time.

John was furious. He was also sad. With tears in his eyes, he told me that he was so sorry that it happened, and that he hadn't done anything to help me, and from then on, he would protect me from Sal. John would be home a lot more often when I was there, and he'd have his friends come over to the house more often so that he didn't have to leave. But right away, he said, he was going to catch Sal in the act, then get the cops to come to witness it. And Sal would be locked up and couldn't hurt any of us anymore.

The windows in Sal's room were rather large, with sheer curtains hanging up, so John was going to leave the house and return and watch outside of the bedroom window, in the bushes, waiting for Sal to make his move on me.

It didn't exactly happen that way.

Somehow, Sal caught sight of John outside of his bedroom window before he made me touch him and then proceeded to beat John to a pulp. Bloodied and bruised, John had enough. He ran to the police precinct for help. But before he did, John forewarned Sal he was in big trouble.

"You're done, you fat slob."

Sal kept calm but ordered me into his bedroom and growled that I had better tell the cops that John was fighting with his friends, and that's how he got the bloody nose and swollen eyes, "or else." He then stormed out of the house, and by the time the squad car cruised by, Sal was driving down the street calmly as if nothing had happened. The cops flagged Sal down and asked him about the incident, but it didn't do a thing. Sal drove away and the cops came to the door and asked me what had happened to John. Who had beaten him up? I told them that as far as I knew it was his friends. They asked me if Sal had *ever* beaten him up and I said no, that Sal was nice to us all and loved us.

The truth is I was scared to death and didn't want Sal to hurt anyone in my family any further—I had just witnessed a ruthless beating of my big brother. Later, when Child Protective Services case workers would visit the house, I lied to them too. They would come, with big folders and lots of questions, and would interview me in Sal's room, in the very place where the abuse repeatedly happened. But Sal threatened that he would kill every last member of my family if I ever said a word, and I knew he could. There was no one else to tell. I wasn't in school often enough to trust anyone, and no one spoke of these things back then anyway.

I had learned my lesson. Never tell a soul. It wouldn't help. Even my brother, John, my would-be savior, couldn't win against the vicious likes of Sal. He was as tortured and trapped as I was. Well, almost. Most of the time, he was living with Marilyn while I was shipped out to Sal and Linda's. When we were together, we made the best of it. I think that John and I subconsciously knew something was off about the way that we grew up, and we both knew that we had to survive.

John, at least, had his father in the picture. I thought that my life was more difficult because I didn't have Marilyn most of the time nor a father, and John was only *physically* abused by Sal. I was getting it from all sides. I was physically and emotionally abused by Aunt Linda, physically, emotionally, and sexually abused by Sal and then neglected by my mother. I'd look at John and think he had it good.

What John couldn't do for me in the short run, he did in the long run. He left me with the knowledge that not all men are bad, nor are they all going to hurt me. And for that, I will always cherish him. He was the most influential person in my life. It makes me sad how it all turned out.

John has never been married. He was engaged once, but that ended as quickly as it began. No kids that we know of, no college. He thought of going to culinary school and I believe studied to become a physical trainer, but at the end of the day, he settled into a job at a convenience store in Philly and is in a constant battle to stay sober. We touch base occasionally, on holidays, and I wonder, if there is anything that I can do to help him, but then, I can't get sucked into his life. John gave me so much, but like everything else in my past, I have to leave him behind.

My life went down a completely different road. I was immersed in eastern Long Island high school normalcy. I was hungry to make up for lost time and had no problem slamming the door shut on a past that only provided me with nightmares.

At East Hampton High School, I went out for the volleyball team and the cheerleading squad. I quickly realized I was more of a guy's girl than a girl's girl. The girls were catty and I had no problem liking boys.

In therapy, Mary told me that abused children go in one of two directions: They are either very promiscuous or very shy. I was neither. I dated several boys in junior high, summer camp, and now high school, but I would only go as far as kissing. I was extremely concerned about disappointing my foster parents, to whom I was now firmly devoted. I would lie to them about stupid things because I didn't want them to think I was doing anything with boys. That, I was sure, would make them think I was as dirty as the people who raised me.

Actually, I never told my parents about any of my boyfriends and cut the relationships off before they could go any further physically. I wasn't ready to be sexual with anyone, and I didn't want to feel like I was being pressured. When I ended one relationship, there was usually another one around the corner. I was never without a boyfriend for too long. I changed boyfriends almost monthly for one reason: I didn't want to get too serious with any of them, nor did I want them to expect anything from me.

In tenth grade, I joined the tech crew building sets for the high school plays. I didn't realize it at the time, but the friend who got me involved in the tech crew actually had a crush on me. I had no romantic interest in him. But it was there, in tech crew, that I met my first love.

Tech crew became my family: Sid, Raj, Justin, and Scott. Then there was me—the only female on the crew. They were my best friends, and this is where I was most comfortable, around boys. I confided everything in Raj. He knew how to make me smile when I was miserable over a bad day, or over a break-up, and then he was there for me when I started to fall for Scott.

I don't know exactly when I started to develop feelings for Scott, but I had them for a while before I confided in anyone. Scott was exactly a foot taller than me, six foot four! He had dirty blond hair and the most amazing blue eyes. Looking back, I should have realized he felt the same way about me. He never missed a football game when I was cheerleading. He hated football but still traveled to every game. And he never missed a volleyball game I was playing in.

Scott was friends with other girls on the squad and on my volleyball team—so, to me, it never added up.

Raj and I were waiting in town one day for Scott to get off of work at an upholstery shop where he was considered to be a "jack of all trades." Raj could tell I was upset. I finally confessed to him that I was hurt that Scott never seemed to notice me. Raj's response upset me even more. He told me that Scott had noticed me and talked about me, but never mentioned whether or not he liked me.

I burst into tears, crying, sending black mascara-streaked tears running down my cheeks. When I took out my makeup bag and mirror to wipe away the streaks, Raj grabbed my foundation and put it on his face, like war paint stripes. He didn't realize that it wouldn't rub off. I was laughing hysterically.

A week later, I could no longer hold back my feelings. Scott and I were at a rehearsal. It was February 24—I remember the date. Scott could tell that something was bothering me. He kept asking me what was wrong and I told him I would let him know later. Scott was relentless, asking me over and over what was wrong. Maybe he just wanted me to make the first move. So I did. I told Scott what I had been dying to say for months, a simple, "I like you."

After blurting out the words, I turned my back quickly and walked away, too embarrassed to look at him and face rejection. A few seconds later, Scott grabbed my arm, turned me around and pressed his mouth against mine. After he kissed me, he said, "Mmm, watermelon."

I was wearing watermelon Chapstick. I laughed. From that day on, we were inseparable.

He was unlike any boy I had ever known. He could always make me laugh. I tried to only surround myself with positive people, and Scott was very positive—always looking on the bright side of things. My relationship with Scott was built on a friendship rather than attraction—I was actually attracted to Scott's personality.

Aside from his ever-present flannel shirts, which he ditched at my request, there was nothing about Scott that I would have changed. I was so lucky to have had him in my life. He was my best friend, and my soul mate—or so I thought.

I was sixteen years old and pretty sure this might be love, but I didn't tell my foster parents. And they didn't ask. They let me go to the movies with Scott and Raj and hang out with them because we had all been friends for a long time—the three of us always together. Scott and Raj were best friends, then I came along and we were three, but I knew now things were going to be different.

BURIED MEMORIES

We were between dress rehearsals for a play and had to take a drive because Scott was watching over a house for a family that was out of town. Scott and I walked around the property to make sure that everything was okay. There was a pool house, so we went inside to check it out, deciding to stay a while before going back to the school.

We were alone and in love. It was the first time I was ever physical with anyone by choice. It wasn't exactly romantic, but for me, it was intensely emotional, to be able to trust and love a man. It was a risk to take and a relief to discover I was capable of both. I had never before felt that close to anyone.

I later learned not to consider the rapes the loss of my virginity, because it was something that I was forced to surrender rather than something in which I willingly participated. Now it could be a choice, as an expression of love. I knew early on in our relationship that I loved Scott. He was easy to love.

I loved Scott with all of my being—every second that we could be together, we were. When we weren't together, Scott would call me at eight at night. It became a running joke in the family that no one could be on the phone at that time because Katie had that time reserved for Scott. When the phone rang, no one else bothered to pick it up. It was always for me.

When it was time for me to think about going to college, I wanted to stay close to home because I didn't want to be far from Scott. He had become my world. My parents, though, had other priorities. When my mother recited the criteria she deemed important in choosing the right college for me, her list was simple: small, secluded, religious.

The search resulted in the discovery of a tiny liberal arts college in central Pennsylvania. I didn't want to go to school this far from home, but when she and I visited the campus, I thought it was perfect. The town was small, and the campus was beautiful—this is where I belonged. I believe that everything happens for a reason. My college choice determined the course of my life.

With my college plans firmed up, Scott then informed me that he was also going to move to Pennsylvania to work with his brother as a roofer with the Amish in Lancaster. I was thrilled, but when we announced the plans to my parents, they did not share our enthusiasm. It wasn't that they didn't like Scott. He had never given them reason to dislike him. They just didn't want me to go off to college with my high school boyfriend following me and tying me down. So instead, we then told them that he was moving to Virginia.

Scott and I then felt horrible that we had lied to my parents, so at some point during my first semester in college, Scott was home visiting his family and went to my house to admit that he had lied, confessing that he had actually moved to Lancaster for a good job opportunity. My parents were not at all pleased, but they respected Scott for coming forward and finally being honest.

With Scott nearby, the transition to college life was painless. I arrived thinking that I was going to be a child advocate one day, majoring in psychology, but I quickly changed my major to business management and accounting. I knew that I would need to earn a living both during and after college and needed something practical.

My therapy was paid for by the New York State Victims' Compensation Fund and Social Services because I was still officially a foster child, but college was paid for by my parents. They had put their monthly foster care stipend toward my college education and paid the rest out of pocket. I wanted to be able to pay them back.

A lawsuit against John Esposito's homeowners insurance for millions was lost; Uncle Tedd was livid. He knew that if I had been called to testify, I stood to collect a large sum that could have helped me in life because I remembered, by this point, that the bunker had been built in plain sight. But the county attorney never called me to testify. He later admitted to Tedd that was a mistake. It was one of the few times I ever saw Tedd get really angry. He felt the county botched the lawsuit and then, to make matters worse, wanted to deduct lawyers' fees, which would have left me with little more than ten thousand dollars. He threatened to go public, and the county agreed to waive the fees. The settlement check was for thirty-five thousand dollars, but it was enough for me to buy a car. There were also a few thousand dollars in John's inmate fund, so I used what was left to pay for the remainder of my college tuition, and I hoped to use the rest one day for a wedding.

I hunkered down with school work, happy that no one seemed to recognize my name, and I tried to see Scott regularly. He would come to my dorm after work to pick me up, and we would spend weekends together in Lancaster. When I needed him, he dropped everything.

During my sophomore year in college, my father's father, Pop-Pop, passed away. He was a special person. Growing up, I loved time with him doing arts and crafts, making bracelets, necklaces, or cross hook rugs, anything creative. Pop-Pop used to make blankets with yarn. He planned on teaching me to make them, but he passed away before he could. Scott held my hand through the services and viewings. He was my rock.

During Thanksgiving break in my junior year of college, I worked at the Coach store on Main Street in East Hampton. I was upstairs helping a customer choose a purse when Wesley, my co-worker, sneaked up behind me, put his arms around me and gave me a squeeze. I was a little annoyed with him because I thought it was unprofessional to hug me while I was trying to make a sale. But when he turned me around, Scott was standing there, all dressed up. He was supposed to be helping one of our friends put a roof on their house, so I knew that something was very odd about his formal attire. Scott took a little box out of his pocket, got down on one knee, and before he even said anything, I began crying. He looked in my eyes, and declared, "Katie Beers, I love you, will you marry me?"

I immediately started sobbing and exclaimed, "Yes!" When I composed myself, I realized that all of my co-workers were upstairs watching with wide smiles; Scott had told all of them that he was going to propose.

Somehow, I finished my shift, staring at the stunning ring on my finger. The ring was a platinum band with seven diamonds—the center stone was huge, with three smaller diamonds on either side. Scott had designed it himself, and it was perfect. So was he. I was on Cloud Nine at the knowledge that I found someone who could love me for me, baggage included.

Scott knew everything there was to know about me, full disclosure, and he loved me in spite of it. Scott got along with my new family as well as my old family, Marilyn and John. Until then, I never thought that I would meet someone who would love me knowing everything about my past.

I was so excited to tell my parents about our engagement. I wanted to deliver the news while we were at dinner that night, but my dad wasn't home and I didn't want him to miss the moment, so I somehow kept it to myself for one more day. The fact is, they already knew. Scott had properly asked for my hand in marriage a few days earlier, and my parents gave him their blessing.

We all vacationed at my parent's house in Florida for Christmas and set our wedding date: September 24, 2005. The date has special meaning. It was the same day of the month as our first kiss.

Five months after he proposed, I broke up with Scott over the phone. Cowardly, I know. But if I tried to do it in person, I would not have been able to go through with it. One look into his beautiful blue eyes, and I would have agreed to anything.

I didn't give him a chance to talk. I knew that if he spoke, he would convince me to stay. It wasn't that I no longer loved Scott because I truly did—I just realized that I had not had the chance to live yet. I wanted a career and a life outside of college before I settled down, got married, and started a family.

Scott wanted a family right away. At twenty-one years old, I was still a child myself. After all, I had to discount the first ten years of my life. I had no childhood worth remembering. All of it was sad and ugly.

I told him that things weren't working out anymore and that I no longer wanted the same things he wanted out of the relationship. I hadn't really lived my life. It was a typical "It's not you, it's me" situation. Scott had done no wrong. I wanted to experience what life had to offer.

But there was more. I never verbalized this to Scott when we broke up, but I also think that our relationship had too much emphasis on the physical. Scott had the sexual appetite of a normal young man and I was indifferent. I just couldn't change that part of me. It was not something that I needed or desired.

The first time that I had sex was intensely emotional, not because I was a rape victim, but because Scott and I were so much in love. But after that, it was something I could easily live without. I rarely initiated it. The truth is, I struggled to find sex pleasurable—and I now understand why. It's one of the long-term effects of it being forced on me so early.

I have seen Scott twice since we broke up in 2004: once when I returned the ring and again, that same weekend, at a bar in Sag Harbor. I saw him walk in the door, and my heart stopped. I was with a few of my girlfriends. Scott walked over and offered to buy us all a round of drinks, and everyone else said "yes." I declined, but I ended up drinking too much that night, anyway. I had to work the next day, and up until that point, I had never called in sick since I was fourteen years old.

I was working three jobs that summer: at the Coach shop as a salesgirl, at a nursery and landscaping store as a cashier and at a restaurant as a hostess. The restaurant job didn't last long. The owner picked the wrong girl to harass. I wore jeans to the job one day and asked him if it were allowed. He instructed me to turn around in a complete circle for him and then said, "If all of your jeans look that good, then yes, you can wear jeans."

Later that evening, as I walked past him, he slapped my butt and said, "Looking good, Katie." I quit the next day. I was no longer a defenseless child.

The nursery quickly made up for the lost hours. This is why I felt horrible about going to work hung over. It was the drunkest that I had ever been in my life. I actually had to ask to pull over on the side of the road to throw up, but I was determined to not compromise my job and disappoint my employer, despite feeling awful and out of control.

My boss at the nursery could tell that I was in no shape to work and sent me home early. My mother asked me what I was doing away from work and I just acknowledged that I wasn't feeling well. All I wanted to do was sleep away the hangover and the sadness I was feeling.

But she is able to read me better than anyone before in my life. She is not my biological mother, but has a connection to me I never knew was possible. When I woke up, she pressed further. I was old enough now to stop lying to her and trust she would react as she always did, with love and support. I confessed that I had had too much to drink the night before after running into Scott at the bar. Rather than lecturing about me drinking too much and missing work, she hugged me and simply said, "Honey, this must be so difficult for you."

I had underestimated my parents' ability to accept everything about me, perhaps because they were so strict with me when I first came to live with them. But the need for their approval has kept me centered and given me a strong sense of right and wrong. Parents came late into my life, but not too late to make a profound difference.

The loss of Scott was my choice, but a heartbreaking one. Scott was my first love, my rock, my best friend—and now, I had rejected our future together. I think the hardest thing about breaking up with him was losing his friendship. He still holds a very special place in my heart and he left me with more than just memories. He gave me the knowledge that, even after a loveless childhood, I was capable of loving back.

THE TAPES

T HE CHIEF HAD A paternal reaction to almost everything I broached about Katie. And I was careful to reassure him that this was Katie's idea, that she was the one who wanted to unearth these well-guarded memories. He looked at me with a measure of distrust, but proceeded anyway, respecting Katie's wishes.

The tape started to grind into the play mode. It wasn't long before a tiny voice startled and shook me.

"Help meeeeee. Heeeeeeeelp meeeeee. Let meeeeee ooouuuuuut."

I leaned in closer to hear. The sound quality was more than adequate. I could hear every bone-chilling word.

"Heeeeellllp...get me outta here." Then, a whimper and a whine, *"heeellllppppp me."*

The voice was young—younger than that of my own children—and stopped my heart. I cradled my head in my hands as I listened.

"Helppppp mmeee...oh pleeease let me outttt." Then, banging over and over again—*"bang bang bang."*

Oh, my God, I thought. This is surreal. An actual tape recording of Katie while she was in captivity!

"You are the first reporter to ever hear this," Dominick deadpanned, as he could see the shattering effects of Katie's blood-curdling screams on my blanched face. He stopped the tape.

"Some people may hear some of the encounter and may be disturbed about how she acts to him. It goes to the 'Stockholm Syndrome' but more important it speaks to a nine-year-old who is deprived of any human contact. And Esposito, as bad as we think he is, for her, it's a human being and you almost have to wonder if she took some comfort in his company and conversation."

He looked up and stopped shuffling papers. "It's upsetting. But not as upsetting now because you realize she survived. But very disturbing that a nine-year-old child would have to endure this kind of misery. She wasn't murdered, we know that. It's a horrible thing to put a child in a situation

THE TAPES

like this."

He returned his eyes to the pile of records.

For the first time, I realized that Katie never told police that, down in the bunker, as a prisoner of John, she was raped.

"A pedophile cultivates a child," he explained. "It's almost a love affair, a courtship, and you hear some of that in some of their exchanges." He stopped the tape and read now from his handwritten transcript.

"See? We could play games and stuff when I get the time, okay?"

"It's a very fascinating, yet very disturbing exchange. He takes her to use the toilet, he says, *'Go ahead—I won't watch if you don't want.'* He says it again. In other words, what the pedophile *wants* her to say is, 'Go ahead and watch.' But she says, *'Good, I don't want you to watch.'* Sexual predators want the victim to fall in love with them."

He read more from the log, a hand written account of every decipherable word on the tapes. I patiently listened, waiting for the tapes to actually roll on.

But instead, he read, *"Leave it alone and I won't hurt you."*

"I know. I'm going to try to do it one day."

"I know you are. I know you are."

"I think," said Chief Varrone grimly, "I think this is, this may be his penis. I think *'leave it alone.'* He may have been rubbing on her. *Leave it alone. I won't hurt you.* And she is crying. And she says to him, 'I'm going to try to do it someday.' So again, this is that cultivation and the victimization." The seasoned detective was choked up.

Emotional lapses were brief. Recovery was swift and Dominick read more of the transcript.

"Do you want to walk around a little bit? You know what I'm going to do. Tomorrow night I'll get some warm water, you know, to wash yourself."

With a slight roll of his eyes, it was apparent that Dominick didn't think John was in the least bit concerned about Katie's hygiene.

"Again, it gets into the sexual aspect where the pedophile wants to wash and fondle the victim. This is a very common technique when they fondle their victims."

The tapes are very short snippets, a very narrow window into what actually occurred down there during the seventeen days of captivity. Dominick said he listened to them for months, hours and hours at a time, donning headphones, going over and over the same small pieces of tape to discern voices and cries. Some parts were so hard to hear, he enlisted the help of a sound lab. And when listening with headphones, he said, "I was there. I was actually in that bunker."

Parts of the tapes were indeed hard to make out, and the Chief was protective of their contents, stopping and starting the machine to add dimension to barely audible voices. He wanted them put in context, and I got it. The tapes are a window into the mind and *modus operandi* of a pedophile, and he saved them all these years only to share them for an instructional and non-exploitive purpose. They are a rare fly-on-the wall perspective that any criminologist would pore over. They also provided a glimpse into the nature of Katie's recovery—the potential disparity between what she remembers now and what she may have blocked out.

There was a part of the tape that actually made the corner of Dominick's mouth curl into a faint smile.

"A fascinating aspect of it that I took comfort in," he said, "was that harassing him, disturbing him, certainly limited the amount of time that he spent with Katie."

"They keep calling me—these guys, every fifteen minutes."

"Every fifteen minutes?"

"From the other house and every time I have to pick up the phone. And they're driving me nuts."

"He's dying for us to pack up and leave. And had we ever done that, then he would have spent a very long time with her. So our presence forced him to realize the contact with her had to be limited.

"Katie sneezes and John says *'Bless you. Getting a cold? Don't get cold—keep under the blanket.'* It's very fatherly—no I wouldn't use the word fatherly—it's a technique he is using to cultivate his victim."

"I don't know what they are going to do to me when they find me, but at least I had you a little while. Give me a kiss, you want a kiss? I'm gonna have to go now, okay?" He wants her to say, 'I want you.' This is classic *classic* pedophilia and child victimization."

Dominick lifted his gaze. "This was an incredible amount of work," he sighed, and pulled out another box of cassettes, another treasure trove of unearthed memories. Debrief tapes. They were Katie's conversations with detectives in the first hours after she was rescued. These, the chief let me

218

hear immediately.

Her voice is tiny. I struggled to adjust my ears to the slightly muffled recording. Then, I could make out her words, butted together quickly with a child's heavy Long Island accent.

"My story is…"

"Tell me something," cut in one of the detectives. *"The first time you heard about the plan of Big John, when was that?"*

Katie said she knew nothing about it, until that moment on John's bed when everything changed. Immediately, her words defied her age.

"He started kissing me. He threw me on the bed, and then he dragged me downstairs into the room by the kitchen, and then I was screaming my brains out and I didn't know what to do, and then he got duct tape and then after he put…" Katie spoke in rapid-fire succession only to be stopped, repeatedly, by the detectives.

"How did you know it was duct tape?"

"It's gray tape." She couldn't be stumped.

"Did he put it on you?"

"He said if I didn't be quiet….And then he threw me in the closet and I hit nails! And then he threw me down the thing and then he came down. He dragged me into that room. He made me make that tape."

"What did he say to you while he was draggin' you?"

"I asked him when I was gonna go home!"

"Did he tell you why he was taking you down into that room?"

"He said he wanted to get me away from the custody battle."

"Between your Mom and Aunt Linda?"

"Yeah….then I made the tape," Katie rattled out verbatim the words "a man with a knife kidnapped me…" as if she had rehearsed the words a million times.

As she told the story, Katie was upbeat. Exuberant. Her sing-song voice had the cadence of a worn out fairy tale, not a horror story.

"He asks me, he said, he's gonna take pictures of me actin' like I was dead so then you guys would forget all about me. But then I said NOOO because I knew you guys was gonna find me."

"Sooner or later we did. So then he wanted to take a picture of you to convince us you were dead? But what about the tape—the tape recording? How did that all come about?"

"He wanted Aunt Linda to think that someone kidnapped me." There was a brief exchange about the size of the tape recorder, then an unexpected sound. Humming. Katie was humming.

"Very, very good," said the detective. *"Now did you keep all of this in your memory or did you have something to write on?*

"I kept it in my memory."

"You did, huh?"

Dominick paused the tape and said, "This was our special victim's detective."

"Boy, you are smart, Katie; I have to tell you, you are a very smart little girl. Now when you made that tape, you were already down in the room. He already had brought you down to the room. And when you saw this room, what did you think?"

"I was scared, plus on the sheets he had down there, they were white like this paper and then down at the end there were little spots of blood! Okay, that's what scared me the most!"

"Yeah... I can imagine," Detective Tyrell exhaled, facing the unshaken little girl.

I had heard of the spots of blood, but from police, not from Katie. When I asked her about this, she drew a blank. She now has no memory of being terrified by blood stains on the sheets in the box.

"He made a hole in the wall so I could get air. I could get my hand out that way, but the boards were heavy. I was bashing the chains against the ceiling."

"Chains? Where were chains? What did he do with the chains?"

"Nothing at first. I was screaming for the police again and again and again. 'I'm down here!' And then, I started bashing against the roof and everything to get your attention. But with all that talking up there, no one could hear it."

"Did he get mad at you for that?"

"Uh huh. And that's what made him put the chain around my neck."

"So after you made the tape, what happened?"

"I made the tape and he said he'd be back at around seven. Then he said he went to a pay phone, called up Aunt Linda, put the tape on her answering machine...which I thought was a pretty dumb idea, because they could trace the call! Plus he said he wanted a little daughter or son."

"He did?"

"Uh huh."

"All of a sudden he wants a little daughter or son? And what did you say to that?"

"I said, so why don't you adopt one? And he said 'cuz they won't let me. And I said like why? And he said 'cuz what happened in the past."

Katie was humming again now.

"So did he come back and say, 'Oh I went to a pay phone'? Why did you think he gave you an explanation about the pay phone?"

"So I wouldn't be scared—but unfortunately I was. I know you guys got reports that I was in Hyde Park."

"Someone thought they saw you there last night. Not so, huh?"

"Well, how could that be if I'm right here?"

"Yeah, right! Some people, when they hear something like this—they get all excited—and call the police. And it's all over the country too. How do you feel about all the notoriety?"

"Not very good."

The conversation was long and meandering, and I was wondering what else has been suppressed in Katie's long-term memory. I was expecting gaps in her adult narrative. People who survive repeated, inescapable childhood sex abuse may lock away their memories in complex amnesias.[38] The tapes seemed to support that theory. In Katie's extended conversations with me, there were parts missing, liquidated either by time or trauma.

There are long spans of silence between questions. Katie was drawing hearts, while the detective was drawing conclusions.

"Why would they want to make a movie about me?"

"Maybe they won't."

"I hope not! I just want to be a normal kid! I had no childhood!"

"You're only how old? Ten years old? You still have a chance for a childhood."

"Three more years and then I'm a teenager!"

"Watch out—watch out!"

"Wait until I get my license. Everyone betta stay off the road!"

"Oh oh! You'll be a good driver. I'm sure you will. As I was telling you before, a question came up about you sitting on John's lap driving his truck. Did you ever do that?"

"Once. A long time ago. When I was with my brother."

Katie had told me she felt guilty about John wanting to touch her, so I anticipated and understood her lies.

"So pretty much—the touching stuff only happened while you were down in that room?"

"Uh huh."

"Okay and had he ever before tried to touch your private areas?"

"No. When am I going to go home?"

"Well, we are going to be chatting with you for a while yet."

"G'nite." Katie put her head down on the conference table and closed her aching eyes.

"No no!! Don't go to sleep on me, Katie! Don't do this to me! How many times did you ask him to let you go—do you think?"

"ABOUT A THOUSAND!!" Katie raised her voice.

"And what was his excuse? Or did he have different ones?"

"He said, 'Next Monday, next Monday. On Monday, I'm gonna kill myself. I'll leave a note somewhere where they will find it.'"

The chief stopped the tape. Katie, he surmised, was avoiding talking about the tough parts. I had a different impression. To me, it seemed the right questions just hadn't been asked yet, but then I reminded myself that she was a ten-year-old girl and this was a delicate process.

There is silence on the tape for several minutes. Different detectives entered the debriefing room.

"Where were we, miss?"

"I don't remember."

She was exhausted, but still had enough steam to continue an upbeat dialogue. The cops now were all chiming in, as Katie demonstrated her grit. She needed no prodding. Eager to share every detail, she plodded on through her exhaustion.

"Whenever I heard him coming, I locked myself."

"Do you know what today is?"

Katie counted on her fingers from December 28 all the way to January 13.

"You missed the whole New Year!"

"I got about two hours sleep every night," Katie yawned.

"Why two hours?"

THE TAPES

"'Cuz I was scared! I was down there," she counted aloud, *"twenty-eight, twenty-nine, thirty—sixteen days I was down there without seeing the outside except the news!"*

"Now," said one of the male detectives, *"Debbie just came in and you had mentioned before Big John kissed you."*

Debbie began, *"Where did he kiss you?"*

"On my lips and on my cheeks," Katie answered matter-of-factly.

"Anywhere else—did he kiss anywhere else?"

"No."

Katie drew a diagram of the bunker. She hummed as she scribbled and the cops made small talk. *"When you grow up, you should be a detective!"*

More detectives entered the debriefing room. This time it was the Police Commissioner, Peter Cosgrove. The detectives told the commissioner that Katie was going over stories. She was talking fast, in good spirits.

"Every time he came and visited you, did you ask him when he was gonna let you go?"

"He said he was gonna kill himself and leave a note pinned to himself. He has a note in his safe and he has a tape of the underground, for when he dies. He has a note behind the big screen TV. The last night he said he was gonna hang himself, I said, 'Good, I'm glad!'"

It was as if I were interviewing her twenty years later, but the details were sharper. The voice was juvenile, the accent more Long Island, but the facts were generally the same. I was listening, my ear literally pressed against the recorder speaker, scouring for details she may have left behind long ago. Katie no longer remembered the blood stains, or the threats that John planned to kill himself. And she never told cops about the rapes.

Debbie then pressed her on the sex abuse, asking how long he would kiss her.

"Four, five minutes," Katie estimated.

"He would just kiss you. He didn't do anything else?"

"Nope."

"What did he say?"

"He said that he liked me, that I was pretty."

"That's all he said?"

"He said he was gonna leave me five thousand dollars."

"How'd you like that?"

"I liked that!"

"He was gonna give you five thousand dollars and he gave you five hundred?"

"I'm gonna buy presents for my family—that's all I do with all my money..."

Katie paused and touched her shirt. *"This is all wet. Because I had it behind the pillow and the walls started to get wet. Because I was underground. My shirt is filthy."*

"You want to have a lady-to-lady conversation here?" When I heard this, I assumed the male detectives had left the room.

"I just thought, maybe you'd want to talk to me. I was asking you before, when John would come down, once a day to give you food, how did you go to the bathroom?" Debbie asked.

Katie described the toilet set-up but then said eventually she couldn't wait for John's once a day appearance.

"I decided the heck with it, and I went under the TV."

Ultimately, the conversation veered into the place detectives needed details most.

"We have to be sure," said Debbie, *"did he ever touch you anywhere in your private places?"*

There was no audible answer. Katie must have nodded.

"He did? Where, when? Do you remember what day?"

With the same melodic kick in her voice, she then mapped out a calendar of molestation.

"I know it wasn't yesterday ... um...last Thursday, last Friday, last Sunday—the first night I was there and the first day ... "

"And what would he do?"

"In my privates—in both places."

"What are your names for those places?"

"My vagina and my butt."

"What would he say while he did this?"

"Nothin'."

"No? What would be his reason?"

"I dunno. He asked me if I had to go to the bathroom and the next thing I knew he was rubbing me."

"With what?"

THE TAPES

"With his hand."

"What did he say while rubbing you?"

"Nothin."

"What did you say?"

"I said stop. He said no."

"How long would he rub you for?"

"About two minutes."

"Did he ever make you touch him?"

"No."

"How did you feel?"

"I didn't like it."

"So he did this a lot?"

Katie changed the subject.

"You're pretty smart, you know."

"Hey, I'm a street-wise kid."

"You certainly are!"

"Living in Mastic, you have to be like that."

"You're a pip. A street-wise kid that's cute to boot!"

"Is he going to jail?"

Dominick came in to check on me occasionally—he could hear Katie's animated little voice. Then I hit pause.

"What do you think?" he asked me.

"I think she sounds chipper."

"Exactly," he said. "What does that tell you? We always knew," he said, answering his own question, "from her demeanor, from her spirit, she'd be okay. She'd be okay."

I then asked the chief if I could listen to the captivity tapes as he had, alone. With a long gaze deep into my eyes and a clear understanding of my motives, he agreed.

The black outdated recorder was easy enough to pilot.

"You didn't realize everybody loved you so much—right?" John's voice on the tape startled me.

"I knnnnooooow." Katie's word was almost sung, with a whine, in several long sorrow-filled syllables. *"That's why I want to go baaack."* Then, a deep slow cry of a child in misery.

"You're looking at TV all the time. Are you sleeping a little bit?"

John's voice was not at all what I had expected. There was no Hannibal Lecter, no madman erupting into psychotic rants. He spoke with the sing-song cadence of a kindergarten teacher and as if Katie were his favorite pupil. But his gentle inflection did nothing to soothe his astute captive.

"No!" she answered emphatically. *"I'm up all night!"*

The tape, forty minutes long on one side and twenty minutes on the other, was, in places, impossible to decipher. The voices remained muffled, even after being enhanced with an equalizer. At times, there was clarity when Katie and John must have been positioned next to the recorder.

"It gets a little hot in there, right?"

"Not really. I like it warm; I'm under a blanket twenty-four hours a day." She wasn't crying now. It sounded as if she were plotting.

"You like it?" He took the bait. *"Maybe tomorrow I'll get some warm water ... "* She ignored the comment.

The tape was voice activated, so there were no gaps. Any pauses in conversation were eliminated and days were strung together with almost imperceptible audio stops and starts. It was impossible to ascertain when one day began and another one ended.

"I'm gonna go. I gotta go," he said breathlessly.

"No, don't go," Katie cried.

"I gotta clean this place up, too, one of these days."

"Gooood night," she said, sounding resigned to the loneliness and isolation she knew followed his departure.

"Ohhh noooo... I missed my birthday." It was a heart-wrenching lament followed by loud unrelenting sobs. December 30, 1992, was Katie's tenth birthday.

"I missed my birthday..... Oh, I missed my birthday...I'm ten years oooooollllllddd," she cried over and over again, to herself, in the underground prison.

Later, I could hear banging, a hammer, and then latches opening.

Next, drilling.

More banging.

Then, crying, *"I wanna be home!"* Screaming, weeping. It was not clear if she were alone or if John were present. There was simply loud, unrelenting weeping. It was eardrum-shattering crying, like an inconsolable baby.

THE TAPES

John's demeanor changed after the next spate of drilling. He was out of breath and Katie asked, *"What do you waaant?"*

"Nothin' Katie," breathlessly he added, *"Something's gonna happen soon."*

Alarmed she asked, *"Is anything gonna happen to you?"* Katie obviously realized without John to lead police to her, she was dead.

"Maybe, but I just want you to know you'll be all right."

"No!" she screamed.

"Don't worry about it, Katie; nothin's gonna happen to you. I promise. I gotta go. All right?"

She screamed again.

"Don't worry about it..."

"I promise, Katie, nothin's gonna happen to you. Okay? I promise, I promise. I gotta go."

"All I want is my family back!"

"I would never hurt you... never," he said for emphasis. I wondered here if he said this for the benefit of the tape. He had to know it was rolling on the shelf beside him, but it made me wonder whether he was fully aware of it all the time. He had created an underground prison for a specific little girl. Was he now carefully writing the script with his own self-preservation in mind?

"Okay?"

No response.

"All right? Gimme the bag. Oh I gotta go."

"When is it gonna happen?" she asked, still alarmed.

"Soon, any day, maybe any minute. All right?"

"Is your brother gonna know?"

"The police will know."

"You're gonna tell them?" she asked with disbelief.

"Yeah."

"Okay, thank you so much."

"Okay, I love you, I want you to know, that's the only reason I did it. Don't be mad at me, okay?"

"I'm not. The police are gonna know?" she asked, unconvinced.

"Yes definitely, okay?"

"Thanks for the ...." What she was thanking him for was inaudible.

"You're welcome, bye bye." Her voice, becoming more muffled, trailed off as the sound of hammering ensued. I was listening to a child being locked into a coffin-like box.

John yelled over the hammering sounds, *"Don't worry about it. I'll talk to you later, okay?"*

The shrill spinning of the drill could be heard as Katie was left alone in the box.

What came next was devastating to hear. It was so troubling, the secretary outside the conference room where I was alone with the tapes knocked on the door and inquired what on earth I was listening to? She thought I had been given access to debriefing tapes only. She, like everyone else, had no idea that actual tapes of Katie's captivity existed.

It was unclear if John was drilling to get into the box, or if he were locking up after a visit. In either case, the piercing sound of drilling was interspersed with God-awful screaming.

"Oh God," she choked on tears, *"Help, help, help, help, help,"* she wheezed amid coughs. *"Help, help, help, help help me, help, help…"* It escalated to top of her lungs, caterwauling that intensified with each breath and each shriek of the drill.

"Let me out, let me out, let me out…."

They were dreadful howls followed by a diametrically opposite friendly exchange.

"Katie, are you okay?"

Banging.

"You have to go to the bathroom?"

The TV droned on in the background.

He was calm, his voice childlike. He narrated for her step by step what he was doing. *"I have to close it now."*

"Alll riiiiight," she moaned.

The grinding of a power ratchet could be heard tightening the bolts, which locked Katie into the upper coffin. A second later on the tape was quite possibly the next day.

"Hey, John, guess what?"

"What?"

"You're just in the nick of time," she said defiantly, *"because I was about to run out of soda! And I couldn't live without soda or something*

else to drink, because or else I would die!"

"I'm not going to let you die."

"I'm just saying if you don't come or if you don't feed me, I could die," Katie said, hanging on the last word.

"Okay. Feel better? If you get cold, do jumping jacks or something." I rewound to confirm he actually said that. Indeed he had.

There was then some explanation as to why he put a makeshift toilet *outside* the box he locked her in twenty-three hours a day.

"I tried to get the bathroom in there but I couldn't," John said.

"You're on the news," Katie announced abruptly.

"I wish I hadn't done that," John answered.

"Why do you have to lie on live TV?"

"What am I gonna tell 'em?"

Fragments of the conversation were discernible now, with John explaining why he was antsy about what was "gonna happen soon." His fingerprints, he told Katie, must be on one of the coins in the phone booth where he made the call to Linda and played the "man with a knife" recording.

"What's gonna happen that's so bad?"

"They found the phone booth that I made the call from—remember the tape recorder? They think it was a tape recorder. You don't want to stay with me?"

"No! I want to go home!"

"All right. If they find you, you wouldn't say... if I let you go, you wouldn't say that we planned it? To stay with each other?"

"No!"

"So it would get me off the hook?" Dejected, he added, *"I know, you wouldn't say that,"* adding hopefully, *"if you said that—it would get me off the hook. And you see how everybody sees things, you really haven't been taken good care of and Mommy doesn't love you and..."*

He paused, but Katie's answer, if there was one, was lost in the hiss of the two-decade old recording. John, though, was loud and clear.

"I know that's not true, but we can lie a little."

Nothing was heard in the way of a response.

"All right," said John, *"I'm just sayin',"* he paused, *"you know what I'm sayin'."*

The tapes moved without pause from hushed conversation to panicked plotting.

"I think I may be in trouble." He lowered his voice, as if others could hear. *"That's why I say somethin's gonna happen—I hope not. I'd rather be with you."*

"I was hoping you'd come down at some point today," Katie answered.

"Remember when they do find ya, Katie, that I love ya. All right?"

Katie burst into tears and her cries nearly drowned out John's attempts at encouragement.

"Remember what I said to you, when you get outa here. You're gonna have a good life because you're gonna be rich. You're gonna tell your story, Katie. Okay? Remember you're going on 'America's Most Wanted.' You're gonna be on that next Friday, if they find you before that." She wept as he obsessed.

"Somethin's gonna happen and if they find that quarter with my fingerprints on one of those quarters. What am I gonna say? I wasn't there? You're gonna go nationwide. You're a very populah kid now, you know that? And when you get out of here…"

"When I get out of here I'm gonna be on TV a lot." Katie seemed to like the idea.

"Everybody's gonna want to see you. You're gonna be a very populah kid. Everybody's gonna say, 'That's Katie Beers. That's Katie Beers.' People are gonna be looking at you from all over the world, not just from New York. I know. Nationwide, maybe worldwide. It's syndicated. You're gonna be very very polpulah. Just remember that I love ya."

"Do me a favor then, when you do get out?"

"What?" Katie whined.

"Tell them that I didn't molest ya."

"Uh huh."

"Good girl."

"Whatchamacallit…Something happened twelve years ago?"

"That's true, but it was … a twelve-year-old kid … I was trying to adopt a kid and …I never really molested anyone except you." The words were clipped at the end, due to the auto-stop feature, distorting perhaps the most crucial line on the entire cassette.

"I may be back at the same time tomorrow, so you're gonna be okay."

"But John ..."

"Wanna wash your face? Want new underwear? I left them in there. They're not wet, they're brand new. Put them on. I know you don't like them, but put them on."

He talked to her as an accomplice, wondering aloud if fingerprints would even stay intact on the coin as it dropped into the pay phone coin box.

"We don't even know," he said. *"It may not even be my quarter in there, I don't know."* John speculated that the phone company may have already cleared out the coin box, and then lamented, "I didn't think they would find the phone."

She listened to his worries, plots to make police believe she was a willing participant, but never was she heard going along with his plans or quelling his fears.

"They're not gonna find me."

"Yes, they will. I think they're gonna have those blood dogs coming."

"They did that already."

"Really?"

"They went through all the garbage; they did all that, three times."

Then, the fragments began to suggest something even more sinister. *"Maybe you want to wear that instead—you can be cool."* I remembered Katie told me that it was when she changed underwear or went to the bathroom, that John would molest her.

"Gotta go?" he asked.

"I can wipe it myself," Katie answered. *"Oh, yeah, by the way, Big John guess what, they have bloodhounds, they're gonna find me."*

"You lose your scent within the hour. They took everything, they took your coat and hat and pocketbook." But then he drifted back to his own fate. *"If they find out I went to the phone booth, I'm gonna say 'Yeah I did.' I played that message because me and Katie were gonna get away from the whole family."*

"NO!" she yelled.

"And I'm gonna say," he paused and reversed himself. *"I won't say that. I'm gonna say where you are. This is my life. You know what I mean. I am gonna kill myself."*

The conversation became hushed here and only scraps of words survived the years.

"If they find me...they'll put you away," Katie said.

"I know," John said.

What came next was barely audible, but it seemed apparent what was going on while the tape recorded Katie's soft whimpers.

"I'll try not to hurt you too much, all right?" John said.

"Oooo," Katie cried.

"I know. The smell."

"Ooohhh."

"You're gonna be okay."

When he was done with whatever unseen act on the child had taken place, he said, *"I'm gonna close it, okay?"*

And as John tightened the bolts to the vault that held her, he shouted over the churning of the ratchet, *"I'll see you in a little while okay? Love you."* Then he added, blithely, *"Sorry!"*

Banging. Hammering.

"You okay? See you tomorrow, baby. What?" Even he had a hard time hearing Katie's words from within the cramped box.

"See you tomorrow," he yelled again. *"What??See you tomorrow!"*

Loud drilling.

Screaming.

Crying. The tape slipped on, into another day.

John was at once trying to play the role of boyfriend, lover, and savior to Katie. He sounded like a nervous wreck, consumed with what he was slowly accepting would be his inevitable arrest. But most of the next twenty minutes of the recording was filled with loud, unyielding, heart-wrenching sobbing.

"Nooooooooo."

"Heeeeeeeeeeeelp."

"Katie, you up. Katie, you up?"

Banging.

"Katie, you up? Get up quick!"

The box door was unbolted and John was breathless again.

"I'm gonna go somewhere. I'm not gonna tell you because you're gonna tell them. It's gotta be where nobody knows. And when I'm gone, I'm gonna call up and say where you are, and that will be it. They'll think

you're dead and then you'll pop up and be very populah."

John paused, and then added, *"I love you."*

As the counter indicated that I was nearing the end of the one hour, I could make out, *"Are you okay?"*

"Noooooo!" Katie responded.

The TV background noise was ever-present.

"I'm sick!" cried Katie.

"Why are you sick?"

I couldn't make out his answer but Katie repeated, this time more convincingly, *"I'm sick!"*

"Want some soup? You want a thin blanket? How you feel—huh? You okay?"

"Oh, John, I wanna go home!"

"I know, you will go home."

There was a conversation about being sick but it was mostly drowned out by the television. I could ferret out a few words spoken by John.

"I'm gonna have to think of a way I can leave and you can go home."

"You can always put me on a plane!"

"If I'm gone, I can't be alone with you. As soon as the detectives get out of here I can see you more and more. Then you can spend more time with me" He wasn't giving up.

"I'm sick!" she said again with urgency.

"I gotta go, all right?"

As he departed, over the sounds of newscasts and hammering, he said, *"Now you be good. I'll see you tomorrow, okay? What? What? I'll see you tomorrow, what? When? I dunno, probably tomorrow night. Soon as we get outa here, I can see you more and more, all right?"*

The bolts were tightened. Now Katie was alone again, crying and screaming. At first, it was hard to understand the word she yelled at the top of her lungs. Then, it was horribly clear.

"Lindaaaaaaa!"

"Ahahahah....Linda...Linda Linda Linda Linda Linda Linda Linda Linda Linda Linda Linda...ahahahahahahahah...."

The endless string of Lindas was an assault on the ears and the soul. My fingers moved quickly to type every word the recorder spit out, but my brain could barely comprehend the anguish behind the blood-curdling screams. There was not even a breath between them. The enunciation of the name "Linda" alternated, some with high-pitched intensity, others uttered with exhausted whimpers.

Then, the words became unintelligible for a long while and, for what seemed like forever, there was nothing but guttural screams. Words reemerged several minutes into the soul-deep sobs. *"Big John, Big Joooohhhnnnn, Biiiiiiig Joooohhhhhn,"* over and over and over.

This went on for at least ten minutes.

"Big John, Big John, Big John..." on the voice activated tape that may have taken hours, perhaps days to record.

It was very hard to bear. Each "John" scream was stretched into four or five syllables and lasted just as many seconds. In between the Johns, there were sorrowful, hopeless gasps.

"Big Jooooohhhhnnnnn. Jooooooohhhnhhhhhnnnnnnnn."

With time, they became more forceful, not less. As her strength should have been waning, her voice neither weakened nor waivered.

And then the drilling began anew.

And the creak of doors opening.

"Katie, you up? Katie?"

"Katie, you up? Katie, Katie, you up? You okay? Sleeping?"

Katie was crying.

"You still sick? You okay? It's good for you to eat. You have to go to the bathroom... or anything?"

The chief appeared at the door while I was listening to the captivity tape, to ask me how I was holding up. "I don't even know if Esposito is aware this tape is on. It records only what's loud enough to be captured.

"It's a window into the interaction between the abductor and the victim, a window you never get first hand. I think his actions are obvious; he is cultivating a love affair. An inappropriate love affair with a ten-year-old."

Katie, though, was doing her own manipulating.

"She's convincing him she's sick. We think this is what finally drives him over the edge, 'Oh, my God, she's gonna die...I better get her out of here.' As for Katie, it was her Cinderella upbringing. It made her a tough person, wise and street-smart way beyond her years. Our nine- or ten-year-old? They never would have made it."

THE TAPES

Drained, I stopped the tape at the end, and opened the large dark blue police case file next to the tape recorder. In it was a Suffolk County Police report dated January 14, 1993.

Katherine in her statement describes the room in which she was secreted. She also stated that during this time, John touched her vagina. Sometimes he touched her over her clothes, sometimes under. This happened when John came down to give her food. Katherine stated that she was chained and handcuffed in this room. This began after the police arrived to search the house. Katherine states she began banging on the ceiling hoping the police would find her. There was a monitor for a closed circuit camera in the secret room so Katherine could see what was going on outside. Katherine went on to say that on 1/10/93 at night John brought her a newspaper. He also promised her 5,000 dollars so she could spend it when he let her go. On Monday he gave her 500 dollars and told her he would give her 500 dollars every other day. On Tuesday 1/12 Katherine told John she was sick and she needed a doctor. He said he couldn't get her a doctor right now. He later told her he was going to hang himself and pin a note to himself telling the police where to find her. Subsequently, Katherine was freed on 1/13/93.

Upon rescue, the report concluded, Katie exploded with glee exclaiming, *"I'm going home? I'm going home!"*

THE WHOLE TRUTH

I KNOW THERE WILL never be *full* recovery for me. But somehow the act of telling the story, revealing the pain that I endured as a child, helps me live with it today. Because I think that letting people know what really happened to me makes good come from bad. Maybe people in similar situations will gain the courage to come forward. This is why, in October of 2007, I finally told the whole truth to New York State Division of Parole.

John Esposito was eligible for parole every two years. When he had served the minimum fifteen years, I traveled with my parents to a hearing in New York City. We were in a conference room with one female commissioner and a stenographer. We all sat at one end of a long table, and now, as a young adult, I was able to deliver a victim's impact statement[39] and say what I had never before uttered publicly.

> *Looking back on it, I wish that it had gone to trial, because I really think with what he did he deserved a harsher sentence rather than just fifteen years. Over the course of the sixteen days, I was abducted; I never thought I was going to get out. He had a video camera and a TV installed so he could see if anybody was coming into his house while he held me captive. I watched the news every single day and that was just pure torture. To see them speculating where they were searching, wondering if I was alive. He would come down at least once a day and either molest or rape me. At least once a day, for the time that I was down there. Then he would just talk to me like nothing had happened. And I would ask him what I was going to do about school. What was I going to do when I was older? Was I going to work? He would always reassure me, telling me that I would be happy when I was eighteen, when I was older and nobody was looking for me anymore. And he would keep me chained in there for twenty-three hours a day.... I*

don't know why he chained my neck to the wall.[40]

My parents had their turn, arguing that it would never be safe to allow John to go free.

"Katie is a survivor," my mother told the commissioner, "and she has a strong spirit and she has overcome her past. She has turned into a lovely young woman. But you have to understand at ten years old, the difficulty she had to overcome, the terror that she had in her life. It will never leave her, and she'll have it the rest of her life."

John was not at the hearing, but when he had his turn at Sing Sing Correctional Facility, he told the board his plan was only to take me for four days, then whisk me away to live happily ever after with him in Mexico or Australia, to rescue me from my miserable life, but everything went wrong.[41] And he told the commissioners that he only chained me around the waist, because I was banging on the electrical box and he was concerned for my safety and that I would start an electrical fire.

The commissioners asked him, "... you didn't have sexual intercourse with her?"

"No. I'm asexual. I can't—I don't have sex."

"Did you kiss her?"

"I didn't do it for sex."

"Where? On the lips?"

"On the face, sometimes the lips."

He told the board he let me go, in the end, because I spilled a soda can on the mattress and he didn't want me to get wet. He made it sound like a hapless camping trip.

And then John pleaded for his freedom.

I'm very sorry for what I've done. Believe me; I know how horrible it was for Katie after also being locked up. I have been locked in a facility almost fifteen years not knowing if I will ever go home, thinking I will never be with my family again. I know how Katie must have felt. It must have been much worse. She was just a little girl. Most of the time she was alone…I know how selfish I was…Believe me, if I could go back and know what I know now, it would never happen, never would enter my mind. I don't know if I deserve to go home. If you give me one chance I know I will not let you down. You can make the rules of my parole very strict, take away my license for life, give me a lifetime curfew, put one of those things on the leg that tells you where I am at all times, give me programs that last for life. If you feel it is necessary, you can castrate me. Whatever you want, I will do at my own cost. For some reason, if I fail you can lock me up and throw away the key. This is how sure I am I will be a good and caring person if released.

Parole was denied. In a report mailed to me, the board wrote that releasing him would be "incompatible with the welfare of society and deprecate the serious nature of the crime against" me.

Two years later, when John was sixty years old, I read in the transcript of his next parole hearing that he continued to deny any sexual contact with me. In 2011, he stated to the parole board that his plan was to raise me as his own daughter.[42]

"You are saying there was no sexual contact?"

"There was no sexual contact."

"So why would she say that? If you are her rescuer, taking her out of her terrible circumstances and trying to raise her as a kind father, why would that person turn around and say that you touched her?"

"I believe that she said that I kissed her, and I did. But it was not sexual."

Forgiveness is a luxury reserved for those who admit their mistakes. I knew that John was sick, and maybe, in his own way, he was looking out for my best interests, but now, I don't feel that he deserves my forgiveness and I don't believe that pedophiles can be cured or rehabilitated.

Again, John asked for freedom.

I'd just like to say I am not the same person I was when I first came to prison. I am a much more social person, a much more humble person, a much more caring person, a much more religious person. I'm less self-centered. I know what I do will affect others, so I think more, much more, before I act. As for my prison record, since coming here, the first year I got my G.ED. I've been a teacher's aide...I have learned much more about carpentry. I got six titles in drafting. I learned to play a musical instrument, which I can cite music fluently now. I play my instrument in church. I have learned that music can take away the loneliness and make me happy. Also, I have been very good in prison...Each quarterly report I get is excellent. Also whatever programs that my counselor told me to take, I did. I have not refused any programs. I have completed everything they wanted me to take. My time in prison has been consistent right from the start. If I do make a mistake, I try to never do it again. I never disrespect any office [sic], inmates or civilians. I am very sorry. What I did was very selfish, and I believe I have been punished enough. I am prepared to be free and I know I can be a plus to society.

The commissioner congratulated John on a well-prepared statement and a few days later, denied his parole, ruling that his release "remains incompatible with public safety."

As I looked through the transcript, I did find something John said to the parole board that may have actually been true.

"The last thing Katie said to me, and it's a fact, my lawyer was there, is: 'John, don't worry. Everything is going to be okay.'"

On that point and that point alone, John was right. I am, somehow, okay.

On the car ride home from delivering my impact statement to the Parole Board, I finally mustered the courage to inform my parents that I wanted to share my story publicly—in a book. My mother, of course, played devil's advocate and wanted to know my justification for it. I told her I want to tell my story, to finally set the record straight. Why should John's lies stand unchallenged?

I also wanted to warn parents and other adults that children aren't going to tell them things when their lives are being threatened. They need to open their eyes and speak up when they suspect a child is in danger. In my case, predators were circling in and around me, and no one helped.

I wanted the thirty-year-old rape victim to know they have to talk to someone. I wanted to let children of abuse know that it isn't their fault and they didn't ask for it.

I grew up way before my time. The abuse that I endured as a child stripped me of my childhood. Because of this, I will not live the type of life that other adults have the chance to live. I try to have a positive outlook on things, I believe that everything happens for a reason, that God doesn't give you more than you can handle, and most importantly, what doesn't kill you only makes you stronger. Yet, it still astounds me that every single adult in my young life stole a piece of my childhood from me in one way or another.

It was around this time that I learned that audio tapes existed of my days in captivity. I was uninterested and adamant that I don't want them ever to be played or heard publicly. I don't want to hear the fear that I experienced. I don't want to ever hear John's voice again. I blocked out much of what happened in the dungeon to help in my recovery. I still remember a lot of it, but for endless hours, I was by myself. I am sure that I talked to myself, cried to myself, and tried to comfort myself. I have no desire to relive that trauma.

But I was equally adamant that I wanted others to know, others to bear witness, so that the whole truth is indisputable.

It was Mary Bromley who called in February of 2009 and left me a short but stunning voicemail. I saved the message. Someone from the DA's office had called her and let her know.

Sal was dead. I immediately called my parents. My mom's reaction was a sarcastic "Boo hoo." That was a death that none of us were going to mourn. Then, I called Marilyn. I wanted to let her know, but I also wanted to make sure she didn't talk to the news reporters if they came calling, as I was sure they would. I didn't want a return trip to the headlines. She was at work, so it wasn't an easy conversation. She received and digested the news during the three minute call while she manned the dispatch desk at Sunset Taxi, yelling orders into a two-way radio.

I asked, "Guess who passed away this morning in jail?"

There was a pause. She had no idea.

"One of the guys I put behind bars."

"SAL?"

I think in the back of her mind, she'd been worried about Sal getting out and threatening one of us. She said simply, "That's great."

I wanted to get her off the phone as quickly as possible. She never really talked to me like a mother—not that I treat her as a mother. I think she said, "Now the bastard can rot in hell." It was something along those lines. She was relieved.

My entire foster family was relieved as well. I felt no sadness. I always hoped someone would kill him in jail. I was actually quite surprised no one did.

I was happy because I knew now that he could never do what he did to me to anyone else. I learned that, prior to his death, he was living in North Carolina with a girlfriend who had a small child. My heart sank. I was disgusted that a woman would let a convicted pedophile into her home and into her life with a child in the house, after what he did to me. He never admitted it, though. Always said I was a liar.

I think if he had shown remorse for what he did to me and how he treated me, I would have felt differently. John publically apologized for what he did, at least for the kidnapping. Now I'm the one keeping John a prisoner.

Sal was the type of man who thought he could do no wrong. He thought he could get away with anything. I used to believe he was just an evil man who liked to do evil things. Now I know that abuse can be a learned behavior. Sexual, verbal, physical, and emotional abuse are acts that deeply scar a child, who may later act out what they learned. When Sal was younger, abuse wasn't recognized or treated. He got firsthand schooling in the subject and repeated the cycle of abuse. I don't think one day you just start abusing a two-year-old.

With Sal, he told me that his dad abused him both verbally and physically. So he just went to another extreme.

With me, the cycle ends. I have learned much about abuse. I went through years of therapy and I know that I will never repeat what happened to me with my children. It is the one thing that I am actually grateful about having been kidnapped. My case was broadcast around the country to a nation that had not yet fully and openly discussed the many aspects of child sexual abuse: children forced into sex by grown men in their own homes, little girls the object of desire of men who pretended to be average Joes. When I was kidnapped, these were no longer unspeakable taboo subjects. I hope what happened to me helped to open people's eyes.

People still ask me what I was feeling when all of this was going on. I wondered what I was doing to deserve what was happening to me. I felt dirty and guilty. Dirty because of the almost daily sex acts and guilty because I must have done something wrong to be so badly punished.

Perhaps there is something to be said for inner strength, a strong will to survive. Maybe I was born a fighter. Or maybe the fact that the abuse started so early made me tough. It's all I ever knew.

Remembering is healing. I'm sure of that now. No matter how hard it is to talk and write about the embarrassing details, they must be brought to light. And then, once they are revealed, they can be shed, like an old skin. And buried. That's why I never want to hear the tapes. I have remembered enough.

THE TEAM

MARY BROMLEY'S FIRST CORRESPONDENCE had me confused. "I have heard the tapes. They were gruesome."

If Katie's therapist had heard the captivity tapes, then Katie must have known of their existence as well, long ago. But Katie told me she was unaware audio tapes existed, until I told her about them. Did she banish that memory as well?

"The tapes," Mary told me, when we finally met, "were shocking."

"She is screaming at the top of her lungs for *Linda*. Sobbing uncontrollably. And she never once cried for her mother. I cannot emphasize enough the impact that these tapes had on me. To hear Katie's cries for help, her fear and loneliness, her fear that John was going to kill himself, the crying for Linda. Over and over and over, she was wailing for Linda."

This, Mary explained, is often what victims of chronic abuse do. They cling to the only provider they know, even if that caregiver is cruel, abusive, or neglectful.

Mary is a psychotherapist with an impressive *Curriculum Vitae*. She trained under the famous Dr. Nicholas Groth, who conducted landmark research on pedophilia, and she later saw the brutality of sexual assault up close. She was a supervisor in the Rape Crisis Program at Saint Vincent's Hospital in Manhattan, counseling rape victims as soon as they were brought to the Emergency Room.

In the mid-eighties, she, her husband and their three-year-old son moved from their Upper West Side apartment to East Hampton. By fast-paced city standards, that was almost akin to dropping out. She opened a professional office on Pantigo Road, smack in the middle of "Bonacker" territory.

Bonackers are Springs, Long Island natives, a breed of their own. Descendants of East Hampton's original seventeenth century English settlers, they arrived, legend has it, at Accabonac Harbor. For the better part of three centuries, hearty Bonackers worked the fishing and clamming boats and potato fields. They kept to themselves on Long Island's south fork and maintained a unique dialect and their own phraseology that leaned more towards New England than New York.

When Mary Bromley arrived, she was most definitely "from away," Bonac-speak for anyone not a Bonacker.

A year into her transplantation, Mary's toddler son came home from day care with a note. "Beware of strangers," it urged, below a picture of a sinister-looking man in a raincoat.

"I had to laugh!" Mary said. "I called the police chief and I said, 'It's nice you are concerned about these things, but actually it's almost never a stranger that abuses a child! It's someone they know, love and trust.'"

The East Hampton Police Department hired Mary Bromley the next day to work with sex abuse victims and detectives.

"There was a huge amount of abuse I was dealing with here at that time," Mary told me, "but we are talking the kind of abuse that people didn't even think of as abuse: kids being lowered into wells, bats in their faces; kids staying home for months shucking oysters and not going to school; kids walking on the 'oyes' to see if it was frozen solid enough for the ice-fishermen who were following them; lots and lots of sexual abuse; lots of domestic violence. So when they hired me, it was for things that were always kept secret, things that were known, but not spoken of."

After working for the East Hampton Police Department for a year, Mary pushed for the creation of a domestic violence shelter. The problem wasn't any more prevalent there than elsewhere, she assured the local Rotary Club, but something had to be done to protect local battered women. Rotary members agreed. They were progressive and forward-thinking, and Mary's practice thrived.

When Katie Beers stepped out of the headlines and into the home of a Springs family, Mary wasn't only the logical choice for Katie's therapist, she was a godsend.

Mary's role was twofold. She was to work with prosecutors to prepare Katie for the criminal trials of both John Esposito and Sal Inghilleri, and she was to introduce Katie to the notion of love and safety. In many ways, they were contradictory goals.

"She needed to be comfortable with me; I had to create a safe harbor for her. But she also had to understand that some of what she told me, I would have to reveal to other people. I needed to create a trusting relationship, which given the history with her mother and the other women in her life was very difficult. She had no trusting relationships with women in her life. None."

Mary's office was just as Katie had described. Large and airy, with big picture windows. Plants and bookshelves lined the room, along with large bamboo roller shades. A bronze bust of Buddha gave the room an ethereal feeling, as did the stained glass panels that hung from strings in front of the vertical windows. The walls were painted light blue; the couches were green leather, and just as Katie had said, Mary sat in a "comfy" chair.

Mary exuded warmth and greeted me wearing rectangular reading glasses, an artistic chunky necklace, and a navy blue print sweater dress. Her hair was auburn and her smile kind and inviting.

"I have notes, drawings, and many, many memories," Mary had written to me in advance of our appointment, "both hers and mine that I hold in my heart, waiting for this opportunity to share with you."

Mary's memory was clear where Katie's had faltered. She held a thick pile of notes, hand-penned in perfect, single-spaced script, recorded, she told me, after each of Katie's bi-weekly sessions over more than a decade. She remembered the smallest details and had deep perspective that Katie, at times, lacked.

"She has a lack of affect, a flatness, have you noticed that?" Mary asked. I had, but hadn't thought much about it. "There is a reason for that," Mary added.

Mary's office was my last stop on a journey that began with an assignment in court some four years earlier. Sal was back in the news, having been returned to New York from North Carolina on a parole violation. I wanted Katie's reaction, but first I had to find her. I dug up her foster parents' address and wrote a letter, requesting that my message by relayed to Katie.

Tedd responded, expressing Katie's desire to write a book. Upon meeting Katie, she readily admitted her memories might contain gaps. Mary Bromley, she said, would be able to fill in the blanks.

Mary, from her comfy leather chair, did indeed have a unique perspective on the story, not only on the days and years after Katie's rescue, but on its ending. The journalist in me wanted a logical ending and concise answers to broad questions. Does profound trauma destroy people or can they survive it? How do they recover? Does recovery from trauma come by remembering or by denying the horrors of the past? I had waited a long time to find out if this indelible story could possibly have a happy ending.

"It is a symptom of Katie's trauma—her lack of affect. She was flat," Mary emphasized. "And when Harvey Weinstein came in, that began to change."

Mary invited Harvey to half a dozen sessions after reading about his kidnapping and learning that he had a house in East Hampton. He had a deep, soothing voice which Mary heard in news reports and she had a hunch the meeting would be mutually beneficial.

"It was so beautiful. He sits there; she sits here," Mary said, gesturing to the green couches, "and he's this big guy with a deep voice, and they got right to it. They were talking about Katie seeing the cops searching for her but being unable to get their attention. And he said, 'How did you feel about that?'"

Mary mimicked his deep voice and then Katie's child voice.

"And she said, 'Well, I just kept waiting and waiting,' and he raised his voice! He yelled, 'Katie, how did you FEEL that the cops couldn't find you?' And she just started sobbing and he yelled, 'GET MAD! GET MAD, KATIE!' He made her get mad; it was the first time she ever had."

Harvey and Katie also compared "notes" on how they survived their ordeal.

"'I was seventeen days; you only had thirteen days!'"

"'Well,' Harvey bellowed, 'I didn't have a TV!'"

"There was so much laughing and crying, laughing and crying," Mary said. "He was a real *mensch*."

"What was incredible," she recalled, "was that they both used the same technique. Harvey was seventy-five and Katie was nine, and both used the same process of 'reviewing their life' moment-by-moment to pass the time in their respective dungeons.

"Harvey had seventy-five years of memories as a tough Jewish guy, Marine, fighter, businessman. Katie had nine years of being a tough, sweet-hearted kid, alone on the streets. They both survived using this technique. They laughed and cried when they realized this fact."

With Harvey's help, Katie got mad and with Katie's help, Harvey got spiritual.

"Did you forgive your kidnappers?" Katie asked him one day.

"No," Harvey answered.

"You have to forgive them!" Katie responded.

It was a simplistic thought, but it spoke volumes. Mary felt it spoke to Katie's innate moral compass and a spiritual nature that wasn't taught, but just came with her.

"When Katie went into that dungeon, she was already unique," Mary said. "She had a strong constitution. You can have a kid that suffers a lot less abuse than she did who would have more trauma. She was born with a strong and practical constitution. But on the other hand, she was sexually abused from the age of two and onward. So her whole landscape was of trauma, sexual abuse, and neglect. She learned to adapt to trauma and abandonment by her mother. She became accustomed to that world view."

The inescapable abuse and neglect had somehow immunized Katie from pain.

"It hardened her, but also after the abduction, she was embraced by a huge team of people which most children don't get. Most children are abused and return to more and more trauma and difficulty, but Katie was rescued and given a team—a therapist, the DA himself, the best case workers, the police, an incredible foster family, and the love and support of all her teachers."

This was quite evident to me. Members of her "team" devoted themselves to a mission. They functioned as Katie's absent childhood parents, attempting to make up for the sins of her past. Even members of the news media had participated in this group rescue, by keeping its distance.

What was Katie like when you first met her?

"Do you remember *Paper Moon*?"

Of course I did. Addie Loggins, the child con-artist from the seventies film. An indelible adorable character.

"That was Katie. Right? Wise, practical, very savvy. *Paper Moon*. And she looked like her, too. I told her I was a new member of her team. It was important for her to know she was not alone anymore."

"The whole world is on my team," a chipper upbeat Katie had announced at her first therapy session.

Katie liked having the whole world on her side. But even the best-intentioned on Katie's team had personal agendas.

"You have to remember, there was extreme interest in this case," Mary explained. "It triggered everyone's worst nightmare, that their own children could be kidnapped, that their children could be sexually abused. It was a mother's worst nightmare. And it also engendered incredible curiosity and interest in her and how she was doing, every step of the way.

"Everybody had an agenda. It was incredible. I kept saying, 'We are not pressuring this kid!'"

During her first meeting with prosecutors, Mary said she was invited into a large "war room." It was filled with crime scene photos tacked to the walls, two dozen detectives, assistant DAs, and the District Attorney himself.

"I walk in and they are all sitting there in a huge room and DA Catterson is sitting there and says, 'What's your name?'

"And I say, 'Mary Bromley.'

"He goes, 'Merry Brommley…Irish?' with a brogue.

"I say, 'Half Irish.'

"And he says, 'Come here, Merry, have a cookie.'

"And I go, 'That's okay, thanks.'

"So he repeats, 'Have a cookie.'

"And I say, 'Really it's cool, no thanks!'

"Well, finally, I realize I have to go over there and have a cookie, because he is establishing control. Power and control, you *are* having a cookie because you work for *me*. You can't believe what it was like. I had to establish guidelines so that Katie wasn't going to be a puppet for his re-election—a poster child.

"Later on, he wanted me to bring her to a staff picnic and I said, 'No!' He called me up at eleven at night, and he said, 'You're not bringing her to the picnic?' And I was laughing. I said 'No, of course she's not going to picnic with all the ADAs.' I thought he was kidding!

"And he said, 'You will regret this.' I never got another case from him."

Katie escaped the stress of those days, Mary said, through sleep. On the way to court or to the DA's office, she would fall asleep almost instantly. Therapy was its own trauma. It was focused, in the beginning, on the effort to recall detailed specifics about having been sexually abused by Sal and John.

There were times it was just too much for her. Katie would crawl up in a fetal position on the floor of Mary's office while Bill Ferris, the assistant DA, would pepper her with questions, and Mary would say, "Enough."

Bill, Mary explained, was a gentle, caring and patient man, an important force in Katie's life, but there were moments she just couldn't endure it anymore.

In the second session, Katie told Mary that she was able to survive being in the dungeon because of Linda Inghilleri.

"...how badly she was treated. Katie implied that nothing could be worse than how she was treated by the Inghilleris. She said she had a slime ball list, that's the way she talked," Mary chuckled, "and Linda was at the top of that list!"

And as they talked, they played games. Katie played checkers the way she survived in the dungeon. She was able to think ahead to her next move.

Katie also wanted to be able to cheat. "She was greedy, starved for winning," Mary wrote in her notes. "She doesn't expect guidance and she doesn't expect to be given a chance. She is amazed that I would be happy for her if she won."

It took Katie three months to call Mary by name, but when she finally did, Mary felt it was a breakthrough. "She has absolutely no memory of any adult trying to protect her in any way."

Now, with the beginnings of a trusting relationship, Mary was able to get past the games and ask Katie about Sal.

"I told her it was okay to be angry at me for helping her to recall incidents of abuse. I made sure she knew she would never lose me if she expressed anger or frustration toward me."

Katie was very anxious that Sal, at his trial, would accuse her of *wanting* "to touch his penis."

Mary believed that he must have said that a lot while he was abusing her. "You want this."

Said enough times, Katie believed it. As a result, she had deep feelings of shame. Mary stressed how beautiful her body and soul were. Katie began to understand the dynamics of shame and guilt, where the offender blames the child.

"She was a very brave little girl," Mary said, for facing her abuser in court and staring him down as she clung to Mary's hand.

For many years, Katie denied to Mary that Sal had raped her.

"Sal terrified her and sexually abused her. I went with what she gave me. What I didn't want to do was suggest anything to her. Because we were going to trial, I had to be very careful not to coach her, not to prep her and to allow whatever was going to come out to come out. I didn't want to give her the possibility of falsely *creating* a memory. I asked her directly. She denied that there was any rape.

"As we went along, a few years later, she remembered that Sal raped her. There was a crystal clear memory of him raping her near a pipe in a basement. But it came out years later.

"Denial," said Mary, "worked very well for Katie for a long time."

Key people in Katie's life made guest appearances on the green leather couch. This was Mary's way of showing Katie that there was a large team behind her.

Dominick Varrone was invited in. "Katie loved seeing him," Mary recalled.

"During the session with Dominick, it came out that Katie felt extreme guilt for the things she had to do to get out of the dungeon, such as being 'nice' to John and 'playing along with him.' She also believed that she should have been able to get out all by herself."

Varrone suggested that Katie might benefit from visiting the dungeon when she was older, to get a better sense of how she could never have escaped on her own."

After a series of heavy sessions, Katie would ask to go out to eat, walk around and people watch at the park. Mary and Katie took mental health breaks. And they lightened the mood through art.

Mary kept the drawings and paintings and pulled them out of a wide bureau drawer. The paint was cracked and the paper hardened into a roll, but when flattened, the images were still vivid.

Two faces of women are painted alongside each other. One is bright yellow and sunny, the other is dark and enraged.

"I asked her to draw a picture. I didn't tell her to do this. This is her view of women. She never drew bodies."

Why would there be no bodies?

"I think she was drawing herself. That part of her doesn't exist. It's been violated so many times, it's cut off.

"Here is the dungeon. She calls it 'my dungeon.' You see how precise she is?"

The painting showed the tunnel and the box where Katie was locked. She painted chains and handcuffs.

"She was very focused on getting it right."

Mary felt Katie's ability to paint the dungeon represented closure.

"It was very moving and emotional for her. She cried and I probably did, as well. One fact stood out as she made the drawing. She had incredible trouble making the toilet. She kept crossing it out and re-doing it. It suggested to me there were very strong feelings connected to the toilet, which she later confirmed—deep shame and humiliation. He watched her relieving herself. In these notes, she tells me that when she saw the police on the TV monitor, she believed they would never come back and that she was going to die and there would be poop next to her on the mattress."

Katie also spent many early sessions making a toy box out of clay and spent a lot of time trying to construct a lock for the box. She called the art therapy "dumb," but Mary felt the lock signified her deep need to protect herself.

Katie drew dark flowers with black and brown appendages and subtitled the work, "Everything but the inside is ugly." Mary felt the appendages were phallic and Katie's need to draw these flowers over and over showed an urge to gain mastery over something that was "dark and ugly."

But there was no mastery of the parts of her life that remained beyond her control. Marilyn was arrested for "labor fraud" and Katie's brother John for burglary. Katie received the troubling news while she was in elementary school, and Mary rushed there to counsel her, finding her in the nurse's office, rolled up in the fetal position, crying deeply.

"After her mother's arrest, she paints a red sky over a dark blue sea. There is no sun. Everything was on fire. Many behavioral problems were reported by her foster parents around this time. We did family therapy, and Katie paints another picture of a bloody sunset."

Mary visited Katie at school several times, and although she would say "hello" to everyone, she could see that Katie was deeply lonely. There was an inner sadness on her face. She was involved in school—cheerful—but in unguarded moments, there was profound loneliness.

The day a teacher showed Katie a picture of Sal on the cover of the *Daily News*, Katie felt sick, fled for her home, and covered all the windows with blankets, "thus recreating the dungeon," Mary wrote.

"Seeing Sal's face. That is what frightened her most. She recreated her own dungeon. Later she states she never saw the newspaper. She just blocked it out."

And that, said Mary, is how Katie coped and initially survived. She went underground.

Problems surfaced. Katie feared going down into the foster home's basement. She fought with her foster siblings, acted out, was oppositional, manipulative, clingy. There was nervous laughter. And when Katie was very stressed, she would suck her thumb.

Mary had to urge Barbara, who attended many sessions, not to take Katie's anger personally. "I would explain to her that it was such a huge gift that Katie was giving to them. She was comfortable enough to be obnoxious."

Barbara, who worked part-time in an accountant's office, and Tedd, a corrections officer, were conservative Christians and ran an extremely tight ship. Katie was their daughter now. Mary explained to Barbara that Katie would likely regress before recovering from post-traumatic stress disorder. Barbara braced herself, and Katie delivered with nervous clinginess, chattiness and anxiety, needing to know where everyone was at all times and what they were doing.

Mary explained to Barbara that this was Katie's way of coping with her anxiety. It comforted Katie to know where everyone was. She suggested that Barbara be more direct and reassure her by saying, "I know you are feeling nervous because you remember being so frightened and alone. You are not alone anymore. We love you so much."

Barbara wanted to shoulder all of Katie's hurt. In one emotional session, she told Katie, "I wish I could take your pain. I wish you could give it all to me. I am strong enough to handle it."

Katie flew into Barbara's arms in great relief and burst into tears.

For Katie too, there was hard work for many years. She had to practice "cognitive behavioral techniques," learning to think before reacting in the household. She was taught to express her feelings to Barbara and Tedd directly, rather than display her anxiety. And she had to slowly peel away useless illusions and view Marilyn honestly.

Mary made a decision early on to include Marilyn in the "team." Katie, she believed, needed to have a therapeutic relationship with her. Going through an adoption process and losing her mother forever, Mary felt, would be too overwhelming and crushing. But Katie needed to face up to her mother's many failures.

As part of the team, Marilyn was invited to therapy sessions. Katie was extremely protective of her mother and constantly made excuses for her, explaining to her foster parents that the reason she never received gifts was because her mother couldn't afford them, and the reason Marilyn was distant was that she "grew up without any affection." Mary recalled that Katie became much calmer and happier with Tedd and Barbara after they showed compassion for Marilyn.

Eventually, Katie began to articulate that Marilyn didn't know how to be a mother. In one pivotal session, Katie informed Marilyn she almost drowned in Ann Butler's pool. Marilyn asked why she never told her.

"Because I never lived with you!" Katie shouted.

John Beers also came very willingly to sessions with Katie, sharing that he was sober and active in an AA program. He truly wanted to make amends to Katie for his behavior before, during and after her abduction.

"He stated he was mostly drunk or stoned during that time," Mary wrote. "He also admitted to a lot of anger towards Marilyn and stated how much he loves Katie."

The sessions with John helped Katie know she grew up loved by at least one person. Shortly after these sessions, Katie and Mary attended John's one-year anniversary in AA. Katie sat stoically, but held Mary's hand throughout as John spoke emotionally about the people he felt he had hurt. Katie said little after the meeting, except how proud she was of her big brother.

Mary knew she could never approve of Katie living again with Marilyn and John, but she did give Marilyn credit for one thing. Marilyn had provided Katie with many of the traits that helped her survive. Marilyn, a cab driver, knew how to get from point A to point B. She knew how to get around. Katie could also navigate her way around the most awful obstacles with extreme acuity. "And," Mary said, "Katie was not psychologically deep."

"This saved her. She didn't over-think things. She had to get the memories out in order to face Sal and John in court, but once that was behind her, she didn't look back. Her normal inclination is to be passive and flat. She was never depressed."

Outbursts of anger and emotion were rare, and came only at the hint of shame and embarrassment, as was the case when Katie found out audio tapes were made by John of her days in captivity.

"How did Mr. Ferris know I was crying in the tapes?" Katie was visibly upset. Mary explained they had to gather evidence, and had to listen to the tapes.

"I assured her they would never be made public. They made her feel 'yucky.' She never heard them back then, but she was quite upset and angry they existed. She knew all about the tapes. She knew I had heard them. Dominick let me listen to them."

If Katie had since "forgotten" about the tapes, Mary said, she wouldn't be surprised.

"Has Katie heard them?" Mary asked me anxiously.

I told Mary that Katie wanted the tapes destroyed. She felt their contents would be helpful in this format, for others to learn from the brutality of her experience, but that she did not feel she needed to reopen her wounds so deeply. They had long ago crusted over. She wanted to tell her story in order to help other children.

"Even at ten years old, she wanted to do that."

Katie asked Mary for "permission" to tell her story to classmates in a seventh grade health class, to "help other kids, who have never been able to ask me anything about what happened."

Mary said yes, but added, "We needed to continue to monitor the results. She understood that sharing her story would not necessarily bring friendship. She also needed to understand that sharing her story could help her find closure."

Eventually, Katie made friends and even ran for student government secretary in Junior High School. She lost the election. Sessions with Mary evolved into more mundane pre-teen and teenaged issues, although Mary was always on the lookout for regression and symptoms of post-traumatic stress.

"Katie gets her first period," Mary's notes read. "She is proud and happy about this."

The two had many talks about sexuality as Katie became a teenager. Mary wanted Katie to have a healthy expression of it. She wanted Katie to be able to talk about it.

"I told her that her body territory had been invaded and how frightening that was, and she would need a lot of reassurances."

Around this time Katie began to discuss boys. "She asks to keep all her feelings confidential, as she knows Barbara would disapprove. I told her everything is confidential unless I suspected she was being harmed in some way. She appreciated this on many levels. Feeling protected and feeling validated."

But Mary expected fears of abandonment and bodily harm. "As she enters adolescence," Mary wrote, "I expect many of these problems to become more apparent."

In a later session, Katie was happy about friendships that were starting to truly bloom. Katie was matched with a "little sister" in a school peer support program. The child had been abused and was also in foster care.

"Mary, I felt just like you," Katie announced happily in a session. "I had to ask her how she felt about everything…questions about her feelings and everything!"

She was proud to be able to help someone else.

Art therapy also demonstrated Katie's progress. She made twelve clay caterpillars with a wide range of emotions: happy, sad, scared, angry, bored, shy, anxious, nervous, amazed, and surprised.

"They were beautiful," Mary said. "I loved that she thought of caterpillars, because after all, they eventually turn into butterflies! She loved working on these critters. The initial point of this project was to 'help little kids find their feelings, especially kids who were abused and had trouble talking about their feelings.'"

Katie also toiled over many sessions to complete the lock on the clay box, but she decided at the end of the project that the box didn't need a lock anymore.

A great moment, Mary said, signifying she had become more trusting, less guarded and capable of helping someone else. "I felt she had a glimmer, for the first time, that no one was going to invade her body. She felt safe. I told her not to keep any more secrets."

Mary phoned Katie when Sal died in 2009, but Katie didn't return her call. "Her whole thing is to go underground. She didn't call me back. We were so close. I couldn't believe it. It was disturbing to me. But that is how she takes care of herself. She erases. She just shuts down."

Katie seems to have done well blocking memories out for many years. In terms of recovery, is it healthier to remember or forget?

On this, Mary was unequivocal. "It's better to slowly remember, much better, because if you are in a safe harbor you slowly let out everything you can, rather than have it ice over. There are other theories, that the effect of trauma is twenty years later. You want people to let it out; you don't want them to keep it a secret or suppress it. Denial worked for Katie for some time, but she had so many secrets to let out, and she took her time with it."

Why would Katie "remember" later, so many years later, that she was raped?

"She was old enough to truly find her voice."

Why didn't it come out earlier?

On this, Mary paused and looked deeply into my eyes. "Carolyn, you know what? That didn't matter."

What did matter, said Mary, was that Katie was slowly releasing her secrets, learning to trust in a world that had betrayed her.

I knew from the landmark work, *Trauma and Recovery: The Aftermath of Violence—from Domestic Abuse to Political Terror*[43] that "atrocities refuse to be buried."

> *While the ordinary response to atrocities is to banish them from consciousness...denial does not work. Remembering and telling the truth about terrible events are prerequisites...for the healing of individual victims.*
>
> *People who have survived atrocities often tell their stories in a...contradictory and fragmented manner which undermines their credibility...When the truth is finally recognized, survivors can begin their recovery.*

Katie is clearer on these memories now. She believes she was guided by shame and humiliation. She told me she never wanted to admit to herself that she had let things get so out of control, that she had *let* someone violate her like that. Somehow, she felt responsible for her fate.

Has Katie broken the cycle of abuse?

Mary is certain she has.

Love, Mary believes, was the lifeline, the essential ingredient. It was provided in abundance by a community that felt a sense of collective guilt over the abandonment of a child.

Motherhood, she warned, is the final frontier. "She will be extremely obsessive compulsive about things to try to keep her children safe. She will have overwhelming anxiety. And she won't connect it to her trauma. She has the tools, but she will need reassurance. The work that I did with her was Stage One of recovery. And being able to go into young adulthood without depression was another stage. But the next stage is mothering. This mothering stage brings up all the mistrust that anyone ever had. She was not mothered. The only mothering she received was after the kidnapping. More and more issues will come up for her. Betrayal. Everyone betrayed her. I hope I didn't."

I told Mary that Katie credits her entire life to her love and that of her foster family. Mary's eyes watered and she tried to smile.

Has Katie recovered? Is telling her story a tool in her recovery?

"We are all recovering from something. Everyone is damaged in some way. I am so glad she is on this path of sharing her story, which is such an important part of her recovery. But," Mary warned, "trauma can, and sometimes does, return.

"The recovery doesn't stop. There is no end of story."

MOTHERHOOD

I MET DEREK AT a college town bar. I was sporting a dazzling engagement ring and he, a pool cue and an attitude. I was happily engaged to Scott and not looking to meet anyone. My college girlfriend, Aileen, and I would go regularly, after we had finished our homework, to shoot pool, and often found ourselves in a game with two cocky, arrogant townies. I figured they were interested in Aileen because they'd always drift over our way and show off trick pool shots.

I really didn't care for Derek or Martin. Neither one was my type. I liked nice guys, and these two didn't seem the "nice guy" type. They acted as if they owned the bar because they were locals and not college kids. Derek owned a successful information technology business and everyone knew him. To me, though, he was simply a stranger.

I always had my guard up at the bar. There were a lot of people that I didn't know, and I didn't want to get into a situation where I was not in control. Control is a major issue for me. Feeling out-of-control launches my anxiety attacks. I need to, at all times, control my "exit strategy."

In high school, I would always be the designated driver. I felt safest when I was behind the wheel. I don't like being cooped up either or in a room where the exits are blocked by something or someone. I don't like feeling helpless.

With my guard up, I have been told I come across as "standoffish." I just don't give people the time of day that I don't know, and that is how I behaved toward Derek.

That didn't stop Derek and Martin from inviting Aileen and me back to their apartment after shooting pool one night. It was hardly a date, and by this time, I felt I knew them well enough to go with Aileen to their apartment. We all got some snacks at a twenty-four-hour gas station and curled up on their couch to watch a movie. Aileen and I ended up staying until four in the morning. Half asleep, with me still completely oblivious to Derek's interest, we exchanged numbers, and I went back to my dorm to catch a few hours of sleep before class.

MOTHERHOOD

When I broke off my engagement that spring, I spent a lot of time shooting pool in between cramming for finals. I didn't give Derek a second thought. He always showed up on the other end of the pool table. He was there to help me forget about school work, the disintegration of my engagement, and at the end of the semester, to help me study for finals and move out of my dorm room to head home.

He was also very easy to talk to. I told Derek about my childhood before I left school that first summer. He casually answered that he already knew. He had "Googled" me.

I liked Derek's down-to-earth style, and I wanted to get to know him better. We began to talk on the phone almost every day. I enjoyed the friendship that was now a budding romance. Our relationship started very quickly after my engagement ended.

I was realizing that I should never have said "yes" to Scott, but I was blinded by the beautiful ring and the promise of a fairytale ending. Derek was more of where I wanted to be in my life. He owned a business and wasn't thinking of starting a family any time soon.

For our first official date, Derek promised to take me to my favorite Italian restaurant, even though it was almost an hour's drive from our rural Pennsylvania town. He was going to pick me up after work at six o'clock, but called right before pick up time to say he was running an hour and a half late. He arrived two hours later than that, apologetically offering the option of rescheduling.

It was so late, we ended up scarfing down subs at a nearby Subway. Not very romantic, but the perfect beginning for two unpretentious people, and a fitting start to what would later evolve.

Derek and I kept in touch most of the summer while I was home in Springs. I went to visit him twice over the summer, but pulled back when I found out he reconnected with an ex-girlfriend while I was home.

It started as a favor. He told me he was just going to be picking her up from the airport after not seeing her for a long time. I didn't understand why he was the one picking her up, and he explained that she had asked him for a ride because her parents were working. I gave him credit for being honest, but I told him that if he spent any more time with her after picking her up from the airport and dropping her off at her parents' house, he could forget about dating me any more.

He spent the entire week with her.

He actually was so upset with her departure, when he dropped her off at the airport, he called *me* to vent! I was in disbelief and I was done. I wanted nothing more to do with him.

This was a deal-breaker for me. I wasn't going to play "second fiddle" to someone who I didn't know, who lived in another state and who Derek told me had broken his heart.

Being a single college student in the Hamptons over the summer was no hardship. My girlfriends and I went out dancing in East Hampton, Southampton, Sag Harbor, and Montauk regularly. I was learning the value of having girlfriends in my life, girls who didn't judge me, no matter how difficult I am to get close to. They understood why I have trouble trusting people.

Caitlin and I were inseparable. I had known her since my freshman year in high school. Then, there was Corinne. Corinne was a year ahead of me, and she was friends with Caitlin. In my mind, Corinne was a threat to my relationship with Scott. She was a new girl in high school, and Scott, being a nice guy, went out of his way to show her the ropes. This didn't sit well with me. I didn't trust her near Scott, even when she was dating someone else. In the end, I recognized my paranoia and understood its origin. Both Caitlin and Corinne would end up serving as my bridesmaids.

When I came back to college the fall of my senior year, I had no intention of seeing Derek again. I didn't need someone in my life who didn't want me. But I had to make one exception. Derek had my television in his apartment and I had to get it back. So I headed over to his place one night and Derek asked if I wanted to stay and watch a movie. There was no one else on campus; I was up at school two weeks early for RA training.

I was very apprehensive when I got to his apartment. I had my guard up, a shield that I had no plan of letting down. I only stayed for the movie so I wouldn't be alone the entire night. That was it. We watched the movie and parted awkwardly. Not so coincidentally, we both showed up the next night at our favorite bar to shoot pool. It didn't hurt that word was circulating that I was suddenly single, and a few of my residents were asking me out. After a few dates, I realized quickly how much I missed Derek and how close we had become. He realized it, too.

I fell in love with Derek's values, his love for his family, his work ethic, and once I got to know him, his personality. He loved me for who I was and didn't judge me. He could put up with my baggage, my emotional, defensive, immature and always on-guard nature. Derek loved me, in spite of my many flaws.

For a long time, the trust issues lingered with Derek. I was exhibiting what Mary would call "self-destructive" behavior. I constantly wondered if he was still in touch with his ex-girlfriend or other women. Every time he got a text message or a phone call, I would wonder if it was her. I was constantly grilling him about it, looking at his phone and his text messages. Derek was patient with me then, and even now, when insecurities resurface.

Derek and me at my college graduation.

I never know if my insecurities exist because of the dysfunctional models of relationships I had growing up, or because I have reason to mistrust. This is one of the pitfalls of surviving child abuse. I never know if my instincts are normal or just recurring mistrust creeping back from beneath the crust.

The awful lessons Sal and Linda taught me also resurface, and this is perhaps the most painful part. I don't like admitting that I am wrong; I get defensive when I feel like I am being attacked. I have a short fuse and don't like being criticized or put down. If someone is criticizing me, I become severely defensive, or alternately, completely shut down.

It could be as simple as Derek saying that there are dishes in the sink—he isn't criticizing me, he is just making an observation. But I take comments like that to heart, and automatically feel like he is attacking my homemaking skills. I put up a wall, or I lash out.

I wasn't thinking about the future that night in 2005 traveling home from a sales training trip for my first job after college. My flight from Minnesota was delayed for hours due to mechanical problems and I missed my connection in Chicago. I could have stayed the night or flown to a different Pennsylvania city.

Derek, who was picking me up, told me to grab the flight to Harrisburg, even though he would have to drive hours to retrieve me and I wouldn't arrive until after midnight. I was at the baggage claim carousel when Derek found me, exhausted from traveling and sporting freshly dyed bleached blonde hair. He gave me a hug and a kiss, and held me extra tight, telling me how much he missed me and loved me, and couldn't picture his life without me.

I had no idea where he was going with this, until he got down on one knee at twelve thirty in the morning, with the baggage circling next to him, and asked me to marry him, presenting me with the most beautiful ring. My immediate response was, "Are you kidding me?" and followed quickly with a resounding, "YES!"

His original plan was to pick me up at the airport on time and surprise me with the ring tied around our Jack Russell Terrier, River's, neck. But the airport was hours from home and the time was late. The execution of the plan mattered little to me. I was truly ecstatic inside. I had a feeling from early in our pool hall days that I would make a life with Derek. We clicked; we wanted the same things out of life, out of a marriage, and out of work.

The next day I awoke in complete bliss! I was so excited, I wanted to tell everyone. Derek's family got the news first; because they live close, we saw them often. I had to wait three weeks to tell my family, because I didn't want to do it over the phone. They truly loved Derek and knew how happy he made me. It was, to me, the start of a fairytale, and the first step in what I never had before in life but always imagined.

Derek and I decided that we would make his home town my home town, and I needed to find work. I became the manager at a small second-hand retail shop, and I liked the job, but I was suddenly managing employees who were my age, as well as existing employees who had been with the company for years and who thought that they should have been promoted to the management position. The store owner didn't give me the support or authority I needed to be successful, so after seven months, I quit.

My second job was working for a cleaning company. I was supposed to be the office manager, but I ended up being a highly paid cleaning person. The owner of the company hired me without consulting with the company vice-president. She would refer to me as a bimbo, for no reason, just in the course of a normal conversation. She told me that the only reason the owner had hired me is because I looked good in a skirt—and was constantly cutting me down, not allowing me to do my job, nor teaching me how to effectively do the job.

I was miserable, not because I was cleaning more than I was office managing, but because I didn't like failing, and at this particular job, it seemed I was given no other option than to fail.

I started my third job right after Derek and I got married. It was in the customer service field for a small custom label water bottle company. I did data entry and fielded calls about products and pricing. I loved customer service. I loved dealing with clients and developing relationships with them. It was a nice Monday through Friday day shift with mandatory overtime in the busy months. I was quickly asked to take on more responsibilities, learning new job functions, such as calculating large order shipping fees, credit, and accounting. And I helped to fill in at the art department—I processed and checked the art that people wanted to put on their bottles. I did everything I was asked to do with enthusiasm. This is why I was so upset and confused when I was laid off, just as I discovered I was pregnant.

It took me over a year to conceive, so I worried there was something wrong with me, perhaps from the abuse I suffered as a child. But that changed one Saturday morning when Derek and I were getting up early to go kayaking with friends.

The plan also included drinking that night. Since I was trying to get pregnant, I would take a home pregnancy test at least once a month, so I would know if I could have a drink. My cycle was irregular, so I tested often. On this morning, I felt hopeful.

The test came back with two pink lines. Positive! I ran upstairs to our bedroom and woke Derek. I showed him the positive test, and his response was tempered. "I'll believe it when we have a doctor's confirmation."

I took another test that morning, just to make sure it wasn't a false positive, and the second test had the same two pink stripes. I was elated! But the thought of motherhood also scared me to death.

My pregnancy was bittersweet and endless, as I was anxious and unemployed the entire time. The Human Resources Manager at work had known that I was pregnant because we were changing health insurance carriers and I had asked if my doctor would still be in-network. But there was no mercy. I was told business was slow and I would have to go.

A real life happy ending.

I hated being unemployed. I had been working since I was fourteen years old, first as a cashier at Barefoot Contessa in East Hampton, the gourmet food shop, then at the YMCA at the front desk, and later in college, teaching in a computer lab. Being out of work made me feel useless. I hated the fact that I was not able to rely on myself. My whole life I was self-reliant, until now.

I was nervous to tell my parents that I was pregnant and unemployed. Derek and I had a trip planned to visit East Hampton to share the good news, but cancelled because money was tight. It was on a webcam that I broke the news that a baby was on the way.

Logan's due date was May 30, 2009, but ten days later, there was no sign of labor. My doctor didn't feel comfortable with my pregnancy lasting any longer, and I was ready to meet my little man. But I was terribly afraid of the delivery. My fear of needles still intense, I avoid any and all things that can cause pain, both physically and emotionally. I had more than nine months of built up anxiety about labor and delivery, and I prayed that I would go into labor on my own, but contractions never came.

Labor was induced and I was unable to get an epidural. I had put off the inevitable needle plunge into my spine for so long, it was then too late. Instead, I received an IV of Stadol, which did little to ease the pain. But that was nothing compared to the emotional pain that followed.

Logan's head was too big, and his umbilical cord was wrapped around his neck. I don't remember much about the panic in the delivery room, because I was wearing an oxygen mask and couldn't see, but Logan's heart rate dropped precipitously and there was a frantic effort to get him out.

Derek looked grim. I was losing my baby. There was no controlling this situation. There was a mad rush to vacuum extract his head. I was told to push and push and I knew his life depended upon it.

Then, finally, there was a baby's cry and sudden calm. I was holding my baby boy in my arms. My life had just changed and it would never be the same. I had a little person who was going to rely on *me* to teach him what was right and wrong. And I knew the difference all too well. I had a beautiful son, and suddenly being out of work didn't sting as badly.

The euphoria was short-lived. Even after we brought Logan home, motherhood was a struggle for me. Logan wouldn't latch on. I knew it was important to nurse him to develop a bond with him that I never had with my mother. I tried everything to get Logan to nurse, but nothing worked. He cried miserably and I felt like a failure.

Sadly, I resorted to pumping, and Derek would give Logan breast milk from a tiny medicine cup. I was jealous that Derek was able to develop that bond before I was. I couldn't even feed Logan from the medicine cup because I was still in so much pain from delivery and a deep, fourth-degree episiotomy. It was difficult for me to get in and out of bed, to sit down, to stand, to walk; I was so out of control.

Derek, it seemed, was the only one who could calm Logan down, and this was hard to handle. I was the mother, but it was as if no one had told my child.

My parents came to visit us to meet their new grandchild. My mother and I talked about the difficulty that I was having nursing and how quickly I would get frustrated. She assured me that it takes time, it is a skill that both Logan and I needed to learn, and that if nursing was something that I really wanted to do, Logan and I would need to work on it as a team.

Finally, on a Saturday afternoon, his tiny lips figured out what to do and a burden of guilt and shame melted away. Logan nursed in my arms for nearly an hour. It was the greatest feeling I ever had. I felt one with Logan and knew that I would never let anything or anyone cause him pain. Now, more than ever, I have no idea how anyone can hurt a child.

I stopped by Marilyn's taxi stand about a year later. I had Logan with me. I didn't warn her that I was coming. She wasn't there; she was out on a call. So we waited. I hid behind a door and Logan was running around the dispatch office in toddler circles. Marilyn walked in and grinned, "Who's this little one?"

"Your grandson," I said, as I moved out from behind the door.

She had a big smile on her face and tried reaching out to hold Logan but he squirmed out of her arms. She gave me a hug. The visit was brief.

I try to be as civil as possible to her; I don't think she is a bad person. She just never learned how to care for children. Grandma Helen gave me hugs and kisses, but it seems to have skipped a generation. As Uncle Bob told me, growing up in that house was awful. I don't know what went wrong. Maybe Helen resented not being able to have biological children of her own.

It took me a very long time to admit that Marilyn neglected me. She wasn't there for me until it was too late.

I live in fear of becoming like her. I used to watch Marilyn work countless hours at dead-end jobs, just to get nowhere; I watched her in very few relationships; I watched her struggle to make money and not make ends meet. I don't want to worry about making our next house payment, affording new clothes for the kids, or birthday presents, and yet I constantly worry about our finances.

Her one trait that may have been worth inheriting was that she always put other people's needs before herself. That is why it was so easy for Sal and Linda to take advantage of her. Sal and Linda were not only predators to John and me, but they abused Marilyn's kind nature. I strive to not be as gullible, nor someone that can be easily taken advantage of. It's a trait that, when taken advantage of, can be disastrous.

People have told me that I look like Marilyn, and each time they do, I get defensive. To me, it is an insult because of the weight. Concerns about my weight will be a constant fear and battle as I know that my genes contain that disposition.

I have never been fat, but there was a time I would look in the mirror and see Marilyn. I'm certain that good eating habits are established when you are a child. This is why my eating habits are horrible. Growing up, an acceptable lunch was a candy bar or ice cream. My children will have a mother who knows about nutrition and realizes how vital it is.

Worst of all, I fear being short with my children. I don't know why, and it kills me that I get frustrated with them so easily. Toddlers don't automatically know things—they need to be taught, and I need to teach. It breaks my heart that I have a temper with him. I want to give my kids the best childhood that I am capable of and I don't want them to remember me being short with them.

I don't ever want my kids to look back on their childhood and think about how angry Mommy got with them. Logan is my life. He is the sweetest little boy ever. He is an adventurer, gets into everything that he isn't supposed to, and doesn't listen. He is being a normal little boy. It is I who needs to learn, from scratch, how to be a mother.

I also live in fear of my family's safety. Financially, I am unable to be a stay-at-home mother. I went back to work at an insurance company before Logan's first birthday. Not being with Logan all of the time, I constantly worry about him. I try very hard to not be cynical, but it is very difficult to not immediately suspect the worst in people. I try to give people a chance to show me that they are not bad—but it is difficult for me not to have my guard up. I find, as a mother, I am always looking at ways that my family or I can be physically or emotionally hurt.

I am cautious about the people that I bring into my life, and that of my family. People are not what they seem. I have had so much hurt and pain that I don't know if I can endure any more, and I don't want to subject my family to even an ounce of that.

One day, I hope to be able to forgive the people who hurt me, but I'm not there yet. I still suffer effects of the abuse. I love my husband more than words can describe, but I care little if we are intimate. I would rather express to my husband that I love him by snuggling on the couch, enjoying a conversation over dinner, cooking dinner together, or sharing the joys of parenthood. These are things I never knew could bring such pleasure. For the first ten years of my life, I never saw any adults being caring or loving toward one another.

As I tell this story, I am nine years old again. And I hurt very deeply for my nine-year-old self, mourning my lost childhood. But I have gained so much since then.

I celebrate January 14th each year like a birthday. It is the anniversary of the day I moved in with my parents. It is the day my life truly began. From the little girl that inched away from Tedd during car rides and lied to Barbara about the smallest things, I grew up to be my mother's best friend and Daddy's little girl. I owe them my life, and I know they feel just as deeply for me. I only remember my father crying twice since I have known him: first, when he dropped me off at college, and later when he walked me down the aisle. I hope the tears came from being proud of the work he did and of what I have become.

While I kept my silence for twenty years, I have been able to anonymously live a life more normal than I ever dreamed possible when, as a little girl, I was curled up in a ball, sobbing to my captor that my future was slipping away.

I gained precious parents and siblings; I was the first person in my immediate family to graduate from high school, and then college. I have a husband I tell I love each night before I go to sleep and mean it, and a home we own. I have had several productive jobs and years of life-saving therapy. I am a loving and learning mother, and I continue my recovery every day.

The first member of my biological family to graduate from college.
My proud father by my side.

RESILIENCE

I AM AWED BY the soul's capacity for recovery. The most traumatic experiences unquestionably alter perspective, yet the original DNA that determines human grit appears to remain intact. My father called that "constitution." A person is either born with thick skin or pulp. Katie has the leather-tough variety. Whether it was bestowed on her by virtue of her unidentified lineage or was the result of unremitting conditioning, I do not know. Add to the mixture dashes of love from Little John and Grandma Helen, and the end product was unyielding courage and a coat of emotional armor that shielded Katie until far better parenting came to the rescue. And it came in abundance in various forms.

This is not unlike the resilience of broken skin. Even the worst wounds heal. When ripped apart, jagged edges come together gradually, each day another band of tissue grows until a scab forms to protect the body from an invasion of germs. It's a fascinating orchestration of biochemical events, but it's also a fragile process susceptible to failure.

Even after the scab falls off, the skin is never exactly the same and can remain tender for a long time, vulnerable to the elements. This is where I found Katie, healed but justifiably altered.

Memory can also regenerate. I used to think that erasing memory would be helpful in surviving such ordeals. The blurring of painful details dulls the sensation. It did for Katie, for a long time. Her foster parents helped to blot out her old world and create a new and vastly improved one in its place, an immeasurable gift. It gave Katie time to grow up, without tragedy defining her, and the ability to revisit her past when she was in a better place—stronger, older, and with loving support.

The memories returned slowly when she was ready to face them. She takes them out only occasionally now, as needed, brushing off the dust to see what lies beneath.

When they come without warning, Katie is usually unflappable. Such was the case when I received a handwritten letter sent from Sing Sing Correctional Facility in Ossining, New York, from Inmate # 94A6357, and shared it with her.

> *Dear Mrs. Gusoff,*
> *You don't understand how it is in prison, everytime something happens about my case out there, I get punished in here. Inmates say bads things to me and I must endur it. Ive had an excellent record throu out that time. I know Im guilty of my crime, but I beleave Ive been punished enough. I mean I didn't kill anyone, and when I started my crime I really thought it would be good for the both of us, now I know I was wrong. The only thing I wish for is to die in freedom, thats all I dream of. I think Katie knows I will always wish her well. I'm sorry for what Ive done, Im sorry I even thought it up. It was a mistake.*
> *If you write this book I will be punished again and again, It doesn't matter if the book shows me in a good or bad light, it will take away all hope for me to die in freedom.*
> *The only way I could possibly give you an interview is if I was free, all other ways would just punish me in here. Im a old man with bad health please don't bring back all the things we both should forget, It cant do any good for Katie, and for me it would destroy all my hopes. Please tell Katie I wish her and the family the very best.*
>
> *Yours Respectfully*
> *John Esposito*

Katie, busy with a toddler son, a new job, and baby on the way, didn't say much in response, other than a snarky comment that again, even now, John is only thinking of himself.

Soon after, like most of my routine communications with her, this one came in the form of an e-mail, with a decidedly unceremonious subject line: Update. It was, however, anything but ordinary.

> *Things are going great here so far, just adjusting to being a mommy of a two-year-old & a newborn! Halee Katherine was*

*born on July 28 at 5:22 pm. She weighed 6 lbs 7.2 oz & was
19 1/4 inches long. She looks exactly like Logan.*

Halee Katherine. I whispered the name aloud and it choked me up. Then, I opened the attachments. The face of a newborn baby girl stared back at me, a beautiful little thin lipped, plump-cheeked angel with almond-shaped brown eyes and full lids that were unmistakable. She looked exactly like Katie.

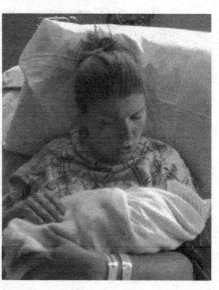

Katie and Halee

I shared the news with Chief Varrone that Katie had given birth to her second child—a baby girl. Like a proud papa, he spread around the department photos of his girl cuddling her newborn in her arms. Coincidentally—perhaps not—his own daughter, Catherine, was due to give birth to a child any day.

"Here," he said, when I saw him next, dropping a few pages of copy paper into my hands—an email thread between him and Katie. It included his note to department heads.

> *To All,*
> *It has been nineteen years since Katie Beers was abducted and secreted underground for seventeen days. It is comforting to know that not only did she survive her ordeal but she went on to have a productive, rewarding life. Please enjoy these photos of her with her second child (who was just born) and please share with officers and detectives who were involved in the case.*
>
> *Thank you,*
> *Chief Varrone*

Katie responded in her simple positive way:

Katie and Halee

Thank you for sharing the pictures! I feel it is important to know that, after everything that I have gone through, I have gone on to lead a "normal" life, which is a big part of the reason for the book—so that it can give people hope that they too can go on to lead productive lives!

Speak to you soon,
Katie

Another note fell into my hands upon the twentieth anniversary of Katie's abduction. It came from a voice now silenced. James Catterson, the DA, passed away in 2007 after a stroke. A year earlier, he had sent this response to a news reporter inquiring, "What ever happened to Katie Beers?"

My contacts with Katie are nil, mainly because I avoided staying in touch with her for a most compelling reason. I feel strongly that she was off on a new life and any contact with the past made her very uneasy. It was best for her to put that part of her childhood as far away as possible, even though it meant severing ties with her champions as well as her demons.
The last time I saw her was at high school graduation, a fine young woman who deserved a clean slate away from whisper,

raised eyebrows and furtive knowing looks of recognition from total strangers. She's graduated from college now and living (I believe) and working outside the Northeast, so be it! I'm still curious as to how she's doing but I'm more concerned about dredging up bad memories for her. I confine myself to my own grandchildren and truly wish that my other "daughter" grows as strong, happy and safe as they.

Thanks for thinking of Katie. She is a compelling and courageous person who desperately needs to escape a past that was thrust upon her by dysfunctional caregivers who let her down. You and I don't need to be added to that long list.

All the best,
Jim Catterson

THE LETTERS

A DUST-COVERED BROWN box came out from beneath the green leather couch in Mary's office.

"This is my Katie Beers box." Mary offered a bittersweet grin.

It contained hundreds of handwritten letters from well-wishers, many of them school children who, in the days and months after Katie's rescue, discussed in classrooms and assemblies the dangers of abduction and child abuse. The headlines were unavoidable, and Katie's fate was a closely-followed drama and teachable moment. Letters arrived in bundles, in crayon, marker, pencil and ink. They were created on construction paper, lined loose-leaf and stationery. Some were illustrated and others typed.

"They are beautiful in different ways," Mary said.

She and Katie had read many of them together, very slowly, a few at each session. Katie saved some for herself, including those from children requesting to be her best friend and from adults who were abused as children, offering support. Mary believes they are a compelling testament to the outpouring of community love that functioned as an essential ingredient in propelling Katie Beers into recovery.

> *Dear Katie,*
> *Welcome to a new beginning! Here is my message of hope to you: That you have the birthday party you have been waiting for. You will have nice clothes, dolls, and a lot of friends. I hope you will have a lot of love and stay with the family that has made the new beginning for you.*
> *Kerri, 6th Grade*
>
> *Dear Katie,*
> *I'm so glad that you survived. And I hope you and your family live happily ever after.*
> *Gina, Grade 5*

BURIED MEMORIES

Dear Katie,
I'm extremely sorry that help didn't get to you sooner. We should
all be thankful that you got out of that horrible place alive. Be
happy and fight what you don't like about life.
Stacey, Grade 5

Dear Katie,
You are safe now. You have your whole life to catch up on things.
Your New Friend, Julie

Dear Katie,
I heard about what happened to you. I felt very bad. I hoped
and prayed every night and day for you. Katie, I feel like I have
known you all my life.
Sincerely, George

Dear Katie,
I hope you find a family that shows you loving care. Don't worry
about the past. Look forward to life.
Yours sincerely, Marlon, 5th Grade

Dear Katie,
I'm so glad you're ok. I prayed for you every night. You're a
very strong and very lucky little girl. You're probably scared
and confused but now finally you'll be cared for. Your mom will
always be your mom but there is more to being a mom than
giving birth. It's time you have a real mom to show you love and
take care of you. I hope to hear good things.
Love, Laraine.

Dear Katie,
I am very happy that you are alive. Everybody loves you. You
are a very special girl.
Love, Jovanka

LIFE AFTER *BURIED MEMORIES*

THE MORE I THINK about it, the more it becomes clear: Recovery never ends. It constantly evolves.

The mind is miraculous. It protects us from ourselves. It harbors memories in a safe place until we are ready to process them. Just when I thought I had remembered all of the evils of my childhood, my mind decided that I was mentally and emotionally prepared to deal with more. And luckily, I agree. I am in a stronger place, better able to come to terms with these new and sometimes recurring memories. They come in flashes, in daydreams, or at times, in nightmares. I do not allow the memories to startle to me. I have been through enough therapy to know how to navigate my response. I must figure out the "root" or cause of the memory—why something painful and long ago forgotten has broken through into consciousness. That part is not difficult. Of course, writing *Buried Memories* provoked a flood of memories. That was my intention and what I believe I needed. Because Carolyn and I had been writing *Buried Memories* for some time, and I started journaling my memories even before that, I was certain that all of the terrors of my childhood had come to the surface. But that is the hard part: I, apparently, had not (and still do not) remember everything from my childhood because newly discovered memories emerge periodically.

The memories that are resurfacing now are from early childhood—rooted, no doubt, in the care of my own children. I could be putting Logan or Halee to bed, or giving them a bath, and I'll get really sad because I look at their innocence and could never imagine them going through the pain and heartache that I went through. Halee is almost four years old. When I was her age, I was running errands and doing Sal and Linda's laundry, activities so completely inappropriate for a child, I now cannot even fathom. As I sit writing this, on a couch with Halee and Logan, Halee is curled up next to me watching the Disney channel, and Logan is spread out playing the blocks game, MineCraft. I take a deep breath and take in the sight of them enjoying their childhood. They are carefree and surrounded by love. This is my immediate goal in life—to keep them safe and innocent.

I am more mindful than ever before of emerging memories. I put them to work to formulate a healing message, as I now speak publicly about my past. But even that has not been a completely smooth ride. The first public appearance I made upon the book release was on *The Dr. Phil Show*. I wasn't quite sure what to expect from this experience; I was encountering all new experiences. First, a production crew came to my home for a videotaped "pre-interview." I was peppered with questions about the day of the kidnapping. This caught me off guard, as I had not been briefed at all about what subjects they would delve into. Since it was Dr. Phil, I assumed the focus would be on my emotional and psychological recovery and about how counseling altered my life after entering foster care. But instead, I felt grilled about the gory details of the most horrible day of my life. Derek and I headed to Los Angeles anyway to tape my appearance on the show, hopeful the pre-interview had been an aberration. To the contrary—I was horrified by the experience. Frankly it felt more like an effort to shock the audience than to help people. It didn't seem like a positive experience for the other guests on the show either.

I felt it going downhill from the beginning video sequence. The production crew put together an introductory video which I had to watch from back stage. I had not had the opportunity to preview it, and it contained a video I had never seen before: pictures of John Esposito, Sal and Linda Inghilleri, and Marilyn, and police footage of the "dungeon." Perhaps I should have been prepared for it, but I trusted my hand would be held as the guest on a psychological advice program, moreover the victim of child abuse. Instead, caught completely off guard, I became emotional and teared up. I had only a moment to compose myself before being ushered out on stage where I could not help but feel like a pawn in the ratings game. I know how television works; you want to give your audience something that they've never seen before, something they cannot take their eyes off of. For the *Dr. Phil Show*, on January 13, 2013, that was me—I was the subject mesmerizing the viewing audience. It felt superficial and sensational.

Dr. Phil also focused intently on the abduction. It seemed to me (and to family and friends later watching the show) that he plugged and discussed his own book far more than mentioning *Buried Memories*. But the part of the show that was most devastating to me was watching the spectacle that came next.

When I had initially spoken with the production staff about the structure of the show, I was advised that it would include another segment; my portion would be followed by that of another abduction victim who was only fifteen years old but was "ready to speak out." I was seated in the studio audience, next to Derek, after my interview was over. I was absolutely sickened by what followed. Sarah Maynard had been kidnapped, while her younger brother, mother, and family friend were all brutally murdered by her abductor. As young Sarah sat on stage next to her father, only two years after living an unthinkable nightmare, she tearfully tried to answer questions but hardly spoke. She did manage to share that she had been only briefly in therapy. It was clear to me that Sarah was not emotionally stable enough to be on this world stage—I could not believe that I was participating in this. I firmly believe that before one can publicly share details of a serious trauma, one needs to have come to terms with it, gone through therapy, and to what extent is possible, to have recovered. Sarah had done none of these. Sarah and her father had also co-written a book about her horrific abduction and the murder of her family members. The more I thought about Sarah sitting in front of a national audience at fifteen years old, detached and visibly traumatized, the more it angered me. It was clear to me that her emotional well-being was not the priority of adults who, it appeared to me, were taking advantage of the situation.

After the taping of the show, I made sure that I "bumped" into Sarah in the hallway. I told her that if she ever wanted to speak to me, or to keep in touch, that she could call me any time. I asked the production staff to please provide Sarah with my contact information. Sarah's father didn't seem pleased that she was speaking to me in the hallway and kind of rushed her off. I've kept tabs on Sarah over the past two years, as much as I can. She made news again in May 2013, when her stepmother was accused of shoving her down a staircase and her father was accused of striking her. My heart sank when I read the coverage. I have never heard from her since that day in December 2012, but I feel such a sense of protection over her because of what she went through, and because I know that recovery cannot be rushed.

I returned home after the experience on *The Dr. Phil Show* with a better idea of what the public wanted to hear, but more focused than ever on the purpose of speaking publicly to help victims heal. Following the show, my family enjoyed Christmas, my thirtieth birthday, and New Years.

———————————————

The year 2013 began with a breathless whirlwind. I left my home in Central Pennsylvania and drove to New York City straight into a media blitz. Carolyn and I sprinted from interview to interview: morning newscasts, national talk shows, newspapers, magazines, network news programs, radio shows, and late night news broadcasts. We didn't solicit all of the coverage—much of it was organic—news organizations heard I had broken my two-decade silence and made contact. I honestly had no idea if there would be any interest in my story after so long. It had been twenty years since I was kidnapped. Carolyn had always assured me I had a timeless message to offer, and for the first time, I saw what she meant. Not only were these interviewers interested in what happened on December 28, 1992, but they were genuinely interested in how I managed to go on to have a happy life—how I recovered.

It was while I was in New York on my first round of media interviews that I decided I wanted to become a motivational speaker. This has given me the opportunity to speak to different groups of people: The National Organization for Victim Assistance (NOVA), churches, colleges, child advocacy centers, law enforcement organizations, victims' groups, libraries, and many more. I have been given so many different opportunities and have spoken to so many different people, not only about the effects of childhood abuse on both the child and family, but also about how someone who has experienced such a trauma can productively move on from what they have endured. No matter the nature of the trauma—a car accident, losing a job, stressful child rearing, domestic violence—I believe that my message of recovery and support is important in many of these life challenges. There is hope that no matter how miserable life seems after a trauma, the support system with which a person surrounds themselves afterwards will help to direct their recovery.

I have since met very caring and compassionate journalists who have shared my story with millions—and with the best of intentions. Anderson Cooper, Greta Van Susteren, Jeff Probst, Soledad O'Brien, Katie Couric, Barbara Walters, Piers Morgan, Jennifer McLogan, Liz McNeil, and MANY others. Thank you!

A true highlight was being contacted by the National Center for Missing and Exploited Children (NCMEC). It is an honor and privilege to call this organization family. I have twice been to the HOPE Awards in Washington D.C., their Congressional Breakfast, and in 2014, I was an invitee of the organization's closed door summit entitled "Time to Bring Them Home." The summit explored strategies for finding long term missing children. At the event, I was given the opportunity to speak following Elizabeth Smart, as well as to have conversations with Ed and Lois Smart (Elizabeth Smart's supportive parents), Terry Probyn, (Jaycee Dugard's incredible mother), and many other influential individuals in the "missing children" community. I have had the opportunity to speak with John Walsh—actor, advocate, NCMEC Co-Founder—and John Ryan—President and CEO for NCMEC. The opinions and advice of these two men have been greatly appreciated and cherished. When I attended the first HOPE Awards in 2013, Jaycee Dugard was being honored. It was deeply inspiring to hear her speak. I am awed by this woman, mother, and survivor. At the 2014 HOPE Awards, the Cleveland kidnap survivors Amanda Berry and Gina DeJesus were being honored. No one knows exactly what these brave women have been through, but the grace and dignity that they exhibited was influential! I had an opportunity to meet them and I was speechless—which doesn't happen too often. They are beautiful, inside and out.

And with all the good that has poured into my life as a result of *Buried Memories*, there has also been one grave disappointment. I have had to let my guard down, a lot, and in one case, I feel deeply burned. I protected my privacy since 1993, for, among other reasons, fear of being taken advantage of. I have kept my walls up and closely guarded the most horrible secrets of my life. I have prided myself with only allowing positive people into my life—people who loved me and who would protect me. I try to make sure that every person I allow to enter my life is someone with good intentions. However, early in the publishing process, a person I had trusted to help Carolyn and me share my story took severe advantage of us. I have high hopes that this new edition of *Buried Memories* will continue to help victims for many years to come. I can go on living a happy life now that this negativity is out of it.

BURIED MEMORIES

My family has also grown as a result of *Buried Memories*. I have unexpectedly gained a relationship with my brother, John, who I had reluctantly left behind in a life I wanted to forget. After its publication, he told me that that reading the book was actually insightful for him. Reading my view on him and the childhood we shared made him want to be a better person. But as adults, John and I were now worlds apart. We knew very little about each other. He had never even met my children.

I decided it was time and apprehensively invited him to Logan's 3rd birthday party. When I discovered that his only mode of transportation was the Amtrak train from Philadelphia to my home in central Pennsylvania and learned he would have to spend the entire weekend, I was ready to cancel the party. Could I have John around that long of a time period? In my home with my children? It was almost like inviting a stranger into my house.

Logan and Halee

Despite my anxiety, the party went on. I picked John up at the Amtrak station and was struck by how good he looked. Short hair and a big smile. We drove to my house. He was chatty and friendly, especially to Logan, and told me how excited he was to be with us. Despite my jitters, having my brother with me and my family seemed less strange than I expected. I made dinner while John played with the kids and chatted with Derek. He even helped to put Logan's new bicycle together. The next morning, as my apprehension disappeared, I made everyone breakfast and John helped prepare for the party. He played with the kids, accompanied Derek to town for an errand, and even made himself comfortable as Derek's enormous family filed in for the party.

Everyone made John feel very welcome—which is difficult for John because he doesn't like large crowds, and our family is large! As I drove him back to the Amtrak station on Sunday, I felt a sense of relief and sadness that the weekend was over. It had been surprisingly comfortable and felt right.

Since spending those two days with John, we are now working on rebuilding the relationship that we lost. We are both open and honest with each other, which is something we never were. I feared he was upset with me because of my lack of a relationship with Marilyn, but now I know this meant nothing to John. He was, and still is, most concerned about me. We now exchange a text or a phone call once a month, and he feels more like "family" than ever before.

There has also been closure. In August 2013, I received a startling phone call from the New York State Parole Board. I had been thinking a lot about John Esposito's upcoming parole hearing—which was scheduled for September. I almost sympathized with Esposito; I can't imagine that since I broke my silence and shared my memories for the first time with the world, that his life in prison had become any easier. In fact, I am almost certain that it had become worse. I have always been told (and in a way, reassured) that prison is a place where child molesters and rapists are treated like the lowest forms of life. When Esposito went to prison, his "on the record" crime was kidnapping; it had nothing to do with molesting or raping me. Had I the opportunity to go to trial, I would have been able to break my silence when I was eleven or twelve years old rather than at age thirty, and the world would have known the absolute horrors that Esposito put me through. Instead, I waited. I recovered. I flourished.

After the book's release, I spent a great deal of time talking to my brother, John, about Esposito's upcoming parole hearing scheduled for later that year—September of 2013. Brother John asked me if I thought that the parole committee would be willing to speak with him regarding the abuse that he endured as a child at the hands of Esposito. This was the first that my brother and I had ever spoken of his abuse by Esposito. I was so proud of him for being able to finally address this with me. It was a big step in his recovery and in our relationship. I told John that I would make some phone calls and let him know if another victim—one who had never pressed charges—would be permitted to come forward at a parole hearing. I spent a lot of time on the phone with several different people from the Parole Board explaining who I was and what I was looking to accomplish. I was finally informed that Esposito's hearing was "too soon"—the committee would not have time to schedule a meeting with John. Instead, he could fax a letter that would be read and "taken into consideration." I was devastated for John; he was finally ready to share his story and hopefully receive some justice, but it was "too late."

I called John with the disappointing news. At least he would be able to write a letter that would be read at the hearing, but he had only two days to accomplish this task. I told John that if he wanted me to, he could email the letter to me and I would get it faxed in. The end of the day came, and I didn't receive an email from John. I called to check in with him and make sure he was okay. He explained that he tried, but he was unable to get his words and feelings down on paper with the care and consideration that it deserved, and he decided that he would wait two more years for the next parole hearing. He would have more time to prepare.

At that moment, I had a gut feeling that if John didn't take advantage of the opportunity now, he may never get the opportunity again. I couldn't pinpoint what the gut feeling was—would Esposito be granted parole? I could not imagine that happening. Or, would he die in prison before his next hearing? I did not know, but I had an instinct that Esposito would not make it to his parole hearing in 2015.

The day that I received the phone call from the NYS Parole Board is etched in my memory. I had just picked up Logan and Halee from the babysitter and was getting ready to walk into Wal-Mart for a prescription to treat a painful root canal surgery I had earlier in the day. A New York telephone number was coming up on my caller ID at 5:15 PM on September 4, 2013. I answered the phone while holding Logan's hand and juggling Halee in my arms.

A pleasant voice on the other end asked, "Is this Katie Beers?"

I answered, "Yes."

She told me she was calling from the New York State Parole Board. My heart sank in my chest. I quickly put Halee in the shopping cart and got

Logan situated. The Parole Board has never called after a parole hearing. Was my gut feeling correct, would Esposito not get to his 2015 parole hearing—because he was being granted parole? I didn't know what to think—there were so many thoughts going through my head. I quickly became sick to my stomach. The voice on the other end asked if it was an okay time to talk. Even though I was pre-occupied, I didn't want to delay the call. The voice apologized for calling so late in the day, but she had news that she wanted to share with me before I found out from somewhere else. The sickness in my stomach started to bubble. I became dizzy and needed to sit down. The voice went on.

"John Esposito passed away in his cell this afternoon."

"WHAT? Wait, did I just hear you correctly?! Can you repeat that?" I wanted to make sure.

The voice spoke, "Of course. Inmate John Esposito passed away in his prison cell this afternoon after his parole hearing."

I continued, "He's dead? Was he granted parole?"

"No, he was not granted parole. Parole was denied based on new facts."

"But, he's dead?" I needed the verification because I was beside myself. I couldn't believe what I was hearing.

"Yes."

Immediately, from within Wal-Mart, I called my brother John to let him know. I wanted him to hear it from me and not from anyone else. He didn't pick up, so I continued to my next call—my mom. I was standing in the toy aisle with the kids—normally, I don't let them pick out a toy when we're at Wal-Mart, but today wasn't just any day.

"Hi Sweetie," my mom answered with her standard greeting to me.

I went through the normal greetings and then blurted out, in the middle of the toy aisle, "Esposito died in prison today."

I suddenly felt a sense of relief—as well as sadness. It hit me hard that he was dead, he would never be granted parole! The sadness that I felt was for Esposito's surviving family. The world lost a monster, but the Espositos lost a brother, an uncle, a friend.

Then, still in Wal-Mart, I called Carolyn and shared the news with her. Carolyn is now a close friend of mine, but I had to first double check with the NYS Parole Board that I could tell her because she is also a journalist, a member of the working press. The Board assured me that I could share the news with her, but asked her to hold off on releasing the information publicly until next of kin had been notified. We waited—and waited. We finally received word that Esposito's family had been informed of his death, and we released the news. My statement to the press was from the heart: "I'm saddened at the loss of a life, but at the same time I'm happy that John Esposito will never be granted parole or have the opportunity to hurt anyone ever again."

As the day went on, and I had time to think about the enormity of the news that I had been given, I could not help but to feel a little happy. This monster, who had stolen a part of my childhood that could never be restored, would not be able to harm another child the way he harmed me. In my mind, he died a long time ago—the day he took what was left of my innocence. I did not mourn his death. Instead, I mourned for the people who had loved Esposito and had lost him one final time. Even though he had abused me so terribly, there were still people in this world who cared for him and were hurting even more now.

As if all of this wasn't overwhelming enough, I was then informed that Esposito had finally confessed to the parole board that he had sexually assaulted me. I almost experienced a sense of relief upon hearing this stunning news. I truly thought Esposito started to believe his own lies— that he had never sexually abused, assaulted, or raped me. If you say a lie often enough, whether out loud or to yourself, you may start to believe it. This can work another way. If you tell yourself that everything is okay, especially in the face of a traumatic event, you can start to believe that too. The problem with this double-edged sword is that eventually, it will come back to you! Lying to yourself after a traumatic event is never a good idea. Memories can take you by surprise, and the deep emotions that you "should" have felt at the time of the traumatic event will be there waiting for you.

I used to be nervous about the day Esposito would finally admit to authorities what only he and I knew. There was no reason for my anxiety. Perhaps it was shame I was feeling. In fact, I never truly believed the day would come. After I had the opportunity to spell out for the Parole Board exactly what acts Esposito subjected me to, and how it affected my life, that nervousness faded away. I learned in therapy sessions not to be shaken by Esposito's failure to own up to his deeds and his made-up excuses. Any pedophile who had just been exposed would do the same thing.

So, when I finally had an opportunity, more than a year after his death, to read what he actually said to the parole board, my relief turned to anger. It started the way his previous three hearings had—the Commissioners asked Esposito his age and length of incarceration. Esposito was six-four years old and going on his twenty-first year behind bars. They asked about the dungeon. He replied, calling it a "comfortable" bunker. The Commissioners seemed to bristle. But then, they veered off to uncharted territory.

Q-Were you attracted to her at all?

A-I think I was, yes.

Q-I think so too, because you admit to kissing her, correct?

A-Yes.

Q-Did you touch her in inappropriate ways during that time? Be honest.

A-I'll be honest. Can I just say something, when I was convicted, my attorney said don't admit to anything but to kidnapping. Now I realize that was a mistake. I shouldn't have listened to him, so, yes, I did touch her. I never said it before.

Q-I know you haven't, because I read your transcripts and you've denied that you ever touched her inappropriately, except you did say you did kiss her.

A-Yes.

Q-But you have been in for a long time.

A-Yes sir.

Q-You're finally confessing up to more.

A-Yes.

Q-But I know you are in only for kidnapping but sir, what you did here, I'm sure there's not an hour that doesn't go by that this victim here thinks about what happened to her.

A-Yes, you're right.

Q- You've been in Sing Sing for how long now?[44]

After providing this first-time admission, a complete reversal of his previous testimony and even the rationale behind two decades of denials,

I was disappointed he was not pressed further. The Commissioners moved on. It was not until later in the hearing they returned to the pivotal issue of his confession.

Q-Sir, how old were you at the time?
A-43
Q-Okay. So, you are 43 and she was 10?
A-Yes
Q- Didn't you think that was little odd, you were attracted to her?
A-Yes
Q- Did you have sexual attractions to younger children all your life?
A-No, no.
Q-And you know, you spoke about her home wasn't a good environment and you were going to be there to rescue her, do you really think—
A-I'm not using that as an excuse. I used it for myself as an excuse, but I realize it is not no excuse. I should have notified the authorities what was happening to her.
Q-Right, but beyond that, beyond trying to be this alleged good Samaritan to save this young girl, you put her through a period of torture and hell and impacted her life, I'm sure forever, and I believe your motivation was sexual in nature. It sounds like you're finally starting to admit that, that's good, that's part of your time in prison. You need to acknowledge the circumstances of your offense, and if you still have those feelings for minor children, that's something that you need to get under control, so if and when you are released into society, you do not re-offend against a young child again. Nothing further.
Q-Sir, we've asked you a lot of questions and you answered them all, is there anything you feel we missed or anything you want to say on your behalf that you feel we haven't covered with you?
A-I would like to say something, if I can, it's a short letter, it's not long. I know you've heard this a million times.
Q- Okay. Hold on one second.
A-Yes.
Q-If you are going to read it, read it clearly and slowly, okay?
A-Okay. Real slowly.

Q-Or if you want to just summarize it and say it in your own words.

A-It's not that long, a page and a half, very quick.

Q-Okay

A-I'm very sorry for the shameful thing I did. There is no excuse for what I did. It was the worst thing I could do, especially to someone I loved, but I would like you to know a few things. The police searched my house twice, once with a search warrant, and they didn't find anything. But later on, the police were there when I released her. I released her, knowing I would go to prison. Also, when I released her, she said she felt cold. So, I put my coat on her. She wasn't scared and she wasn't crying. Then she said to me, John don't worry, everything is going to be okay. The police and my attorney heard her. My point is, at the time of this terrible ordeal that she went through, Katie was not angry with me. She actually tried to make me feel good. Why would she do that? I mean, it shows she still cared about me. While—

Q-Sir, I think it's inappropriate that you are putting those statements on the record.

A-Why? That's what she said, that's what I'm saying. It just shows that I wasn't mean to her, that's all I'm trying to say. I know what I did was wrong, but I wasn't brutal. I didn't beat her up or hurt her that's all.

Q-Sir, you left her in a bunker, ten years old. I have a ten year old at home and he still has the light on in his bedroom and he's scared to be alone. Thanks for coming in. We'll inform you in writing.[45]

It did not take long for the board to reach a decision: parole denied. They noted, "During the interview you showed little remorse and tried to rationalize your unlawful conduct."[46] I do not know if John lived long enough to read their remarks and learn his fate. He died in his cell later that day.

Even while finally admitting to a small portion of what he put me through, he was still minimizing it—trying to make it seem as it wasn't all that bad—when in reality, it was much worse than anyone could ever imagine.

I almost wonder if John's death was not as sudden as it seemed. Perhaps he knew he was dying and that is why he finally made admissions—a sort of deathbed confession. I will never know.

Another brush with death, more recently, forced me to confront a different demon. Marilyn was admitted to the hospital in grave condition in 2014. I got the news from my brother, in a somber phone call. It was not the first time that she was being admitted, but it was the first time he was letting me know. He said he was seriously worried this time she was going to die. She was not able to breathe; tests showed a blockage. I tried calling her doctors, but no one would give me information because she had not listed any next of kin on her medical forms. By the time I was able to get through to her directly, I demanded permission to speak with her doctors. She complied—but the conversations with doctors felt as if I was talking about a stranger.

"I'm Katie Beers, you're treating my biological mother there. From my brief understanding, she's not doing well and I need to know if I should rush to Long Island to 'make my peace.'"

I also told the doctor that Marilyn and I didn't really have any sort of relationship, but that if we were nearing the end, I needed to know because I was over six hours away. The doctor told me I had time, so I consulted the one person whom I can always count on—my mother.

"I don't know if I should travel to Long Island. What if she's dying?!"

My mom assured me, "whatever decision you make, Sweetie, will be the right one."

"But, I really don't know how to feel. I mean, she's my biological mother, but the relationship isn't there. There are things that I'd like to say to her--truthful conversations that I'd like to have with her, but I don't know if I'm ready for those conversations--conversations about WHY. Why did she put John and me in the toxic situations that she did, and why did she think it was okay for her to not be a mother to me, other than giving me a five-dollar allowance when I'd see her once a week?!"

My mother told me to sleep on it, and see how I felt in the morning. I have two young kids to think about, and cannot abandon my duties at the drop of a hat. I learned the next day that Marilyn would be okay from this episode, but only if she started to take care of herself and made some drastic health changes. The doctor told me that I needed to have a serious conversation with Marilyn about taking care of herself. I had to bluntly explain that I am her biological daughter and that currently, that is as far as the relationship extends.

The things I wanted to say to her never got said. I don't want to hurt her by clearing my own mind. If I say what I really want to, I fear that it will damage her even more. I don't want that on my conscious.

Since this nearly life changing experience for Marilyn, she has made an effort to contact me a few times. Her lack of communication just further demonstrates to me her inability to be a parent. If it were an opportunity to grow or learn or build—it was a missed one.

The only lingering thought I have about Esposito is this: If it hadn't been for the kidnapping, two days before my tenth birthday, I would not have been given a world of opportunities. When I say that the abduction was the best thing to have happened to me—it was. It truly was. The horror of being kidnapped provided me with some of the worst experiences in my life, but the abduction itself was a "saving grace." I did not have the courage yet to speak out about the abuse I was enduring from Sal and Linda, and I did not understand that neglect under Marilyn was a form of abuse. I cannot say for certain whether I would have told Child Protective Services workers about the abuse, had they simply asked me point blank, but I do know that the right questions were never asked. So I never answered. The abduction by the pedophile known as John Esposito brought my horrible childhood—filled with abuse, neglect and rape—into the public arena. It launched a much needed conversation about child protection, and the responsibilities of teachers, police, and community.

I am, actually, grateful that I am the one who experienced my childhood, and not someone else. Everything happens for a reason—this I am sure of. And, my childhood happened to me, so that I can speak out and know, at the end of my days, that the little girl still within me did not suffer in vain.

With every public appearance I make and every speech I give, I do so with the knowledge that I am helping someone. When I started this journey, I had no idea what I was getting myself into. I had zero expectations because I did not want to be let down. Far from being let down, I have been reassured that my story of recovery is something that needs to be shared. Today, I am truly content. I have an incredible husband, children I cherish, and an absolutely amazing support system. Without all of these people rallying behind me and encouraging me, I would not be here. I am enjoying life to the fullest, being a mommy, a wife, a daughter, and a friend.

When I was a child, living through hell, I always dreamed of being a wife and mother, but I never believed it would be possible for me. So, thank you, to everyone who has ever said an encouraging word to me, supported me, believed in me. Without you, I could not have even imagined…a whole new world.When I was a child, living through hell, I always dreamed of being a wife and mother, but I never believed it would be possible for me. So, thank you, to everyone who has ever said an encouraging word to me, supported me, believed in me. Without you, I could not have even imagined…a whole new world.

Christmas 2014 (Photo by: Lights, Camera, Smile Photography)

Halee & Logan, 2013

John Walsh, Katie, and Derek at the Hope Awards 2014

ENDNOTES

1 Arthur Herzog, *17 Days: The Katie Beers Story* (New York: Harper Collins: 1993).

2 "Police Query 2 in Search for Girl,10," *New York Times*, December 31, 1992

3 Herzog, *17 Days.*

4 Paul Vitello, "Sidney R. Siben Publicity Hound," *Newsday*, May 12, 2001.

5 "Fearing for Katie As Search for Missing Girl continues, Abuse Charges Surface," *Newsday,* December 31, 1992.

6 "Katie's Case County Probed her Treatment," *Newsday*, January 6, 1993.

7 The result of the hearings was a scathing grand jury report in which Child Protective Services was criticized for lax monitoring, inconsistent record keeping, and poorly trained caseworkers. In response, in 1997 Suffolk County opened a Child Advocacy Center, a kid-friendly haven where children can share details of sexual abuse without the intimidation of a police precinct or prosecutor's offce. CPS workers now receive more intense training and carry digital cameras to better document evidence of abuse. And a task force comprised of police, prosecutors and CPS caseworkers meet monthly to share information and try to identify sex abuse patterns. The Katie Beers case is credited with spawning this child advocacy center movement.

8 Herzog, *17 Days.*

9 "Going Nowhere with no Big Leads", *Newsday*, January 5, 1993.

10 Jonathan Rabinowitz , *New York Times*, January 9, 1993.

11 Paul Vitello, "A Tangled Young Life," *Newsday*, January 5, 1993.

12 Joe Treen and Maria Eftimiades , New York: St. Martens Press, *My*

BURIED MEMORIES

Name is Katherine: The True Story of Katie Beers, the Little Girl Who Survived an Underground Dungeon of Horror, p.182.

13 "A Day of Tension ," *Newsday*, January 14, 1993.

14 Paul Vitello, "Sidney R. Siben, Publicity Hound ," *Newsday*, May 12,2001.

15 "Katie Freed after 16 Days, *Newsday*, January 14, 1993.

16 Herzog, *17 Days*.

17 "Katie Freed from Bunker," *Newsday*, January 14, 1993.

18 "Waiting was Agony for Katie's Kin," *Newsday*, January 14, 1993.

19 "Let Katie Breathe," *New York Post*, January 21, 1993.

20 Editorial, *East Hampton Star*, January 28, 1993.

21 "Joy and Relief over Child's Rescue," *Newsday*, January 14, 1993.

22 "Disgusting Marilyn Beers is a Mother Alright," *New York Post*, January 22, 1993.

23 Herzog, 17 Days.

24 "Disgusting Marilyn Beers is a Mother Alright," *New York Post*, January 22, 1993.

25 "Beers' Makeover ," *Newsday*, February 5, 1993.

26 "Katie Beers likes New Home," *New York Times*, January 21, 1993.

27 "Weighting Katie's wishes vs Public, " *Newsday*, April 9, 1993.

28 "Always on Sunday," *New York Post*, June 29, 1994.

29 "Eternal Child," *Newsday*, February 14, 1993.

30 Minutes of Parole Board Hearing, Division of Parole, State of New York, April 28, 1998.

ENDNOTES

31 Minutes of Parole Board Hearing, Division of Parole, State of New York, August 7, 2002.

32 Minutes of Parole Board Hearing, Division of Parole, New York State, May 26, 2004 and June 6, 2006.

33 "Police Team was Ready," *Newsday* December 31, 1992.

34 Mike McAlary, "Little Katie Beers gets Chance to be Just a Kid, *New York Daily News*, April 25, 1994.

35 Dave Cullen, *Columbine*, New York: Twelve (2003).

36 Dr. Judith Herman, *Trauma and Recovery: The Aftermath of Violence—from Domestic Abuse to Political Terror*, New York: Basic Books (1997).

37 Jim B. Green , *Colleen Stan:The Simple Gifts of Life*, Bloomington: iUniverse (2007).

38 Herman, *Trauma and Recovery.*

39 Victim's Impact Statement, Division of Parole, State of New York, October 5, 2007.

40 Victim's Impact Statement, October 5, 2007.

41 Transcript, Division of Parole, State of New York, November 14, 2007.

42 Transcript, Division of Parole, State of New York, September 20, 2011.

43 Herman, *Trauma and Recovery.*

44 Transcript, Division of Parole, State of New York, September 4, 2013.

45 Transcript, Division of Parole, State of New York, September 4, 2013

44 Transcript, Division of Parole, State of New York, September 4, 2013.

ABOUT THE AUTHORS
CAROLYN GUSOFF

Photo by Jeffrey Neira

Carolyn Gusoff is an Emmy award winning broadcast journalist who has covered the Long Island beat since 1987. She is currently seen on air at WCBS-TV in New York. As a reporter for WCBS, Fox5 New York, WNBC and News 12, Carolyn has covered some of the most high profile news stories in New York City and its suburbs, including the kidnapping of Katie Beers. Carolyn has a Master's Degree in Journalism from Columbia University and a Bachelor's Degree in English and Government from Cornell University. She lives with her husband and their two children on Long Island.

ABOUT THE AUTHORS
KATIE BEERS

EAC Garden Party July 2014

Katie Beers is a married mother of two, and currently works as a motivational speaker as well as in a family-run insurance business. Katie has a Bachelor's degree in accounting and lives in rural Pennsylvania with her family. *Buried Memories* is her first book.

ACKNOWLEDGMENTS

FIRST AND FOREMOST, I'D LIKE to thank my parents, Barbara and Tedd, for their unconditional love, support and encouragement. Without them, I would not be the daughter, woman, wife, and mother that I am today. They both taught me what it was like to have a loving and stable relationship. They have been my rock for nearly twenty years.

My siblings, Rebecca, Jesse, Cassandra, and Jay—they welcomed me into their home and treated me as their little sister. I was so lucky to be placed in a home with four wonderful, loving kids for me to play with, grow with, and learn from. Whether it be helping me with homework, fixing my hair, or spending time with me, these four were amazing! I have learned so many things from my siblings and continue to learn from them daily.

My husband, Derek, has been another influential person in my life. He has taught me that it is okay to be myself. He loves me regardless of my many flaws. I am so grateful that I found him and that he has introduced me to the life that I live. For him, I will forever be grateful.

My children, Logan and Halee, are the two sweetest children ever. From the moment that Logan was born, I have truly known what unconditional love is. He is the greatest son and big brother. I don't know how Derek and I got so lucky! Halee is a little angel—she loves her mommy, daddy, and big brother very much. A smile from Halee could brighten even the darkest of days.

I would also like to thank Judge David Freundlich, the late District Attorney James Catterson, and Assistant District Attorney William Ferris. They fought so hard for my cases and what they felt was in my best interests.

I still keep in touch with Judge Freundlich who officiated the custody case when it was closed to the public. He is such an amazing man with a huge heart. DA Catterson and ADA Ferris handled my trial with such care and concern. I was so blessed to have both of them on my side and handling the trial.

A heartfelt thank you to Chief Dominick Varrone, the Suffolk County fourth precinct, the FBI and all of the volunteers who searched relentlessly for me. Also, all of the people who prayed for my safe return. Without all of you, my story may have been more tragic.

BURIED MEMORIES

I would like to thank the Suffolk County Sheriff's Department, especially the Suffolk County Correction Officers Association for sending me to Disney World. The Correction Officers Association's generosity made it possible for me to live out every little girl's dream. I would also like to specifically thank former Sheriff Patrick Mahoney, and Undersheriff Edward Morris for their support. And Sergeant Bud Conway for his generosity. He gave me my first bike, which I rode all over Springs.

Mary Bromley is more than a therapist. She is an ally and a friend. I knew that Mary was a safe person for me to talk to, and she still is! Without Mary, and her genuine care for my well-being, I don't believe that I would have ever been able to recover from the trauma that I endured as a child.

Peter Lisi, the principal at Springs School; Mrs. McGintee, my fourth grade teacher; and the entire staff at Springs Elementary School from January 1993 to June 1997, all played instrumental roles in my recovery. Mr. Lisi was not only my principal, but he was a family friend. I remember in fourth grade when I was called to his office. I thought that I was in trouble, but he gave me a dollar because I was working very hard on improving my speech. I had a deal with my dad that for every word I said properly, he would give me a dime, and for every word I said improperly, he would deduct a dime. When all was said and done, I was a "rich girl" and no longer had my grammar issues! Mr. Lisi will always hold a special place in my heart. Thanks to Mrs. McGintee and the entire McGintee clan—Mrs. McGintee helped me through fourth grade, whether it be with schoolwork, or someone to confide in, I knew that she was there for me. Mr. McGintee was my first softball coach, and one of the very few first men that I knew that I could trust!

My caseworkers from CPS—Ginny, Athena, and Valerie. These three women helped me so much through my visits with Marilyn.

The wonderful people of East Hampton for circling the wagons to protect me. A special thank you to Billy Joel, of East Hampton, for welcoming me and my family into his home. He played his upcoming song "River of Dreams" for me, and it is now my favorite song of all time!

I'd also like to thank my in-laws for welcoming me into their homes and hearts with open arms. Derek's family is amazing. I'm so lucky to have such a close-knit family when I'm so far away from mine.

I'd like to thank my amazing friends for putting up with me after all of

ACKNOWLEDGMENTS

these years. I love you all very much and wish that we got to see each other more often. More specifically, Caitlin, Corinne, and Devyn—you are like sisters to me, and I thank you for putting up with me and my craziness!

Finally, it is difficult to find the words to thank Carolyn Gusoff for helping to make my longtime dream of writing a book come true! Without Carolyn, I do not think that I would have been able to achieve this dream. The road has been long, and it has not always been easy to relive the memories. But Carolyn, through her hard work, sensitivity, and deep connection to my story, found a way to make this journey possible and therapeutic. I am so happy that I had an opportunity to get to know her.

—Katie Beers

ACKNOWLEDGMENTS

WHILE WRITING THIS book, there were times I suspected a conspiracy against its completion; I fended off waves of plagues, spates of disease, and near-disaster. Katie kept me focused. She wanted her story told and believed it possesses a relevant and timeless message. I agree. There have been longer episodes of child captivity since her 1992 kidnapping, but Katie's story speaks, with the benefit of hindsight, to a different theme: human resilience.

It was impossible to write a book about a child who grew up without one positive male role model and not think repeatedly of mine. I dedicate this effort to my late father, Gerry Gusoff. No day has passed without the presence of you in my heart.

To my loving family—my mother, Ileen Gusoff; my mother-in-law, Sandra Turk; my sister, Pamela Cott; my brother-in-law, Noel Cott; and nephews, Ben Cott, Michael Cott, and Daniel Cott: It took a village. Thank you for being such an essential part of mine. My sister taught me how to read and write when I was four years old and has been teaching me about compassion ever since.

To my beloved and supportive friends and colleagues: I feel blessed to have too many dear friends to list each one. My book lock-down days are over. We have serious catching up to do!

To my agent Carol Leff, who has been with me from the start—and I mean the Fort Myers, Florida start: I thank you for always being a pillar of support and a trusted friend.

To Mary Carroll Moore: You taught me how to change gears from one hundred words to one hundred thousand. Thanks for helping me find unique structure and a voice.

To Jill Marsal of Marsal Lyon Literary Agency: How fortunate I feel that I found you. From the start, you recognized the value of Katie's story and its timeless message. Your unwavering support, encouragement, and skill guided us through this journey. Katie and I can never thank you enough.

To Megan Trank and Beaufort Books: It is my hope that Katie's story will help to educate, inspire, and enlighten readers for years to come. I am grateful to you for keeping true to *Buried Memories'* original form while ensuring it lives on.

ACKNOWLEDGMENTS

My thanks to Jerry Fields for coming to the rescue with his artistic talent and input. And to Robert Zimmerman and Ron Edelson—public relations geniuses. Your expertise was invaluable.

To Simone Mets, my first reader: I can't thank you enough for your insightful feedback.

To Grace Caporino: Your determination is a model to me, and your encouragement was deeply appreciated.

To Sandra McLane, who transcribed many long interviews for this book: Thank you for giving the children hot dinners and warm attention.

To my children, Graham and Amanda, who have patiently and lovingly watched me engage in an odd game of "Survivor" for years—a life and schedule as journalist mom with sacrifices and challenges but also priceless payoffs. Guys, this is one of those confetti moments and you both are my greatest joy.

To my husband, Jon Turk, my editor, critic and love: I've been down to my king, alone in the corner of the board. You've always pulled me back from check mate. Thank you for being my life coach and beloved partner.

This book is narrative non-fiction. It is derived from extensive interviews, personal observation and memories, research, letters, hundreds of published reports, court, and prison transcripts. I have tried to the best of my ability to accurately recreate events that took place more than twenty years ago.

I am indebted to many people including Dan Forman, Jennifer McLogan, Jeff Schamberry, Drew Biondo, Bob Clifford, Keith Lane, Stephen Goldstone, John Albertson, Joe Garufi, and Marilyn Beers. But this book would not have been possible without the cooperation and participation of two very important people in Katie's life: Dominick Varrone and Mary Bromley. They were generous with their time and insight. They are as much a part of Katie's survival as her unique constitution.

Finally to Katie: Thank you for trusting me with your incredible story. You inspired me twenty years ago with your strength. Now that I know you, I admire you infinitely more. I have learned that human cruelty comes in many forms. Thankfully, the same force that makes people imperfect also gives us the capacity for repair and recovery. Katie has demonstrated this with her life.

This is a success story.

— Carolyn Gusoff